CHINA
BECKONS

To John Gardner —

my very good friend —

fraternally

Jeff

CHINA
BECKONS

*An Insight to the
Culture and the
National Language*

Clifford H. Phillips
[Lei Houtian]

 THE UNIVERSITY OF ALBERTA PRESS

First published by
The University of Alberta Press
Athabasca Hall
Edmonton, Alberta
Canada T6G 2E8

Copyright © The University of Alberta Press
1993

ISBN 0-88864-240-7 paper

CANADIAN CATALOGUING IN PUBLICATION DATA

Phillips, Clifford H., 1920-
    China beckons

    Includes bibliographical references and
    index.
    ISBN 0-88864-240-7

    1. Chinese language—Textbooks for
foreign speakers—English. 2. Chinese
language—Business Chinese. 3. China—
Civilization.
I. Title
PL1129.E5P55 1993   495.1'82'421
C92-091250-8

Typesetting by The Typeworks,
Vancouver, British Columbia, Canada

Printed on acid-free paper.

Printed by Best Gagne Book Manufacturers,
Louiseville, Quebec, Canada

CONTENTS

FOREWORD

Canada's relations with the People's Republic of China have had a long and productive history that has been characterized by unusually strong political, cultural and economic ties. Though China continues to be among Canada's top five export markets, our inability to expand our current exports further and to increase our export of manufactured goods has been hampered by our lack of understanding of the language and culture of that country. To increase our interaction with China requires that we do business on Chinese—not Western—terms, and this requires a thorough understanding of the workings and nuances of the Chinese way of life—in all its aspects. However, many business people unfamiliar with the ways of the Chinese are often frustrated in their attempts to enhance their trade efforts.

Clifford H. Phillips, also known by his Chinese name, Lei Houtian, is an acknowledged authority on China, having lived in that country and studied its people and language for a lifetime. Those of us who have been privileged to work with him have been impressed by his insightful knowledge of China and his ability to view situations clearly from the sometimes conflicting perspectives of a Chinese national as well as a foreigner.

China Beckons: An Insight to the Culture and National Language is a highly useful and practical guide to understanding the language and culture of China that is written in an informal, engaging, often witty, and instructive way. It will prove helpful to anyone travelling to China who wishes to gain a better appreciation and understanding of this fascinating country and its people.

Dr. Morris Maduro
Director, Asia-Pacific International Division
Federal and Intergovernmental Affairs
Government of Alberta

ACKNOWLEDGEMENTS

A comprehensive list of all the people to whom I am indebted is obviously not practical. I am well aware that numerous friends and associates, and occasionally the captive audiences of long-suffering students, have helped to bring about this work. I am conscious of the benefits derived from past experiences, textbooks and teachers from whose well of wisdom I have drawn copiously.

It would be remiss of me, nonetheless, not to name a few who have made concrete contributions of their time and energy. I am particularly honoured that Dr. Morris Maduro, the Director of the Asia-Pacific International Division of Federal and Intergovernmental Affairs in Edmonton, consented to provide the Foreword. I am most grateful to Isabel Milne for her painstaking work of improving the presentation, and to Gwen Simpson who typed the work. Although much of the material was incomprehensible to them, their remarkable attention to detail made my job so much easier. My heartfelt thanks are due to Victor Radujko for proofreading the drafts, and to Mr. Xin Shuhua and Mr. Joseph Chen who checked the texts of the dialogues. My wife, Enid, contributed very generously with her support and interest.

The audio-cassette was recorded with the help of Joseph Chen, Victor Radujko, Li Wei, Linda Ma and Janet Yu, to all of whom I am much beholden. The music I chose is from the opening bars of "Moonlight on the River in Spring." Credit for the recording of the cassette, together with my sincere appreciation, belongs to Don Spence who runs the studio of the Video Video Production Services for the University of Alberta.

Lastly, I wish to acknowledge the financial support by the Alberta Foundation for the Literary Arts, a beneficiary of the Lottery Fund of the Government of Alberta, who funded in large measure the cost of producing this work. I alone am responsible for any errors, omissions, or other shortcomings of this book.

PREFACE

Oh, East is East, and West is West, and never the
 twain shall meet,
Till Earth and Sky stand presently at God's great
 Judgment Seat;
But there is neither East nor West, Border, nor Breed,
 nor Birth,
When two strong men stand face to face, though they
 come from the ends of earth!

"The Ballad of East and West"
Rudyard Kipling, 1865-1936

Some years ago, Mr. Yang Hui, Deputy Director of the Culture and Education Office of the Heilongjiang Provincial Government and President of the Heilongjiang Institute of Advanced Education, kindly suggested that I should take up Civil Engineering with a view to building a bridge to link our two countries and cultures. Hopefully this work may provide a step towards building such a bridge, in which case, Mr. Yang's advice will have been well taken.

Travellers who take the time to learn the basics of the language of the country they are visiting derive many benefits. Learning to speak Chinese will prove to be no exception. Many urban Chinese speak English, but an English-speaking visitor speaking Chinese creates a good impression. This extra effort by a foreigner is bound to be appreciated by the Chinese people, furthering good relations and better understanding between cultures. This must surely be a reward in itself!

China Beckons: An Insight to the Culture and the National Language is designed to instruct business travellers, tourists, and professionals who wish to associate closely, either socially or in a business situation, with the Chinese they meet during their trips. By presenting common situations in the dialogues, basic vocabulary necessary for a person travelling in China can be learned easily. Although many of the expressions presented may appear simplistic, most communication consists of such trivial phraseology. The background explanations offered in the context of each situation furthers better understanding of the Chinese culture and promotes courteous communication.

The book is divided into two parts. Part I: Practical Instructions on Learning Chinese consists of the essential introductory material to acquaint the reader with the rules of Chinese. Part II: Situational Dialogues is composed of fifteen chapters with Chinese dialogues followed by explanatory notes. A vocabulary section follows each dialogue.

Conversations in Chinese can be conducted in fairly simple terms, based on the situations illustrated by the dialogues, but the reader must become familiar with the basic rules of the language. The first chapter begins with explaining Chinese dialects and the National Language, Putonghua, followed by a section on sentence structure. The next section on sounds and tones should help the reader to pronounce and learn (preferably with the assistance of the audio cassette) the expressions used in the dialogues. The Chinese used in the text is presented in Pinyin, a romanization of the Chinese language, based on sounds, not ideographs. A full explanation of this system is given in the first chapter. Also included in Part I are chapters on everyday expressions, numbers and counting.

In Part II, each chapter begins with an introductory section explaining the subject, followed by individual situational dialogues. The Chinese dialogues have corresponding literal English paraphrasing for immediate comparison and are followed by a more idiomatic translation. The paraphrasing is discontinued after Chapter 13 but literal translations are provided in the Rationale and Interpretation section. The short conversations exemplify the manner of address and speech in certain situations, but these examples are not exclusive.

Since the Chinese people rarely expect foreign visitors to be acquainted with their language, the general design of the dialogues is based on the premise that, as a rule, the reader will initiate a conversation in Chinese. Consequently, it is the reader (R) who begins each conversation, with the Chinese (C) providing the answer. Occasional departures from this pattern will be obvious.

The explanatory notes in the Rationale and Interpretation section include examples of alternative usage. Typical sentence structures are also explained briefly in this section.

The vocabulary sections are supplemented with additional terms at the end of the chapter which may be substituted as required. The side-lines which are placed against many of the terms in the vocabulary are used to indicate the compounds such terms may form. Where double side-lines exist, they indicate that such compounds are used in conjunction with each other, and these double compounds are annotated under the Rationale and Interpretation section.

The audio cassette is provided to demonstrate the acceptable pronunciation of words, and for practising the tones that are a basic feature of the Chinese language. The cassette is recorded with the Beijing accent, albeit without the burr for which that accent is known. If possible, the assistance of a Chinese speaker can help improve pronunciation and help teach good speech habits.

Basic Elements are explained in detail in a separate appendix and there is a list of Suggested Readings, should the reader's interest be roused to learn more. A comprehensive Glossary concludes the book, although the supplementary vocabularies are not included in this section.

Much has been written about China in scholarly as well as fictional publications; surprisingly, little seems to have been done to prepare the visitor for the initial impact upon arriving in China. Peripheral contact may have been made through local Chinatowns or Chinese restaurants catering to overseas Chinese. But these places are also influenced by western demands, so while you may think you are getting "a touch of Chinese," is it after all a "westernized touch." The visitor is seldom ready for the authentic Chinese atmosphere to be encountered.

The Chinese people are as curious about visitors in their midst as the visitors are about them. Too close a scrutiny by either side sometimes can be disconcerting, and it is inherent in human nature to be rather judgmental. Prejudices exist undeniably between most cultures, therefore an open mind is all important.

With the help of the information on Chinese courtesies and mannerisms and the distinctively Chinese attitudes and proprieties, the reader will be better prepared for a visit to China. This book can provide only a glimpse of what to expect when dealing with the Chinese on their own ground. Nevertheless, a little light on the subject may be better than no light at all. One's own observations and experiences are bound to make the strongest impression.

ABBREVIATIONS

Throughout this work, the following abbreviations are used for the purpose of assisting cross-reference.

alt. pron.	alternatively pronounced
Bas. El.	Basic Elements
Ch.	Chapter
Dial.	Dialogue
e.v.	equational verb
Ev. Expr.	Everyday Expressions
extn.	by extension
MW	measure word
N & C	Numbers and Counting
Pinyin Rom.	Pinyin Romanization
Prol.	Prologue
PW	place words
QW	question words
R & I	Rationale and Interpretation
Supp. Vocab.	Supplementary Vocabulary
S-V-O	Subject-Verb-Object
Vocab.	Vocabulary
☐○○	The use of this symbol indicates portions of the text recorded on the audio-cassette.

PART I

PRACTICAL
INSTRUCTIONS
ON LEARNING
CHINESE

ONE

INTRODUCTION
TO CHINESE

"Every blade of grass has its
drop of dew."

The Chinese language is an independent member of a large family of languages known as Sino-Tibetan, which includes, among others, Thai, Tibetan and Burmese. It is one of the oldest of living languages and has undergone continuous change and development. For thousands of years the Chinese have had a written language consisting of characters or ideographs, each of which represents a concept (as words do in English). As the peoples absorbed by the Chinese had no similar system, it was inevitable that this written language should become the common vehicle of expression.

CHINESE DIALECTS

Although there is only one written language, there are a great number of spoken dialects, many differing so much as to be mutually unintelligible. The dialects may be classified broadly under five main groups:

(a) Mandarin—variations are spoken by people living around and north of the Yangzi River and along several of its numerous tributaries.

(b) Cantonese—the group of dialects spoken in and around Guangdong Province, and by most overseas Chinese.

(c) Hakka—spoken in North-eastern Guangdong and South Jiangxi, and among Chinese living in Malaysia and Hawaii.

(d) The Fukienese group of dialects, the most prolific—spoken by

3

Chinese in Malaysia and Taiwan. This group includes not only the Foochow, but also the Amoy-Swatow dialects.

(e)   The Wu dialects—sometimes called the Central or Shanghai dialects.

This is a simplified break-down of the ethnolinguistic groups in China and ignores a number of minority groups, not the least of which are the Mongols and Manchus in the north or the Miao in the south.

THE NATIONAL LANGUAGE (PUTONGHUA)

Mandarin or, as the mainland Chinese refer to it, Putonghua is the dialect spoken universally throughout the country and is the official language used by China at the United Nations. Younger generations of overseas Chinese are also beginning to adopt it. The majority of their forebears from the south speak their own local dialects, since the edict to learn Mandarin was not in force when they left home. While the written language is universally readable by Chinese, there is a considerable variety of spoken dialects over the land. Consequently, a decision was made many years ago that the language of the capital, Beijing, should be the basis of the vernacular common to all Chinese. Thus, Mandarin/Putonghua is the language foreigners should learn.

Mandarin was first referred to as Guanhua (official language), and was later known as Guoyu (the national language), the term still in general use by Chinese in Taiwan and outside China. Since 1949, however, what is still called Mandarin in English is now referred to in the People's Republic of China as Putonghua (the common speech). Only the name has changed, implying the political changes which have taken place since 1911 when China became a republic.

Putonghua is an uncomplicated language to learn, except for the tones. It is a logical language and the grammar is reasonably simple. However, because of the special nature of Chinese grammar, English grammatical terms are avoided in this book as much as possible. Chinese makes sense through its syntax; word order is all-important. Thus, emphasis is given to sentence structure, with the significance of the construction explained in terms of the Chinese rather than the English language. This is also one reason for presenting the literal English version in chapters 4-13. Western fixed parts of speech may tend to confuse if over-used, for in Chinese a word may change its grammatical function. The etymology of Chinese words is often self-evident.

SENTENCE STRUCTURE

Chinese is generally expressed in sentences based on the pattern of:
   subject (S)—verb (V)—object (O).
Certainly modifying words or phrases, and even clauses, may be attached to the key parts of a sentence (in the appropriate position), but rarely with the complicated forms of English construction. Articles do not exist. There are no special forms to indicate gender. Since the Chinese language is not inflected there are no declensions or conjugations. Perspective in terms of past, current, or proposed actions is indicated not so much by tense as by a suitable selection of auxiliary verbs. Many Chinese words change their functions where necessary. It is better to accept these Chinese words at their own face value than to relate them to English terms. The special role of verbs in Chinese substitutes largely for the lack of inflection. This is more fully explained in the Appendix *Basic Elements*.

1.1   SOUNDS AND TONES

It is essential to master good speech habits. Pronunciation based on accurate hearing is vital, especially because Chinese is a tonal language which is intrinsically different from English.

WHAT IS GOOD PRONUNCIATION?

Pronunciation habits vary in accordance with different languages, since varying motions of the organs of speech are involved (such as the tongue in relation to the palate), and these motions may occur in different sequences relative to each other. Since no two speakers sound identical, pronunciation is hard to define. Speech habits have to be developed in such a way that what one says makes more of an impact than the way it is said. The natural tendency to substitute one's familiar articulation for unfamiliar new speech sounds must be resisted, so that one's speech organs may be trained to produce correct articulation.

FEATURES OF CHINESE PRONUNCIATION

It is useful for the student of a language to comprehend the kinds of new sounds which need to be mastered. In English, when two words sound almost but not quite alike, they differ either in a consonant or a vowel sound, or possibly both. Thus, for example:

pin and din *begin* with different consonants, apart from which they sound alike;

bit and bin are similar, but they *end* with different consonants;

pin and pan differ only because of their vowels.

The same may be said about Chinese. In Mandarin, **lan** (blue) and **nan** (male) start with different consonants, while **neng** (ability) and **nong** (agriculture) have different vowels.

Nor does the similarity end there, for both English and Chinese terms of more than one syllable may have different meanings, depending on which syllable is stressed. Thus, the noun **permit** (stress on the first syllable) is differentiated from the verb **permit** (stress on the second syllable). Similarly, in Chinese, we find that the word for luggage (**xingli**) takes the stress on the first syllable, but otherwise sounds the same as the word for salute (**xingli**), which takes the stress on the second syllable. As a guide to where emphasis should be placed, a spot is shown under the particular syllable to be stressed, for example, Putonghua. The stress can be applied to another syllable in different circumstances, but in a general sense this guide should prove useful.

TONES

Tones are what gives the language, in whatever dialect, its distinctive musical quality and cadence. It is imperative to recognize and pronounce tones correctly, since an incorrect tone can alter the meaning of a term, sometimes drastically.

In English, tones and voice inflections are used to give emphasis. Without them, speech would be monotonous, but still understandable. Chinese words also require emphasis and modulation; however, if spoken in a monotone, without the tonal ingredient, they would be more than likely misunderstood, if not virtually incomprehensible. In Chinese, tones are essential to distinguish words which otherwise sound alike. There are,

FIGURE I.I

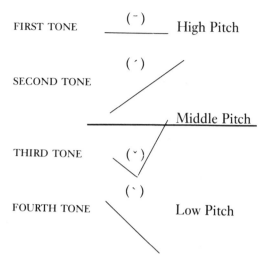

FIRST TONE ——————(ˉ) High Pitch

SECOND TONE (ˊ)

Middle Pitch

THIRD TONE (ˇ)

FOURTH TONE (ˋ) Low Pitch

indeed, many homophones in the language which rely on the context to indicate the term intended. (This, of course, is not a problem when dealing with written characters!)

In Mandarin, there are four principal tones which are clearly distinguishable. In the text a distinctive mark has been placed over each syllable. Sometimes a syllable in a sequence of sounds may be toneless or neutral, in which case no mark is placed over the word. Examples of the four principal tones may be shown using the word "yes":

FIRST TONE (indicated by ˉ over the word) Consider how one would answer one's name in a roll call—"yēs"—a high monotone.

SECOND TONE (indicated by ˊ over the word) Imagine responding to a knock on the door—"yés?"—a high rising tone.

THIRD TONE (indicated by ˇ over the word), as if registering some degree of doubt—"yěs" or yè-és—a falling-rising tone.

FOURTH TONE (indicated by ˋ over the word), as in an emphatic confirmation—"yès!"—a short falling note.

Figure I.I also demonstrates the four tones and corresponding levels of pitch. The sounds and tones illustrated in Figure I.I and the words given in Exercise I.I are demonstrated in the accompanying cassette. Pronunciation of these words is shown phonetically in the left column.

◯◯   Exercise 1.1

WORD/(PHONETIC)	TONES			
	1st	*2nd*	*3rd*	*4th*
ba (**balm**)	bā	bá	bǎ	bà
chou (**chosen**)	chōu	chóu	chǒu	chòu
dai (**diver**)	dāi	dái	dǎi	dài
fu (**food**)	fū	fú	fǔ	fù
gen (**gun**fire)	gēn	gén	gěn	gèn
leng (**lung**fish)	lēng	léng	lěng	lèng
li (**lee**way)	lī	lí	lǐ	lì
mai (**micro**be)	māi	mái	mǎi	mài
qiu (**chew**)	qiū	qiú	qiǔ	qiù
liu (**lieu**)	liū	liú	liǔ	liù
shou (**show**boat)	shōu	shóu	shǒu	shòu
xin (**shin**bone)	xīn	xín	(not used)	xìn
zhao (**jowl**)	zhāo	zháo	zhǎo	zhào

By way of illustrating the tones using a Chinese word, take the word **shou** given at the end of Exercise 1.1. It sounds exactly like "show" in English.

FIRST TONE: **shōu**, meaning to receive, as said in "Shōw me the way to go home."

SECOND TONE: **shóu**, meaning ripe, said as in "Have you something to shów me?"

THIRD TONE: **shǒu**, meaning a hand, as said in "Wouldn't you rather see a shǒw?"

FOURTH TONE: **shòu**, meaning thin, as said in "Shòw me!"

1.2   PINYIN ROMANIZATION

Chinese characters—ideographs—convey only meaning, even though there are phonetic elements in the characters recognizable to scholars of Chinese. It became necessary to devise a romanized convention in order to indicate how Chinese characters sound. The method of romanization used in this book is known as Pinyin, which means literally "spelling sounds" and, in essence, is the Chinese term for transcription. A number of these conventions exist, however the Pinyin system was devised by the Chinese authorities to assist in the elimination of illiteracy and officially adopted by mainland China in 1958. Other romanizations were contrived by foreigners for their own use. Although quite useful, they do not enjoy the official status of Pinyin. In linguistic terms, while calligraphy indicates the meaning of words, romanization concentrates only on pronunciation. Initially, the latter must come first when learning Chinese despite its shortcomings.

Learning Chinese script would introduce an entirely different and more difficult—not to mention time-consuming—element so it is not used in this text. Nevertheless, to learn Chinese properly some knowledge of its calligraphy is necessary. Mr. Lin Yutang, whose works of the 1930s and 1940s received international acclaim, once said: "Painting is the flower of Chinese culture, and the recreation of the scholar. Calligraphy gave it the technique and Poetry lent it the inspiration."

SPELLING

A standard greeting such as Hello in Mandarin sounds like "knee-how," which may seem a satisfactory way of representing it; however, such a method is far from adequate! There exists an official Chinese phonetic alphabet, but it is easier to adhere to a spelling convention using the Roman alphabet known to all English speakers.

A Chinese syllable is generally considered to consist of an initial sound (or, simply, an *initial*) and a final sound (or a *final*). Most initials are consonants. The word **tan** in Chinese uses **t** as its initial, while the final **an** is a word in its own right, just as in English with the word **mark**, **m** is the initial, while **ark** is also a word. A few words in Chinese exist with vowels as initial letters but these are classified under finals. Where one syllable ends with a vowel and the next begins with one, the appropriate separation may be indicated with an apostrophe, e.g., **Xi'an**. Without the apostrophe, the word **xian** is pronounced as one syllable. Apart from the finals which end in **n** or **ng**, it is very rare for the ending of one syllable to be mistaken for the initial of the next syllable. The usage of **x** and **zh** need not be an enigma. The Chinese convention differentiates between **x** and **sh** only because the former is used before certain **i** and **u** vowel combinations. Otherwise, the pronunciation for both is virtually **sh**. Similarly **zh** and **j** are pronounced alike for an English speaker, thus it is as in **j** for judge, never as in French, i.e., juge. Lastly, the letter **v** is never used, and **q** is more often seen preceding an **i** than a **u**.

◖◯◯◗   *INITIALS*

These letters are pronounced as indicated:

B	as in	**bad**
[1]C	as in	**its**
[1]CH	as in	**charge**
D	as in	**dog**
F	as in	**fun**
G	as in	**gum**
H	as in	**hail** (except in words commencing **hu . . .**, when it is pronounced as in **when**)
[2]J	as in	**jeer**
K	as in	**key**
[2]L	as in	**law**
M	as in	**man**
[2]N	as in	**note**
P	as in	**putt**
[2]Q	as in	**chew**
[1]R	as in	**run**
[1]S	as in	**sand**
[1]SH	as in	**show**
T	as in	**top**
[3]W	as in	**wipe**
[2]X	as in	**sheep**
[2,3]Y	as in	**you**
[1]Z	as in	**adze**
[1]ZH	as in	**jaw**

---

[1] Only these seven initials ever precede the palatal vowel -i referred to in the following section on finals.

[2] These six consonants, on the other hand, are the ones used before the other palatal vowel, Ü.

[3] While **W** and **Y** are used as initials, they are in fact regarded as part of an associated final. This concept is explained in the section on finals.

◯◯ *FINALS*

Finals, together with the initials, make up the total number of phonetic spellings used to portray some 400-odd Chinese sounds encountered in Mandarin. These finals consist mostly of vowels, singly, or in groups of two or even three. All vowels are pronounced as in Italian, except when indicated as French or German. However, a number of finals, being resonant, end in **n** or **ng**. A far smaller number of finals end with a retroflex **r**, which may replace one or other of the resonant endings.

A	as in	father
AI	as in	**aisle**
AN	as in	**end** (when preceded by initial **Y**)
AN	as in	**khan**
ANG	as in	**ang**st (German)
AO	as in	**now**
E	as in	**earn**
E	as in	**yet** (when preceded by initial **Y**)
EI	as in	sleigh
EN	as in	**under**
ENG	as in	**sung**
ER	as in	**fur**
¹-I	as in	**urn** or **soeur** (French - see note below)
I	as in	**yeast** (preceded by **Y** if initial)
IA	as in	**Asia** (i + a)
IAN	as in	**yen** (i + an)
IANG	as in	**young** (i + ang - same as above)
IAO	as in	**miaow** (i + ao, preceded by **Y** if initial)
IE	as in	**yes** (i + e)
IN	as in	**pin** (preceded by **Y** if initial)
ING	as in	**sing** (preceded by **Y** if initial)
IONG	as in	**yung** (German - substitute initial **Y**)
IU	as in	**few** (i + ou = 1st or 2nd tone)
IU	as in	**yoke** (slight change in 3rd or 4th tone)
O	as in	**awe**
ONG	as in	**yung** (German - when not preceded by **Y**)
OU	as in	**though**
U	as in	**rude** (preceded by **W** if initial)

²Ü	as in	feud	(French U as in nuance, or German Ü, when preceded by initials J, L, N, Q, X or Y)
UA	as in	wapiti	(u + a, substitute W for U if initial)
UAI	as in	wife	(u + ai, substitute W for U if initial)
UAN	as in	Don Juan	(u + an, or ü + an when following J, Q, X or Y)
UANG	as in	long	(substitute W for U if initial)
UE	as in	ewer	(u + e, only approximate, silent R)
UI	as in	weep	(1st or 2nd tone)
UI	as in	tray	(3rd or 4th tone)
UN	as in	tune	(u + n, when preceded by J, Q, or X)
UN	as in	until	(u + n, when preceded by other initials)
UO	as in	wall	(substitute W for U if initial)

---

[1] The sound for -I in this usage is best exemplified by aural means, as it is vocalized as a buzzing vowel—in effect a sixth vowel in the Chinese syllabary which has no accurate equivalent in English. It does not stand alone, always being preceded by one of the following seven initials: C (e.g. CI), CH (e.g. CHI), R (e.g. RI), S (e.g. SI), SH (e.g. SHI), Z (e.g. ZI), and ZH (e.g. ZHI). Except when preceded by the three sibilant initials C, S and Z, this medial—i.e., a semi-vowel bordering between a vowel and a consonant—is virtually impossible to say without a slight retroflex, which is the reason for the dual representation of this sound.

[2] -Ü is only shown thus when preceded by the initials L or N, as the combination might otherwise be mistaken for LU or NU.

Particular attention is drawn to the use of W and Y. Except when these letters are used with certain prime simple vowels (i.e., A, E, and I with Y only; O and U with W only), the sounds of the finals alter. While W and Y are shown listed with the initials, they are used as finals in conjunction with the simple vowels.

The retroflex suffixes r and ér call for certain modifications of the finals preceding them:

i.   for finals A, O, E, U, and NG: simply add r
     e.g., kǒu-kǒur, fèng-fèngr

ii. for finals AI, AN, and EN: drop the last letter and add r
     e.g., kuài-kuàr; yǎn-yǎr, mén-mér.

iii. for finals I and Ü after consonants: add **er**
e.g., **jǐ-jǐer, lǚ-lǚer**

iv. for finals -I, IN, UI, and UN: drop the last letter and add **er**
e.g., **zǐ-zěr, jīn-jīer, zhǔn-zhǔer**.

SUMMARY

Chart 1.1 summarizes the Pinyin convention. The Initials are shown in alphabetical order across the top and bottom, while the Finals are similarly listed alphabetically down the left. All the possible combinations of these two components of a Chinese syllable are indicated by X in the appropriate squares. The main purpose of this chart is to assist with correct spelling to add new words or expressions.

These basic ground rules should facilitate the memorization of a selection of essential expressions. These have been chosen as a foundation for one's initial vocabulary, and are listed in Chapter 2, Everyday Expressions.

Chart 1.1 Summarized Table for Pinyin Spelling of Putonghua

INITIALS

FINALS	B	C	CH	D	F	G	H	J	K	L	M	N	P	Q	R	S	SH	T	W*	X	Y*	Z	ZH
A	X	X	X	X	X	X	X		X	X	X	X	X			X	X	X	X		X	X	X
AI	X	X	X	X		X	X		X	X	X	X	X			X	X	X	X			X	X
AN	X	X	X	X	X	X	X		X	X	X	X	X		X	X	X	X	X		X	X	X
ANG	X	X	X	X	X	X	X		X	X	X	X	X		X	X	X	X	X		X	X	X
AO	X	X	X	X		X	X		X	X	X	X	X		X	X	X	X			X	X	X
E		X	X	X		X	X		X	X	X	X			X	X	X	X			X	X	X
EI	X	X		X	X	X	X		X	X	X	X	X				X		X			X	X
EN	X	X	X	X	X	X	X		X		X	X	X		X	X	X		X			X	X
ENG	X	X	X	X	X	X	X		X	X	X	X	X		X	X	X	X	X			X	X
ER	X																						
I	X			X				X		X	X	X	X	X				X		X	X		
-I		X	X												X	X	X					X	X
IA								X		X				X						X			
IAN	X			X				X		X	X	X	X	X				X		X			
IANG								X		X		X		X						X			

IAO	x	x			x	x	x	x	x	x	x	x	x		x		x	x		x	x
IE	x	x			x	x	x	x	x	x	x	x	x		x		x	x		x	x
IN	x				x		x	x	x	x			x		x		x			x	x
ING	x				x		x	x	x	x	x		x		x		x	x			x
IONG							x		x		x		x		x		x			x	x
IU	x				x		x	x	x	x	x	x	x		x		x	x		x	x
O	x	x	x				x		x	x	x	x		x	x		x			x	x
ONG	x	x	x		x	x	x	x	x	x	x	x	x		x	x	x	x		x	x
OU	x	x	x		x	x	x	x	x	x	x	x	x	x	x		x	x		x	x
U	x	x	x	x	x	x	x	x	x	x	x	x	x	x	x	x	x	x		x	x
Ü	x	x					x	x		x	x				x		x				
UA	x		x				x				x		x		x			x		x	x
UAI	x		x				x						x		x			x		x	x
UAN	x	x	x		x	x	x	x	x	x	x	x	x	x	x		x	x		x	x
UANG	x		x		x			x	x	x			x	x	x			x		x	x
UE	x	x			x		x			x		x	x		x			x		x	x
UI	x	x	x		x	x	x	x	x	x			x		x		x	x		x	x
UN	x	x	x		x	x	x	x	x	x			x		x	x	x	x		x	x
UO	x	x	x		x	x	x	x	x	x	x	x	x	x	x		x	x		x	x

TWO

EVERYDAY EXPRESSIONS

"Teaching with examples is better than teaching with words."

The common expressions supplied in this chapter should prove useful for general purposes and as "icebreakers." They are recorded on the accompanying audio-cassette. In keeping with the introductory chapter dealing with sounds and tones the next logical step in learning to speak Chinese is to learn commonly used expressions.

Notice that the tones given with certain words tend to vary, usually in the case of the third tone. (See Note at the end of this chapter.) These tones should be taken at their face value and memorized as indicated.

The dot under certain syllables of some words serves to show where to place the accent or emphasis. Both these features appear throughout the book to assist in developing the right cadence when speaking Putonghua.

Good morning!	**zǎo**	
	early	
Hello! Hi!	**nǐ hǎo**	(**ni** normally 3rd tone,
	you fine	said here in 2nd tone.)
Goodbye	**zàijiàn**	
	again meet	

See you shortly	**huítóujiàn** *turn head meet* or **yìhuěrjiàn** *one moment meet*	
Excuse me!	**duìbuqǐ** *facing not rise*	(I cannot raise my eyes to your face, i.e., look you in the eye.)
Never mind!	**méiyou guānxi** *not have consequence* or **méi shénme** *not anything*	(i.e., nothing)
Not important	**búyàojǐn** *not need urgency*	
Thank you	**xièxie nǐ** *thank thank you*	(i.e., thanks)
You're welcome!	**búxìe** *not thank* or **xiǎo yìsi** *small meaning*	
Don't stand on ceremony	**búyào kèqi** *not need courtesy*	(a common expression meaning "Be at ease!")
Please come in	**qǐng jìn** *invite enter*	(**qǐng** meaning to invite, by extension means please)
Please sit down	**qǐng zuò** *invite sit*	
Please wait a moment	**qǐng deng yiděng** *invite wait a wait* or **qíng děng yìhuěr** *invite wait one moment*	
Please have some tea	**qǐng hē chá** *invite drink tea*	

Please have a cigarette	**qǐng chōu yạn** *invite inhale smoke*	
May I smoke?	**wǒ kéyi chōuyạn ma?** *I may inhale smoke, eh*	
You may!	**kéyǐ** *may*	(permission granted, also applies to other situations)
I don't smoke	**wǒ bụ̀ chōuyān** *I not inhale smoke*	
I don't drink	**wǒ bụ̀ hējiǔ** *I not drink wine*	(wine covers all alcoholic beverages)
I'm thirsty	**wó kẹle** *I thirsty*	
I'm hungry	**wǒ ẹ̀le** *I hungry*	
I'm tired	**wǒ lẹ̀ile** *I weary*	
I'm not well	**wǒ bù shụ̄fu** *I not comfortable*	
I don't understand	**wǒ bù dọ̌ng** *I not understand*	
Please may I ask . . .	**qǐng wẹn** *invite enquire*	(these words precede any polite request)
Where is the toilet?	**qǐng wẹn cèsụǒ zài shénme dịfang?** *lavatory at what place*	
Where is the luggage?	**qǐng wẹn xíngli zài shénme dịfang?** *luggage at what place*	
Where is the telephone?	**qǐng wẹn diànhụà zài shénme dịfang?** *telephone at what place*	
Do you speak English?	**qǐng wẹn nǐ huì shuō Yị̄ngyǔ ma?** *you able speak English, eh*	
Is there an interpreter?	**qǐng wẹn yǒu fānyị̀ méiyǒu?** *have interpreter not have*	
How much money?	**qǐng wẹn dụōshao qián?** *much little money*	
May I take a photo?	**qǐng wẹn kéyi zhàoxịàng ma?** *may reflect image, eh*	

Note how changes of tone have been indicated in some of the expressions. They mainly take place when several words of the third tone are spoken in sequence. Since the sequence is difficult to utter, the first of the third tone words is uttered in the second tone to improve the cadence. For example:

kěyǐ   is pronounced **kéyǐ**;
nǐ hǎo   is pronounced **ní hǎo**.

THREE
NUMBERS AND COUNTING

"Measure the extent of expenditure against the limits of income."

Just as it is necessary to practice scales when learning to play a musical instrument or to sing, it is useful when learning a language like **pǔtōnghụà** to practice its special sounds in conjunction with its tones. This helps develop a good accent and a sense of the cadence which arises out of the combination of the sounds and their associated tones. Learning numbers can achieve this object, having the additional benefit of laying a sound foundation for counting money, telling time, and referring to distances or temperatures.

CARDINAL NUMBERS

NUMBERS 1-99

1	yī	6	liù
2	èr	7	qī
3	sān	8	bā
4	sì	9	jiǔ
5	wǔ	10	shí

11	10 (+) 1	shiyī[1]	20	2 (x) 10		èrshí
12	10 (+) 2	shièr	21	2 (x) 10 (+) 1	èrshiyī
13	10 (+) 3	shisān	22	2 (x) 10 (+) 2	èrshi'èr
14	10 (+) 4	shisì	23	2 (x) 10 (+) 3	èrshisān
15	10 (+) 5	shiwǔ	29	2 (x) 10 (+) 9	èrshijiǔ

30	3 (x) 10 **sānshí**	55	5 (x) 10 (+) 5 **wǔshiwǔ**
33	3 (x) 10 (+) 3 **sānshisān**	88	8 (x) 10 (+) 8 **bāshibā**
44	4 (x) 10 (+) 4 **sìshisì**	99	9 (x) 10 (+) 9 **jiǔshijiǔ**

---

[1] The plus and times signs, and the ampersands below are shown only as indicators of the manner in which the digits are linked. Also note that the tens take a full second tone (´) when they stand alone; otherwise they are toneless and therefore not stressed (e.g., rather as -ty is not stressed when saying twenty-five, forty-eight or eighty-one).

NUMBERS 100-1,000,000

Hundred -		**bǎi**
zero -		**líng**[1]
100	i.e., one hundred	**yìbǎi**
101	one zero one	**yìlíngyī**[2]
or	100 (&) zero one	**yìbǎilíngyī**
102	one zero two	**yìlíngèr**
or	100 (&) zero two	**yìbǎilíngèr**
110	100 (&) one ten	**yìbǎiyìshí**[3]
111	100 (&) one eleven	**yìbǎiyíshiyī**
112	100 (&) one twelve	**yìbǎiyíshi'èr**
120	100 (&) 2 (x) 10	**yìbǎi'èrshí**
125	100 (&) 2 (x) 10 (+) 5	**yìbǎi'èrshiwǔ**
130	100 (&) 3 (x) 10	**yìbǎisānshí**
579	500 (&) 7 (x) 10 (+) 9	**wúbǎiqīshijiǔ**
1000	one thousand	**yìqiān**
1008	1000 (&) zero eight	**yìqiānlíngbā**
2105	2 1 zero 5	**èryīlíngwǔ**
or	2000 (&) 100 zero five	**èrqiānyìbǎilíngwǔ**
3080	3 zero 8 zero	**sānlíngbālíng**
or	3000 (&) zero (&) 8 (x) 10	**sānqiānlíngbāshí**
9876	9000 (&) 800 (&) 7 (x) 10 (+) 6	**jiǔqiānbābǎiqīshiliù**
10,000	ten thousand	**yíwàn**[4]
10,007	10,000 (&) zero seven	**yíwànlíngqī**
12,900	10,000 (&) 2,000 (&) 900	**yíwànèrqiānjiúbǎi**[5]

70,009	7 (x) 10,000 zero nine	**qíwànlíngjiǔ**
100,001	10 (x) 10,000 zero one	**shíwànlíngyī**
123,456	12 (x) 10,000 (&) 3,000	**shi'èrwànsānqiān-**
	(&) 400 (&) 5 (x) 10 (+) 6	**sìbáiwǔshiliù**
1,000,000	100 (x) 10,000	**yìbǎiwàn**

---

[1] Regardless of the number of zeros appearing between other digits, it is not necessary to indicate them all. Thus, 1008 is given as **yīqiānlíngbā** and 70,009 is **qíwànlíngjiǔ**. **Líng** serves the same purpose as and in "one thousand and eight;" alternatively the number could be rendered as "one zero zero eight."

When digits are quoted in succession, as in a phone number or ticket number, the **líng** is repeated as often as zero occurs. The number 590-6003 is, for example, rendered thus: **wǔjiǔlíng-liùlínglíngsān**.

[2] Attention is drawn to the change of tone for **yī**. Putonghua is not overloaded with exceptions, but this is one of several which do exist.

(a) On its own **yī** (1) takes the first tone, as shown.

(b) Preceding a word in the fourth tone, or a toneless word, **yi** takes the second tone (e.g., **yíwàn**, or **yíge**).

(c) Preceding words in the first, second, and third tones, **yi** takes the fourth tone (e.g., **yìzhāng**, **yìhuí**, **yìběn**).

Similarly, with the figures **qī** (7) and **bā** (8) a change of tone takes place; preceding a word in the fourth tone both these numbers change to the second tone (e.g., **qíyuè** or **básuì**).

[3] Normally the figure ten is not referred to as "one ten," although it is naturally preceded by a digit in ensuing counts, e.g., **èrshí** (two ten) for 20, or **wǔshí** (five ten) for 50. When counting between 110 and 119, it is usual to say **yìshí** (one ten) after the hundred has been said, i.e., 113 is *not* **yìbǎishisān**, but **yìbǎiyīshisān**, so as to have the same cadence as when saying 123—**yìbǎi'èrshisān**. (In other words, this is roughly equivalent to the English practice of saying: one hundred and ten, one hundred and twenty, etc.)

[4] While the Chinese have a specific word for 10,000, i.e., **wàn**, they have no word for a million. Although in English it is not uncommon, for example, to say twelve hundred in place of one thousand, two hundred, this is not the practice in Chinese. Once the **wàn** point has been reached there is no other course to take. 100,000 becomes **shíwàn** (i.e., 10 **wàn**), and one million is **yìbǎiwàn** (i.e., 100 **wàn**), and a hundred million becomes **wànwàn**.

[5] Note the use of **èr** in this series of numbers. **Liǎng**, which is sometimes interchangeable with **èr**, is inappropriate if any figure precedes 2000.

ORDINAL NUMBERS

To change cardinal numbers to ordinals simply precede the cardinal figure with the word **dì**. For example,

first	**dìyī**	[first] hundredth	**dìyibǎi**
second	**dì'èr**	[first] thousandth	**dìyiqiān**
third	**dìsān**	[first] millionth	**dìyibǎiwàn**

By its very nature, an ordinal number will precede a noun, or a measure word or specifier. Moreover, it follows that where certain cardinal numbers (particularly 1, 7, and 8) change tones, the same change will apply to the equivalent ordinal number.

MONTHS OF THE YEAR

Months of the year are readily named by adding **yuè** (month) to the appropriate number. For example,

| January | **Yíyuè** | October | **Shíyuè** |
| March | **Sānyuè** | December | **Shi'èryuè** |

When **yuè** is used to indicate a period of time however, it stands alone and the MW **-ge** is used:

| three months | **sānge yuè** | fifteen months | **shiwǔge yuè** |

EXERCISE 3.1

As an amusing exercise in both counting and tone practice, this rendering of an old round is recommended. The tune should be familiar, but the English version has been modified to correspond to the Chinese words.

Shíge lǜ píngzi guàzhe qiángshàng (repeat)
Ten green bottles hanging on a wall
Yàoshi yíge lǜ píngzi kěnéng diàodexià
If one green bottle possibly might fall
Jiù shèngxià jiǔge lǜ píngzi guàzhe qiángshàng.
Would leave nine green bottles hanging on a wall

(Decrease count of bottles down to one)

Yíge lǜ píngzi guàzhe qiángshàng (repeat)
One green bottle hanging on a wall
Kěshì nèige lǜ píngzi yàoshi diàodexià
But that green bottle if it should fall
Nà jiù méi lǜ píngzi guàzhe qiángshàng!
There'd be no green bottle hanging on a wall!

PART II

SITUATIONAL
DIALOGUES

FOUR

ON GETTING ACQUAINTED

> "Be kindly with everyone you may meet, who knows under what circumstances you may meet again!"

People of diverse nationalities and cultures have different ways of identifying themselves. The usual way in which Chinese identify a person or place (as, for instance, an address) is to work from general to specific points of identification. Therefore in China it is customary for the surname to come first in one's personal name. However, a number of Chinese living outside China place the surname last in conformity with western practice but this can lead to confusion!

Chinese personal names usually consist of three characters, although occasionally two or four characters may be encountered in a full name. The surname is akin to the family or clan name, of which there are more than 350 in common use. The Chinese sometimes refer to their own kind as the **láobǎixìng** (*old hundreds* [of] *surnames*). The surname is generally a single character, although two character surnames do sometimes occur. When referring to your own name, you are advised to give it in the accustomed manner, spelling it, if necessary. An educated Chinese will usually be happy to oblige with a Chinese surname for substitution, if so requested, but almost invariably this will be an approximate transliteration of the sound of one's name, rather than a direct translation, should a translation even be possible. A surname like White could easily be translated as **Bái**—a Chinese surname of the same meaning; a surname like Gowan or Govenlock, however, would more than likely become **Gāo**, representing the first syllable.

There may appear to be a paucity of surnames in Chinese, the opposite applies to their given names. These are often of an auspicious portent, suggesting in the case of daughters, something poetic, such as physical beauty (e.g., Golden Lotus or Precious Pearl), and for sons, integrity or mettle (e.g., Luxuriant Harvest or Vastness of Talent). Parents sometimes maintain a tradition of having either the first or second syllable of a given name common to all their children (e.g. Ài- in Àidé and Àilián); this common feature would thereby identify a specific generation. Many Westerners are aware of the poetic or artistic qualities of Chinese names and are prone to ask for a translation. This practice, however well intended, is questionable.

Chinese may often have different names at different stages of their lives, such as "milk" names (i.e., familiars—almost nicknames—used in family or close circles), or "book" names acquired later in academic conditions. These names, quite apart from the individual's proper names, may persist through the years within a close circle of friends. Moreover, other practices—too numerous to list here—exist, including the tendency prevalent among Southern Chinese to prefix the word **ah** to a male's surname or given name. In the case of a female, a syllable of her given name only is so prefixed. Other prefixes, such as **lǎo** (meaning old) or **xiǎo** (meaning young or little), may also be used in **pǔtōnghuà**, which practice, of course, is evident among friends of any nationality.

4.1   ESTABLISHING IDENTITIES

R: **Qǐngwèn, nín guìxìng?**
Invite-query, your honorable surname?
May I ask your [sur]name? or Please tell me your [sur]name.

C: **Wǒ xìng** _____ (surname). **Nín ne?**
I surnamed _____. You eh?
My [sur]name is _____. And yours?

R: **Wǒ shì** _____ (state your surname).
I be _____.
I am _____.

Zhèi shì wǒ-de míngpiàn.
This is my namecard.
This is my card.

Wǒ-de míngzi jiào _____ (state given name).
My name call _____.
My name is _____.

Nǐ jiào shénme míngzi?
You call what name?
What is your [given] name?

C: **Wǒ jiào _____** (given name).
I call _____.
I'm called _____.

VOCABULARY

qǐng	to invite; extn.—a request, hence "please"
wèn	to ask, enquire, query; to ask after
nín	you—formal alternative for second personal pronoun **nǐ**
guì	expensive, costly, dear; valuable; extn.—honorable
xìng	surname—used as a noun or equational verb [e.v.]
wǒ	I, me (App., Sec.2)
ne	an interrogative particle
shì	verb—to be [e.v.]
zhèi	this
-de	possessive or connective particle
míng	name, denoting proper names as well as names of objects
piàn	a thin piece or slice; hence a card
-zi	toneless suffix used with nouns (App., Sec.1b)
jiào	to call, or called by the name of _____; ask, order; get
nǐ	you (singular; App., Sec.2)
shénme	what, question word [QW]

RATIONALE AND INTERPRETATION

The Chinese are universally renowned for their courtesy and strongly developed sense of hospitality. It is no coincidence that the first word learned in this chapter is **qǐng** (please). Since common courtesy does much to enhance human sociability, more than casual emphasis is placed on etiquette because the Chinese have, for the most part, a sense of dignity and propriety which differs at times from the rest of the world. One last point: **qǐng** never appears at the end of a Chinese sentence! **Qǐng wèn**—"Please may I ask . . ." or, obviously, "Please tell me . . ." is a stereotypic polite phrase used to precede any request for information.

Nín guìxìng—"What is your honorable surname?"—a stylized formal expression. In reply, the honorific **guì** is dropped, since it would not be fitting to apply it to oneself. On becoming better acquainted, one may feel inclined to take a cue from the Chinese associated with and substitute the common pronoun **nǐ** for the formal **nín**. In the egalitarian atmosphere now prevailing in China, the use of **nín** is considered somewhat old-fashioned, since it was popular with the pre-revolutionary generations. However, personal discretion should dictate which is appropriate (for example, towards an older person, particularly senior officials or dignitaries of some social distinction, **nín** might still be more advisable).

Attention has been drawn in the introductory chapter to the peculiar role of verbs in the Chinese language, and to the way Chinese parts of speech tend to vary from our own. **Xìng** serves as a verb as well as a noun, as indicated in the Vocabulary. At first, it may appear to be a noun, but in effect it acts as a verb (i.e., *to be* surnamed), thus creating an equation between the person and the surname.

The interrogative particle **ne** is used particularly in connection with elliptical questions, where it is unnecessary to repeat the entire question. "Eh" has been used in the literal translation simply to imply the query and indicate the ellipsis.

Shì as the verb *to be* equates I with whatever surname is put in the blank space, and this with card. A further example of the use of **shì** is shown in Dialogue 4.2, where **nǐ** is equated with **Liú Xiānsheng**. Other aspects of the use of **shì** may also be introduced at this stage, since its function should be distinguished from that of the verb "to be" in English.

(a)   Firstly, **shì** is not as essential in Chinese as *to be* is in English. What is meant is that numerous Chinese words, known as equational verbs [e.v.], include "to be" and an adjective. For example:

Tā hǎo!   not   **Tā shì hǎo**
(He good/well!)   *(He is good/well)*

because **hǎo** in this context does not mean simply "good" or "well," but "*to be* good" or "*to be* well."

(b)   **Shì** is not normally used for verbs describing actions or qualities, e.g., "It *is* cold!" or "*Are* they clever?" or "*Is* she pretty?"

(c)   **Shì** may also be used in certain circumstances to provide emphasis.

Míngpiàn—visiting card, business card, or calling card.

Many Chinese words can have a variety of meanings—usually associated, although somewhat tenuously at times. While the Vocabulary lists a number of such meanings, only the rendering used at the time will be explained here. **Jiào** in this case means to call or to be called (the verb *to be* does not enter into it as such).

The use of a question word [QW] such as **shénme** is explained in the Appendix. Its use as a pronoun really does not affect the Chinese sense. The main consideration is the positioning of the word in the correct place according to syntax or nuance.

Míngzi means essentially the same as **míng**. Chinese consists largely of compound words of two or more syllables, to prevent problems with potentially misleading homophones. Many compound nouns are created by combining synonymous or antonymous syllables, or by adding the suffix -**zi**. Since the suffix would be awkward and superfluous in a compound such as **míngpiàn**, it is simply discarded.

4.2   GREETINGS AND COURTESIES

From the ensuing exchanges, it will be noticed that titles, such as Mr., Mrs. or Miss (as well as Doctor or Professor), all follow the name of the person identified (in keeping with the general practice of going from general to specific).

R: **Qǐngwèn, nǐ shì Liú Xiānsheng ma?**
Invite-query, you be Liu Mr., eh?
May I ask, are you Mr. Liu?

C: **Dụì, wǒ shì Liú Rènhuá.**
Correct, I be Liu Renhua.
Right, I'm Liu Renhua.

R: **Qǐngwèn, tā búshi Wáng Tàitai ma?**
Invite-query, she not-be Wang Mrs. eh?
Tell me, isn't she Mrs. Wang?

C: **Tā búshi Wáng Tàitai!**
She not-be Wang Mrs.
She's not Mrs. Wang.

Tā shì Huáng Xiáojiě
She be Huang Miss.
She is Miss Huang.

[then indicating a third party]

Tā shì Wáng Tàitai
She be Wang Mrs.
She's Mrs. Wang.

R: **Dụìbuqǐ, nín shị Wáng Tàitai bushì?**
Facing-not-rise, you be Wang Mrs. not-be?
Excuse me, are you Mrs. Wang [or not]?

C: **Wǒ jịù shì. Nín guìxịng?**
I indeed be. Your honorable surname?
Indeed I am. Your [sur]name?

R: **Wǒ xìng Hụá. Wáng Tàitai, nín hặo!**
I surnamed Hua. Wang Mrs., you well!
My [sur]name is Hua. How are you, Mrs. Wang?

C: **Hén hǎo; nịn ne?**
Very well, you eh?
Very well, and you?

R: **Wǒ yé hǎo, xìexie!**
     I also well, thanks!
     I'm fine too, thanks!

With identities established, greetings naturally follow. **Nín hǎo**, meaning "Hello" or "Hi!" may be couched in the less formal manner of **ní hǎo** (as already indicated in Chapter 2, Everyday Expressions). Phrased as a question, i.e., **"Nín [or nǐ] hǎo ma?"** the expression takes on more the meaning of "How do you do?" or "How are you?" In either event, the response is **Hǎo**, i.e., "Fine"; or **Wó hǎo**, i.e., "I'm fine." If you are meeting a Chinese again after a long time apart, this might be the time to use that somewhat hackneyed expression, "Long time, no see!"

 Háo jiǔ bú jìan! It's been a long time [since we met].
 (*Good while not meet*)

Much could be written solely on the subject of Chinese etiquette, but space precludes more than a superficial reference from time to time where it seems appropriate. In general terms, it is the height of bad manners to cause embarrassment, or—for that matter—to display much embarrassment if it can be avoided. The Chinese are a cheerful people, a fact long noted by observant foreigners. They are by no means as insensitive or inscrutable as some writers imply; often what is seen to be cheerfulness in the face of a difficult situation, to say nothing of adversity, is really no more than a forced smile to hide embarrassment—if not a broken heart! Moreover, if Chinese appear cautious replying to a direct question, it would not be fair to infer any lack of sincerity. They are much more likely to want to give an answer which will please rather than disappoint. Chinese people will often go to great trouble to make a favorable impression, but they need to have time to understand the attitudes or requirements of their foreign visitors.

VOCABULARY

liú	a common Chinese surname
xiān	before, first
shēng	to give birth; raw, unripe, unfamiliar, strange
ma	an interrogative particle
duì	correct [e.v.]; face to face, opposite, towards; concerning
bù	not

tā	he, she, it (App., Sec.4)
wáng	king, monarch; extn.—grand; a common surname
tài	highest, greatest, extn.—too, extremely
huáng	yellow; a Chinese surname (often confused with **Wáng**)
xiǎo	small, little, young; minor
jiě	elder sister; a general term for young women
qǐ	to raise, start; stand up; rise
jiù	with regard to, concerning; then; at once, only; as soon as, right away; just, exactly
hǎo	good, fine, nice; easy; very; in order to; O.K.
hěn	very, very much, quite, rather, much
yě	also, too, as well; still; either; at all
xiè	to thank

RATIONALE AND INTERPRETATION

Xiānsheng, as a title, always follows a man's surname. The basic meaning of **xiānsheng** (*first born*) is teacher, although—possibly much as the English word Master became Mister—it has taken on the meaning of Mr., Monsieur, sir, or gentleman, as well as husband. Note that in this compound the second syllable is toneless, and consequently unstressed.

Duì is a word which may be used in over a dozen different ways. One of the most prevalent is to indicate assent or agreement. Since there are no direct Chinese equivalents for the English words Yes and No, this is one of the logical alternatives used to answer a yes-no type of question. Had the person not been Mr. Liu, his answer would begin with **Búduì**.

Liú Rènhuá is an imaginary full name used for the purpose of the exercise. A Chinese might well provide his identity in full in answer to such a question, but he would rarely add his title.

Búshi...ma? In this context it implies "Are you not..." as if expecting an affirmative response (in this instance, of course, incorrectly); hence the subsequent correction: "Not so, she is Miss Huang!"

Tàitai. This is a title of respect following a married woman's surname (i.e., Mrs.). From this we get Madam, Madame, lady, or mistress of the home.

Xiáojiě is the title for an unmarried lady (i.e., Miss). Literally meaning *little sister*, it is a formal term of respect with which to address a girl, even if her name is not known, just as one would use the term young lady in English. Like all other Chinese titles, it always follows the surname it modifies. However, another term you may hear is **nǚshì**, a more formal address for women (regardless of marital status), often used in business or professional circles, in the sense of Ms., or—in general terms—ladies.

Duìbuqǐ is one of the everyday forms of apology. As such, it is not intended to be any more abject than the English expression "Beg your pardon," "Excuse me," or "Sorry."

Shì...bushì is a split choice-type question. Choice-type questions generally have no need to be split, and for the sake of consistency a beginner should not attempt this often. Although in English it might sound rather abrupt to say "Are you Mrs. Wang or not?", in Chinese there is none of this nuance of possible irritation implied by "or not" at the end of a question.

Jiù is a typical Chinese word serving over a dozen purposes, with a different English rendering in each case. It is also frequently used in connection with time clauses. To avoid confusion each variant is best considered as it appears. Here, the point "Yes, indeed, that's *just* who I am!" is made, thereby eradicating any doubt from the preceding question.

Xièxie—"Thanks." A number of Chinese transitive verbs, particularly monosyllabic ones, are apt to be duplicated as shown here. This must not be done indiscriminately, and examples will be explained as they occur. **Xiè** is one, since it is rarely heard on its own. Indeed, for all their courtesy, the Chinese use this expression less often than English speakers do its English counterpart, preferring to acknowledge kindness with other expressions as appropriate. **Xièxie nǐ**, that is to say "Thank *you*," is even less prevalent!

SUPPLEMENTARY VOCABULARY

nánrén	man, i.e., male person; also mankind
nǚrén	woman, i.e., female person
qīnqi	family members, relatives
fùqin	father
mǔqin	mother

fùmǔ	parents
nǚér	daughter
érzi	son
gēge	elder brother
dìdi	younger brother
jiějie	elder sister
mèimei	younger sister
zhàngfu	husband
qīzi	wife
àirén	spouse

FIVE

ON
OCCUPATIONS

"To one who knows how,
nothing is difficult."

The standard pattern when addressing someone is as follows:
  (a) The surname
  (b) The given name (which is not essential except for differentiation
       purposes, i.e., to distinguish between several persons with the
       same sounding surname)
  (c) The title or rank of the individual.

Furthermore, it is common practice, after initial use of the full formal
identification, simply to use the rank, much in the same way we would
tend in formal circumstances to refer to "Your Worship" or "Her Lady-
ship." Obviously, the same procedure applies to introductions.

Time was when physical contact was generally avoided as much as possible. Nowadays, however, Chinese are far more prone to shake hands
than they used to be, and a proferred hand is rarely ignored. Indeed, often
both hands are used for a handshake, since the use of one only is still regarded as being somewhat slovenly. Note the way Chinese usually offer a
cup or a glass of refreshment, or make a presentation using both hands—
often accompanying the gesture with a bob of the head, if not a slight bow.
A custom which is now prevalent is a hand-clapping welcome on the arrival of visitors at a function—a spontaneous and sustained applause, and
never a steady rhythmic hand-clap. In such circumstances, should you be
the subject of the applause, it is courteous to return the compliment by
applauding back.

5.1   MAKING AN INTRODUCTION

R: **Qǐng gàosu wǒ, nèige rén shì shéi?**
Request inform me, that-[MW] person be who?
Please tell me, who is that person?

Wǒ bú rènshi tā.
I not recognize him.
I don't know him [or her].

C: **Duìbuqǐ! Nín liǎng-wèi hái méiyou jiànguò ma?**
Facing-not-rise! You two-[MW] yet not-have meet-past eh?
Sorry! Have you two not met yet?

Tā shì wǒmen-de shìzhǎng.
He be our municipal-head.
He is our mayor.

Tā xìng Lǐ.
He surnamed Li.
His [sur]name is Lee.

Lǐ Shìzhǎng, wǒ yào jièshào wǒmen Jiānádà lái-de zhèi-wèi péngyou.
Li municipal-head, I want introduce our Canada come-of this-[MW] friend.
Mayor Lee, I want to introduce this friend of ours from Canada.

VOCABULARY

gào	to tell, inform, notify, declare, announce
sù	to tell, relate, inform; complain, accuse
nèi	that [pron.]
gè	a general-purpose measure word [MW] relating to most nouns
rén	person, people; man; adult
shéi	who, whoever; someone, anyone, (alt. pron. **shuí**)

rèn	recognize, know, identify; admit
shí	know; knowledge
liǎng	two; both, either; extn.—a couple, a few, some
wèi	place, location; extn.—position [in society]; MW for polite use regarding people, except subordinates and children
hái	still, yet; even, even more; (alt. pron. **huán**)
méi	no, not (used only to negate **yǒu**)
yǒu	to have, possess; there is, exist; extn.—some
jiàn	to see, catch sight of; extn.—to meet, encounter
guò	to cross, pass; across, past, over, after; to exceed
-men	suffix indicating plurality
shì	market, fair; municipality, town
zhǎng	senior, elder, extn.—head, chief; to grow, develop, increase; to form; (alt. pron. **cháng**)
lǐ	a common family name
yào	essential, important; extn.—to want; shall; supposing
jiè	interpose; upright
shào	carry on, continue
jiā	to add, plus, increase
ná	to hold, take; seize
dà	big, large, great; major, main; (alt. pron. **dài**)
lái	come; arrive; future
péng	friend
yǒu	friend, friendly

RATIONALE AND INTERPRETATION

Gàosu is a compound meaning to tell or to inform.

Nèige rén shì shéi? is slightly more precise in meaning than **tā shì shéi?** which means "Who is he (or she)?" (Note that Chinese sometimes pronounce this interrogative pronoun as **shuí!**) The generic word **rén** means a person of either sex, as well as having the general sense of mankind, taking the measure word [MW] of **-ge**. (The use of measure words is explained in the Appendix, Section 5a.)

Rènshi means to recognize or to know, and is used in much the same way those words are in English. The compound is pronounced with the accent on the first syllable, the second being toneless. Regarding the cognition aspect of the word, it conveys the meaning of understanding, or knowledge, as well as acquaintanceship.

Nín liǎngwèi. The singular formal pronoun **nín** also serves as the plural. Had the usual informal **nǐ** been used, the plural version would have been:

Nǐmen liǎngwèi or, more basic still,

Nǐmen liǎngge rén (you two people).

Liǎng is the alternative word for the figure **èr** (two), the latter being the word used for the cardinal number; therefore only **èr** can be preceded by **dì** to form the ordinal number "second." **Liǎng** is generally connected with things or persons. For more on the use of **liǎng** and how it differs from **èr**, see Appendix, Section 4.

Wèi—this term is used here as a measure word [MW]. Whereas **gè** is the general purpose MW used when referring to persons or people (i.e., **rén**), it is rather blunt for conventional courtesy. Etiquette demands that a more formal expression be used for any but familiar or close relationships. Hence **wèi**, a more formal rendering, is substituted for **gè**, appropriately enough since the subject of the dialogue turns out to be an official of some consequence—i.e., the mayor.

Méi—this word negates only the verb **yǒu**; all other verbs are negated by **bù**.

Yǒu—this verb, meaning to have, is also negated thus:

méiyǒu	to not have, to be without
wǒ méiyǒu míngpiàn	I have no [business] cards
tā méiyǒu tàitai	He does not have a wife

Yǒu is a very hard-working word in Chinese. Besides meaning to have, it performs a variety of functions with its secondary meaning of there is, or there are, and hence by extension there exist[s]. For example,

yǒu rén	There is someone, or
	There are people

In this dialogue **yǒu** serves yet another function; it indicates completed or past action, standing in the very position occupied by the English word have when it is used as an auxiliary verb. The same applies to the negative form **méiyǒu**, often abbreviated to **méi** alone. In the case of the verb **lái** (to come), for starting with current action and proceeding backwards, examples are:

	wǒ lái	I'm coming
	wǒ bùlái	I'm not coming
	wǒ méiyǒu lái	I have not come
or	wǒ méi lái	I haven't [didn't] come

Since all verbs other than **yǒu** are negated by **bù**, should **méi** appear before any verb it stands for **méiyǒu**, acting as a negative auxiliary verb indicating past activity.

Jiànguò—this compound means to have met. **Jiàn** (to meet) is modified by **guò**, which means to cross [over]. Used here as an auxiliary verb, **guò** indicates past action as by extension it signifies to pass, or the past.

Shìzhǎng indicates the head of the municipality, i.e., the mayor. When used as a person's title, it comes after the surname.

Jièshào is used as the verb to introduce, when presenting people to one another. Otherwise, it has the meaning, by extension, of referral or recommendation.

Jiānádà—Canada, the Chinese transliteration of the word. Names of countries are usually rendered in one of two ways: a full transliteration—as in this case; or a transliteration in an abbreviated form, followed by the word **guó** meaning country or nation. The names of some other countries are dealt with in subsequent chapters.

Lái-de—literally *come-of*, meaning from in this context, i.e., from Canada. The particle -**de** has many important functions in Chinese syntax. Here, it is used in forming a relative clause. In this example we find "... our friend [who has come] from Canada," with -**de** being linked to **lái** (to come). Notice that the clause precedes the noun friend which it describes, unlike the English form.

Péngyou—friend! An emotive word in any language, it is particularly so with the Chinese. Let us therefore use the word **hǎo** (good), to modify **péngyou**:

hǎo péngyou	Good friend[s]
nǐ shì wǒ-de hǎo péngyou	You are my good friend

Other pronouns or personal names may be substituted to adapt this basic sentence to suit a number of occasions.

The syntax in the Chinese phrase equivalent to "this friend of ours from Canada" is noteworthy. Being the object of the verb to introduce (i.e., **jièshào**), the whole phrase comes after the verb, in keeping with the standard Chinese sentence format of S-V-O. The progressive build-up of the phrase is as follows:

péngyou	The general word for friend, the main object
zhèiwèi péngyou	This friend. **Zhèige péngyou**, while basically correct, is not as polite as saying **zhèiwèi péngyou**
wǒmen zhèiwèi péngyou	This friend of ours, or simply our friend. (**-de** is omitted from **wǒmen** because the possessive particle is obvious, and is repeated a moment later)

Continuing to work our way from the general to the specific, we now have a relative clause to insert between **wǒmen** and **zhèiwèi péngyou** (i.e., **Jiānádà lái-de**, meaning who has come from Canada).

Chinese people place great store in good personal relationships and in friendship, which is called **yǒuyì**. In the word **péngyou** the accent is on the first syllable, while the second syllable is toneless. In contrast, the word **yǒuyì** has almost equal balance, with the accent, if any, placed on the second syllable **yì**, which also means friendship. Finally, one more example of **péngyou**:

xiǎo péngyou   literally: *little friend[s]*

The Chinese generally dote on children, and this is an expression commonly used by adults towards children, whether addressing them directly or indirectly. It would be equally suitable for you to use this expression in connection with children.

5.2   PROFESSIONS AND OCCUPATIONS

It has often been maintained that bureaucracy was invented and developed originally by the Chinese! Although, it is by no means exclusive to them, the West has its own styles of administration to contend with. However, it would be futile to try to make comparisons; it would be better to accept the fact that the Chinese do things in their own way—as in so many things—and the best course is to conform to their ways when travelling in China.

With their vast population of over a billion, the Chinese are organized by units (**dānwèi**). Regardless of their role in society or their place of work—the urban neighborhoods with their offices and factories, or the vast countryside with its many rural work teams—all Chinese belong to a **dānwèi** of some sort. Each **dānwèi** is responsible for its own administration, seeing to it that its members are housed, fed and clothed, as well as ensuring that their needs are furnished for work purposes. Any foreigners residing and working in China are also assigned to a suitable **dānwèi** that is responsible for them in the same way. Each **dānwèi** or unit is run by officials known as **gànbù**. The usual English translation is cadre, which does little to convey the person's function. Probably a better word would be simply leader, since a **gànbù** is a civil service type of functionary, ranging from a Party member to an ordinary manager. **Gànbù**, according to their place in the hierarchy, make the decisions and hand these down to the lower echelons. They brook little argument! Another word in this connection is **guānxi** (roughly meaning connections). If one does not belong to a **dānwèi**, he will have no **gànbù** responsible for him either. Thus he will be devoid of any valid connections, or **guānxi**, and without influence from some source or another, it is scarcely possible to achieve anything in China. Foreigners working in China would be the responsibility of the host organization, known as **jiēdài dānwèi**, i.e., the unit [responsible for] reception. It is this close-knit network of connections or bonds which binds together the different segments of the community, and anyone without the protection and patronage of a **dānwèi** and the associated **gànbù** is bereft of **guānxi**. A Chinese, not to mention a foreigner, in such circumstances could be in dire straits, very easily attracting the attention of the Ministry of Public Security (**gōngānbù**).

R: **Qǐngwèn, nǐ zuò shénme zhíyè?**
Invite query, you do what occupation?
May I ask your occupation?

C: **Wǒ shì gōngchéngshī.**
    I be engineer.
    I am an engineer.

R: **Nǐ zài nǎr gōngzuò?**
    You at where work?
    Where do you work?

C: **Wǒ zài shìzhèng-gōngchéng zuòshì.**
    I at town-administration engineering work.
    I work in municipal engineering.

    Nǐ-ne? Nǐ zài shénme dìfang gōngzuò? Shǔyú shénme dānwèi?
    You eh? You at what place work? Belong to what unit?
    And you? What line do you work in? What unit are you connected with?

R: **Wǒ búshi shíyèjiā. Wǒ shì zuòjiā.**
    I not be industrialist. I be writer.
    I'm not an industrialist. I am a writer.

    Wǒ shì gēn Jiānádà Fǎnghuá Yóuhǎo Dàibiǎotuán yíkuàr lái-de.
    I be follow Canada visit-China friendly delegate group together come-of.
    I came with the Canadian Goodwill Mission to China.

VOCABULARY

zuò	to do, make, engage in; to write, compose
zhí	duty; position, post, job
yè	line of business; occupation, profession; industry
gōng	work, labour, industry; skill, craft, extn.—worker
chéng	order, procedure; rule, regulation; a surname
shī	a skilled professional; teacher, master
zài	at, in, on
nǎr	where [QW]

zhèng	politics, political affairs, extn.—administration, management
shì	matter; affair; business, job, work
dì	Earth, land, ground; extn.—fields, place, position
fāng	square; upright, place, region; a surname
shǔ	category, genus; extn.—belong to; subordinate
yú	at, in, by (preposition of general use); a surname
dān	single, alone, only; extn.—odd; simple; bill, list
shí	solid, true, real, honest, extn.—fact, reality
jiā	family, household; home; extn.—specialist
gēn	heel; extn.—to follow; extn.—conjunction *and* or *with*
fǎng	to visit, call on; seek out
huá	splendid, magnificent; flowery; literary term denoting China
dài	generation; extn.—to substitute, take the place of, instead
biǎo	outside, external; to show; express; extn.—chart; watch
tuán	round, circular; extn.—group, society, organization,
yī	figure one [1]; same; whole; once, as soon as
kuàr	piece, lump, chunk; slice; synonymous to dollar ($)—basic monetary unit in China, pronounced **kuài** (without suffix **r**)

RATIONALE AND INTERPRETATION

Zuò is, in fact, one of two homophonic characters with very closely related meanings, but for our purposes the two may be considered as one. As shown in the Vocabulary and in the pages to follow, this active verb has a wide application.

Zhíyè is one of several compounds used to mean occupation, line of work or a job. This dialogue attempts to show a few distinctions between the following near-synonyms, such as:

zhíyè	occupation or vocation
shíyè	industry or trade
gōngyè	activity or work role in industry

The last two compounds are virtually interchangeable; however, the Chinese tend to ascribe a particular connotation to the word **gōng**. Until recently, literacy was a rare achievement for a majority of Chinese. A man of letters was one to be looked up to, for the Chinese have always set great store by education. In fact, an educated Chinese person has a distinct advantage over one who has to rely on more physical abilities to earn a living. It is not hard to understand why the intelligentsia were often envied for their place in society. In their turn the intelligentsia have often stood aloof from the common people, often creating a rift in the Chinese hierarchy. Until the advent of the industrial revolution, similar attitudes were to be seen in the West between professionals and those who worked in trade or commerce or as manual labour. So, while **yè** is common to all three of the examples above, the first syllable is what gives the strongest indication of the compound's meaning. By the same token, while **gōngzuò** means work in the broadest sense, as either a noun or a verb, the term **zuògōng** (reversing the compound) has distinct manual connotations. **Zuòshì** implies the superior task of using the brain, and thus also a better income, and consequently a better place in society.

Gōngchéngshī means an engineer—a not-surprising compound, when we consider that this is a person who puts order and procedure into a works project.

Zài nǎr means at which place, or where, and as a QW sets the question. **Zài** is commonly used as a preposition, despite its primary meaning of to exist or to be living. It must not be confused with its homophone **zài** meaning again (as in **zàijiàn**). **Nǎr** is a combination of **nǎ**, a QW meaning which or what, and what is in effect the abbreviation of **lǐ**, meaning within or inside. Thus, together they yield the QW for where.

Shìzhèng refers literally to town or municipal administration, and here acts as an adjective municipal, modifying **zuòshì**, meaning to work, or to have a job doing.

Zài shénme dìfang. This phrase was first introduced in Chapter 2, Everyday Expressions, and represents another way of asking the question where (**zài nǎr**). The QW **nǎr** is well understood in and around the vicinity of Beijing, but the form **zài shénme dìfang** (at what place) is understood far more widely. **Dìfang** means a place when the **fāng** is toneless; otherwise, **dìfāng** means only locality or local, and is thus used much less frequently. Both **dì** and **fāng** are commonly used characters found in numerous compounds. Together, as **dìfang**, they signify not only place, but space, room and, by extension, part (e.g., **zhèige dìfang búduì**—"This part is not right"). The use of **dìfang** in this dialogue has yet another significance, i.e. line of work or type of business as opposed to, literally, a place of work. The point is emphasized by the question which follows.

Shǔyú is a compound of the words **shǔ** (category) and **yú**, a preposition signifying at or in. The meaning of this term is to belong to, to be part of, or to come under.

Dānwèi combines the two words **dān** meaning single, and **wèi** meaning place, and signifies a unit. For the purpose of this dialogue, **dānwèi** means unit in an administrative sense. It may also be used to mean a unit in terms of measurement, but not in this context.

Shíyèjiā is an industrialist. **Shíyè** means, in general terms, industry (e.g., manufacturing). **Jiā** has the basic meaning of home or family. For example, in the past, when skills and crafts were often passed down through generations from father to son, it is not hard to see the extension of this idea to one who is skilled in a particular line of work. Thus **jiā** has the added sense of a specialist.

Zuòjiā means a writer or author. The Chinese consider a writer or author as one who is a specialist in doing things—or in getting things done; in other words, **zuòjiā**. Other examples abound of this special use of -**jiā** (the equivalent of -ist at the end of many English words). Only a few are shown here:

zhuānjiā	specialist or expert
kēxuéjiā	scientist
dàodéjiā	moralist
yuányìjiā	horticulturalist
huàxuéjiā	chemist

An alternative terms for a writer is **zuòzhě**, literally one [who] makes, or a maker [of books].

Gēn is used here as a conjunction meaning with. The Vocabulary shows **gēn** as having the primary meaning of a heel, although it is commonly used as a conjunction. Since heel by extension implies to follow, it is used in Chinese to indicate a link between nouns, and to mean and or with. In English, it is considered courteous to say "you and I," whereas the expression **wǒ gēn nǐ** is normal in Chinese. Despite the opposite word order, there is no difference in the degree of courtesy, since the

Chinese version literally means "I follow you" (i.e., you first followed by me). Context will indicate the appropriate English equivalent: "You and I," "I . . . with you," or "I follow (or accompany) you."

Fǎnghuá is a literary expression meaning to visit China in a formal sense. The first syllable is derived from the compound fǎngwèn, meaning to visit or to call on. Huá, the second syllable, stems from an ancient character denoting China, and represents what is known in the vernacular as Zhōngguó, or the Middle Kingdom. Traditionally the literary form of the language is not the same as the spoken form. Until about seventy years ago, Chinese literature was virtually a different entity. Steeped in antiquity, it changed little over the millenia, bearing less resemblance to spoken Chinese of any dialect than, say, Chaucer's *Canterbury Tales* bears to modern English. After China became a republic, a literary reform took place, thanks to student movements and the leadership of Dr. Hu Shih and other professors of Peking University. The everyday language came to be represented by characters and báihuàwēn, meaning writings in the vernacular or, more literally, plain speech script was adopted. This enabled people to write in Chinese in the same style as they spoke, rather than in the classical style of ancient literature. Admittedly the earlier form still has a lasting influence, as seen to a slight extent in journalese as well as in more formal or educated rhetoric. Huá, then, performs a special function. Instead of fǎngwèn Zhōngguó (which is good báihuà), the expression fǎnghuá is used when a degree of formality is required, for instance, as in an official title. This practice is similar to the formal English practice of using the Latin word Sino- when referring to China or things Chinese. Despite what has just been said, however, Zhōng (for Zhōngguó) is just as likely to be used as Huá. For example, the full title for mainland China is:

Zhōnghuá Rénmín Gònghéguó
China People Republic
The People's Republic of China (PRC)
This should never be confused with:
Zhōnghuá Mínguó
China Republic
The Republic of China (ROC) which is Taiwan.

Yóuhǎo can be used as a noun or an adjective. It is used here in the title of the delegation to indicate goodwill; otherwise, **yóuhǎo** means friendly, or amicable.

Dàibiǎotuán is a delegation or mission. By itself, **dàibiǎo** is the term for a representative or delegate. It can also be used as a verb meaning to represent, and therefore, by extension, can mean on behalf of or in the name of. Thus, by adding the term for group (**tuán**), we have the compound for delegation or, in this instance, mission.

Yíkuàr is a commonly used compound meaning together (*one piece*). As shown in the Vocabulary, the word for piece is **kuài**; and the suffix (retroflex **r**) is appended only for this compound. In the Appendix, Section 16, a selection of common terms starting with **yī** (one) is shown, three of which are habitually spoken with the suffix **r**. **Yíkuàr** is the first example of the use of one of these expressions. While not exclusive to Beijing, the use of the retroflex **r** is very noticeable as a distinguishing feature of that city's speech. (**Pǔtōnghuà** is based largely on the dialect spoken in Beijing.) The retroflex suffix **r** sometimes—but not always—replaces the suffix -**zi**, without which a sizable number of polysyllabic nouns would be monosyllabic. These two suffixes may not be used indiscriminately. Guidance concerning the use of the suffix **r**—or **ér**—is in Pinyin Romanization, Section 1.2.

5.3   MODES OF ADDRESS

R: **Qǐngwèn, wǒmen-de zhǔrén shì shéi?**
Invite query, our host-person be who?
Tell me, who is our host?

C: **Wǒmen-de zhǔrén shì Mù Jiàoshòu.**
Our host-person be Mu professor.
Our host is Professor Mu.

Tā zài Běidà shì Tǐyù-xuéyuàn yuànzhǎng.
He at North Great be body-educate-college college chief.
He is the head of the Phys. Ed. faculty at Beijing University.

Yĭqián tā shì wŏ-de lăoshī.
Previously he be my tutor.
He was my former tutor.

Wŏ géi nĭmen jièshào yíxià.
I give you introduce one time.
I'll introduce you.

Thanks to the Confucian influence bred into Chinese culture over the past two and a half millenia, the Chinese people have through the ages venerated their ancestors and their elders. **Lăo** is a term of both respect and affection. Just as in English one refers to an old friend or old chap, so the Chinese say **lăo péngyou** or **lăoxiōng**. Older husbands may refer affectionately to their own wives as **lăopó**—[my] old lady—with no disrespect, just as the lady in question might refer to her husband as **lăotóuzi** —[my] old man. In the latter case, however, there is also a sly implication, since the term can also be used to indicate an old fuddy-duddy or old codger! Wrinkles or gnarled features, grey or white locks, or a broad expanse of forehead, are all accorded due deference by the well-mannered Chinese people, who intend no disrespect when asking of an elderly person his or her "honorable age."

VOCABULARY

zhŭ	host; owner, master; main, primary; to manage, direct
mù	tree; extn.—timber, wood, wooden; surname
jiào	to teach, instruct; religion
shòu	to award, confer, give; teach, instruct
běi	north
tĭ	body; substance, extn.—form; system
yù	give birth to; raise, extn.—educate
xué	to learn; imitate; school, college
yuàn	courtyard, compound, extn.—designation for certain government or public places
yĭ	to use, according to . . . , with, so as to, as well as
qián	front, extn.—forward, ahead; before, first [in succession]
lăo	old, aged; of long standing, extn.—constantly; tough

gěi	to give; to cause; for, to
xià	below, down, under, beneath; extn.—next, latter; to descend

RATIONALE AND INTERPRETATION

Jiàoshòu is the compound word for the title of professor. Note that the title always follows the surname.

Běidà is the abbreviated way of referring to Beijing University, being an acronym made up of two syllables representing the full name of **Běijīng Dàxué**. This is not so very different from our own practice of substituting initials or syllables for the names they represent, as in U of A for the University of Alberta, UNO for United Nations Organization, or sitcom for a situation comedy.

Tǐyù is a short form for physical culture, or physical education, much as Phys. Ed. is in English. It is the abbreviated compound of **shēn***tǐ* (body) and **jiào***yù* (education).

Xuéyuàn means college, academy or institute, and is used also to indicate a faculty (e.g., **yīxuéyuàn** means Medical Faculty). Here it is used in conjunction with Physical Education.

Yuànzhǎng—this indicates the Head of the Faculty.

Yǐqián—adverb meaning formerly or previously.

Lǎoshī—this compound (old master) means teacher, and may be used as a term of respect for one's tutor.

Yíxià. Like **yíkuàr**, this compound starts with **yī** (one). This particular expression has no particular English equivalent, but generally denotes the carrying-out of an action. Here it has the meaning of "... this once, then." Note that the second tone is applied to **yī**.

SUPPLEMENTARY VOCABULARY

kuàijìshì	accountant
yǎnyuán	actor, actress
nóngxuéjiā	agriculturist, agronomist
yìshùjiā, měishùjiā	artist
yínhángjiā	banker
shāngren	businessman
lǐngshì	consul

gùwèn	consultant
wàijiāoguān	diplomat
zhǔbànzhě, qǐyèjiā	entrepreneur
xīnwén jìzhě	journalist, newsman
lǜshī	lawyer
zhìzàorén, zhìzàoshāng (Co.)	manufacturer
jīxièshī	mechanic
yīnyuèjiā	musician
zhèngzhìjiā	politician/statesman
wàikè-yīshēng	surgeon
jìshùyuán	technician
zhùlǐ	assistant
dàilǐ	deputy/vice-
zhǔxí, huìzhǎng	(chairman, president Association or Society)
dǒngshì	director (i.e., committee member)
guánlǐyuán	manager
zǒngjīnglǐ	managing director, chief executive
zhíyuán	staff (in general)
cáiwùyuán	treasurer
jiàoyù	education
xuésheng	pupil, student
xuéxiào	school
xuéqī	semester
zhuānjiā-tǎolùnhuì	seminar

SIX

THE PASSAGE OF TIME

"Time passes like the flight of an arrow, and the sun and moon course through the sky like shuttles."

The Chinese employ two different types of calendar. Traditionally the lunar calendar, and its connections with the phases of the moon and the seasons of the year, have in large measure not only dictated the determination of time periods in conjunction with the seasons, but also controlled how the farmers dealt with their crops. China is mainly an agrarian nation; this vitally important aspect of Chinese tradition is still retained by the peasants. Moreover, the Chinese way of referring to the calendar and the progression of years persists in most schools today, alongside the Gregorian (or solar) calendar. The lunar calendar was formally established about 1800 years ago, during the Han dynasty, at a time when astronomy, mathematics, botany and zoology were also emerging. This calendar was divided into 24 periods, and, in a sense, served as an almanac. Each period had its established title, such as Spring begins, Heat ceases, and Great cold.

The Chinese, in step with international practice, use the solar calendar for most purposes. With their customary economy of words, the Chinese rarely use A.D., much less B.C., any more than we do. The word sequence for a full date in Chinese consists of year-month-date; but it should be noted that the year portion may be omitted, as is often the case in English.

6.1   CALENDARS

[○○]   R: **Jīntiān jǐhào?**
Present-day how many numbers?
What's the date today?

C: **Jīntiān jiǔyuè èrshiqí hào.**
Present-day nine-month twenty-seven number.
Today is September 27th.

R: **Nàme xiàxīngqī jiù dào-le shíyuè-fèn.**
Like-that next-star-period then reach-ed ten-month-part.
In that case, next week it'll be October.

C: **Kěbúshì-me! Shíyuè yīhào shì Guóqìngjié. Nèige jiérì wǒmen dōu fàngjià xiūxi liǎng tiān.**
But-not-be eh! Ten-month one-number be nation-celebrate-festival. That [MW] festival-day we all release-vacation rest two days.
So it is! The First of October is our National Day. For that festival we all get two days off for a break.

R: **Wǒ kànkan nǐ-de yuèfènpái, xíng buxíng?**
I look-look your moon-portion tablet, permit not-permit?
May I look at your calendar?

Wèishénme yóu liǎng yàng-de shùzi?
Why have two kinds-of numbers?
Why are there two kinds of figures?

C: **Nèi zhǒng dà shùzi shǔyú yánglì. Běnnián jiù shì Gōngyuán yìjiǔbāqī nián.**
That variety big numbers belong to solar-calendar. Current year just be general-unit one-nine-eight-seven year.
The large numerals are connected with the solar calendar. This year is 1987 A.D.

Xiǎo hàomǎ yǒu yīnlì guānxi. Zhè liǎngge bùtóng.

Small numbers have lunar-calendar relationship. This two-[MW] not alike.

The small numbers have a significance for the lunar calendar. The two are different.

The cosmic **yīn-yáng** principles are interwoven throughout Chinese philosophy, and they figure prominently in Chinese culture. The concept is one of dualism: **yīn** is the negative and **yáng** the positive principle of universal life. Antithesis figures largely in Chinese speech (see Appendix, Section 12). Thus we have **yáng** representing the Sun (although it may also represent Heaven, Light, Male or masculine gender, positive, etc.). It is symbolized by the Dragon. This provides the basis for the compound **yánglì**, meaning the solar calendar. In opposition to **yáng** there is **yīn**, which stands for the Moon (and it may also stand for Earth—the antithesis of Heaven, also Darkness, Female or feminine gender, negative, etc.). Its symbol is the Tiger. From **yīn** is derived the compound **yīnlì**, for the lunar calendar. These fundamental principles are applied as well to the Chinese system of geomancy known as **fēngshuǐ** (*wind water*—the two elements which shape the Earth). A western application of the **yīn** and **yáng** principles is found in the field of electricity.

VOCABULARY

jīn	today, present-day, modern, now; extn.—this [coming]
tiān	sky, heaven; extn.—day, season, weather, [MW]
hào	name; extn.—mark, sign; number, date; size
jiǔ	nine
yuè	moon; extn.—month
shí	ten
qī	seven
nàme	in that case, like that
xīng	a star
qī	period of time, phase, stage; extn.—to expect, await
dào	to arrive, reach; extn.—to go to, leave for; up until
le	perfective particle (alt. pron. **liǎo**—see Dialogue 6.3)

fèn	share, portion; [MW] copy (as for newspapers, etc.)
guó	country, state, nation; a surname
qìng	to celebrate, congratulate; a surname
jié	joint; section; festival, holiday
rì	sun; extn.—day; time
dōu	all, every; already (alt. pron. **dū**—capital)
fàng	to set free, release; give way to; expand; add
jià	holiday, vacation, leave of absence; (alt. pron. **jiǎ**—false)
xiū	stop, cease, rest
xī	breath, rest; news
kàn	to look at, see; examine; consider; [it] depends on
pái	plate, tablet, sign; card; extn.—brand
xíng	permissible, O.K.; to go, walk; to act; (alt. pron. **háng**)
yàng	appearance, shape; kind [of], sort, manner
shù	numeral, figure; extn.—several; (alt. pron. **shǔ**—to count)
zhǒng	species, race; breed, seed; type, kind, sort
yáng	masculine or positive principle in nature; sun; open, overt
lì	calendar; experience, undergo
běn	[plant] stem; extn.—origin; current, [MW] volume
nián	year, annual; period in history; harvest; a surname
gōng	public, state-owned; general; male (animal)
yuán	first, fundamental; chief; unit, component; a surname
bā	eight
mǎ	number indicator; [MW], yard (measure)
yīn	feminine or negative principle in nature, moon, shade
guān	to shut; extn.—barrier, Customs; concerned with; a surname
xì	system, series; extn.—link; faculty, department
tóng	same, alike, similar; together; with

RATIONALE AND INTERPRETATION

Jīntiān jǐhào? The compound **jīntiān** means today. **Jǐhào** (*how many numbers*) is a common expression used for asking the date or a door number (of a room, or house). Here, of course, **jīntiān** makes it obvious that **jǐhào** refers to a date. Although in English the reply gives an ordinal

FIGURE 6.1.A

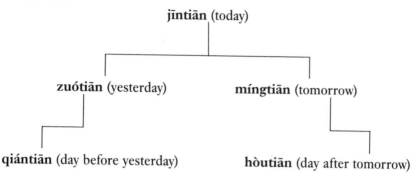

figure, in Chinese the use of **hào** after the figure is the correct form of response concerning a date, rather than **dì** before the figure (see Chapter 3, Numbers and Counting). Only in the case of a particular day in a sequence would it be appropriate to use **dì** before and **tiān** after the figure in a response. For example:

Tā jǐhào lái?	What date is he coming?
Tā wǔhào lái.	He comes on the 5th.
Tā něitiān zǒu?	Which day does he go?
Tā dìsāntiān zǒu.	He goes on the third day.

Note that the time reference follows immediately after the subject, regardless of whether the sentence is a question or a statement. It is not essential—any more than it is in English—to state the month when saying the date. Just as one might reply "Today's the 15th," so the answer in Chinese might be "**Jīntiān shiwǔhào.**" Note that the Chinese use the words **nián** (year), **yuè** (month), and **hào** or **rì** in giving a date. **Hào** (number) is used in speech, but the traditional **rì** (day) is more appropriate in writing. **Tiān** (sky) also means a day, and is used to denote a period of time (i.e., 24 hours) rather than a date. So **tiān** may act also as a MW in the sense of -time, as in **báitiān** (daytime) or **hēitiān** (nighttime).

The method used to describe various points in time in terms of days is summarized in Figure 6.1.A.

Months are referred to numerically (see Chapter 3, Numbers and Counting). For example:

Èryuè—February
(*two month*)
Sìyuè—April
(*four month*)

Bayuè—August
(*eight month*)
Shiyíyuè—November
(*eleven month*)

Xiàxíngqī. Bearing in mind that Chinese calligraphy was traditionally written vertically down the page from right to left, it is easy to understand the use of **xià** (to descend) to mean [the] following or next. **Xiàxíngqī** is the expression for next week. There is a subtle difference between this expression and **xiàge xīngqī** which refers to a week hence or a week's time, rather than specifically next week. The difference is particularly apparent in an expression such as **xià sānge xīngqī**, which means [for] the next three weeks, where the use of a number requires a MW. This applies equally to the use of **shàng** (to ascend) when referring to previous occasions.

Two terms are used to denote a week. Until about forty or fifty years ago, the term used to signify a seven-day period or one week was **lǐbài** (*ceremony worship*), doubtless because of foreign missionary influence. From the seventeenth century onwards the Jesuits had a great deal to do with updating the Chinese concept of astronomy and its relationship to calculations of time. Thus the days of the week used to be referred to, for example, as follows:

lǐbàiyī	Monday	**lǐbàiwǔ**	Friday
lǐbàièr	Tuesday	**lǐbàiliù**	Saturday
lǐbàitiān	(*worship day*) Sunday		

Although one may hear **lǐbài** still used, the modern practice—particularly in mainland China—is to substitute the term **xīngqī** (*star period*), thus giving:

xīngqīsān	Wednesday	**xīngqīsì**	Thursday

Sunday, **xīngqīrì** (or **-tiān**), is the day of rest. Note that where weekdays are concerned the number comes after, but where months are concerned, it comes first. Also when asking for the day of the week, the word order is **xīngqījǐ** (or **lǐbàijǐ**), and not the other way round.

Figure 6.1.B shows the method used to describe points in time in terms of years (**nián**), months (**yuè**), weeks (**xīngqī**), or days (**tiān**).

Jiù dào-le. The term **jiù**, often used as an adverb in colloquial Chinese, also serves a variety of characteristic functions. It has the meaning of

FIGURE 6.1.B

PERIOD	ONE BEFORE LAST	LAST	PRESENT	NEXT	ONE AFTER NEXT
Year	qián-	qù-	jīn-	míng-	hòu-
Month	zài shàng yíge-	shàng-	zhèige-	xià-	zài xià yíge-
Week	zài shàng yíge-	shàng-	zhèige-	xià-	zái xià yíge-
Day	qiàn-	zuó-	jīn-	míng-	hòu-

thereupon, then, or after a while. In this case it signifies next week, as then the month of October will have been reached. This also explains the use of **dào**, meaning to arrive [at], with **-le** indicating affirmation of what will have happened in a week's time.

Fèn is often added at the end of the name of a month to give the nuance of a space of time or a period. This relates closely to the English manner of referring to "the month of . . . ," in this case October. To omit the word **fèn** would not be incorrect, but to use it is more idiomatic and euphonic.

A further point in regard to years, months, weeks and days is that only references to **yuè** (months) and **xīngqī** or **lǐbài** (weeks) make use of a MW, namely **-ge**. **Nián** (years) and **tiān** (days) act to some extent as MWs, and therefore are never preceded by any other MW, much less **-ge**. The following examples illustrate this concept:

shíliù nián	sixteen years
dìwǔ nián	the fifth year
sānge yuè	three months
dìliùge yuè	the sixth month
bāshi tiān	eighty days
dìshí tiān	the tenth day
yíge xīngqī	one week
dìsìge xīngqī	the fourth week

Kěbúshí-me! This is a popular exclamatory expression in Chinese, meaning "Exactly!", "So it is!" or "You've got that right!"

Guóqìngjié (*National Celebration Festival*), the National Day of the Chinese People's Republic, is October 1st. For brevity **jié** may be omitted. This is the anniversary date of the proclamation made by Chairman Mao Zedong in October, 1949 at **Tiānānmén** in Beijing establishing the People's Republic. The National Day is one of the three main official public holidays celebrated on the mainland. The other two are January 1st (not to be confused with the Chinese New Year, which is called the Spring Festival—**Chūnjié**—and fixed by the lunar calendar), and May 1st (Labour Day). Note that a large number of Chinese who do not live on the mainland and are of a different political persuasion, celebrate what is known as the **Shuāngshíjié** (*Double Ten Festival*). This relates to October 10, 1911, when China was first formally declared a republic; this is the National Day celebrated in Taiwan. The Republic of China has a unique method of referring to years. The figure 1911 is subtracted from the current year, to arrive at what is termed *years of republic*. For example 1990 is **Mínguó qīshijiǔnián** (*republic 79 years*).

Jiérì is the compound for a holiday or festival. **Rì** is a word whose primary meaning is sun, and like **tiān** (sky), it is used as a synonym for day. Even though the two characters are virtually interchangeable in meaning, **rì** is a slightly more literary character than **tiān** and is, on the whole, not as commonly used.

Fàngjià (*release vacation*) means to have—to take—or to go on a holiday. In Chinese syntax, it is possible to split the two words of this compound with a modifier such as Summer, or with a number of days, as in an expression such as **fàng sāntiān jià** (take a three-day holiday).

Xiūxi is an expression which virtually means the equivalent of *catching one's breath* or stands for a period of rest or to rest. Since the seventh day of a working week is a day of rest, **xiūxi** is important to the Chinese. It is enshrined in the rights of every Chinese citizen. Although they are justly considered to be an industrious and hard-working people, the Chinese know how to pace themselves according to their climate and diet. While they may sometimes give the impression of virtually perpetual motion, there will always be a portion of the labour force taking a rest, a break, or even a brief nap. The Chinese understand the benefit of a siesta as well as anybody; consequently the pace of modern development as exhibited by western influences has little appeal if it is likely to deprive them of **xiūxi**! Whenever possible, a period of **xiūxi** is a time for enjoyment. If the suggestion is made to **xiūxi yìhuěr** (rest for a while), it is usual to accept.

Kànkan means to look at. Verb duplications are explained in the Appendix, Section 11.

Yuèfènpái is the compound generally used to mean a calendar, although the Chinese also use other words to differentiate between types of calendars.

Xíng-buxíng. Here is a question phrased using a V. not-V. construction. **Xíng** means, in this context, capable or O.K. A question thus phrased anticipates a favourable reply.

In colloquial Chinese, **yàng**—meaning kind [of], sort, or manner—is an extremely useful word. It is less often used in its basic sense of appearance. Consider the following examples:

yàngzi	kind, fashion; sample, pattern, style
yàngr	as above, but in Beijing patois
yàngběn	sample book
yàngpǐn	sample, specimen.

Yàng is also used in such expressions as:

zhè yàng-de rén	this sort of person
shénme yàng-de dìfang	what kind of place
sān yàng-de lǚguǎn	three types of hotel
tā gēn wǒ yíyàng	he is like me
(*he with me one kind*)	
yíyàng bú-yiyàng	alike or not
(*one kind not one kind*)	
bù yíyàng	unlike, not alike
(*not one kind*)	

Shùzì is the term used to signify a number, numeral, or digit. Meaning literally figure character, it is synonymous with the term **hàomǎ**.

Zhǒng is used here as an alternative to **yàng**. **Zhǒng**, meaning variety or type, is not used as commonly as **yàng**, which, having a broader application, is often appropriate when **zhǒng** is not.

Yánglì, the compound for the solar calendar (as opposed to **yīnlì**, the lunar calendar), refers to the Gregorian calendar. Many calendars printed in Chinese show both sets of dates together, generally using Arabic numerals in the former case, and Chinese numerals in the latter.

Běnnián indicates the current year or this year; however, it would not be incorrect to say **zhèinián** or **jīnnián**.

Gōngyuán (*general unit*) is an expression relating to A.D., when reference is made to the Christian era, while **gōngyuánqián** refers to B.C.

Hàomǎ means number or figure.

Yīnlǐ, the lunar calendar, overlaps the Gregorian calendar to some extent, as it is based on the phases of the moon. The lunar year, depending on the appearance of the new moon, has a variable thirteenth month, which gives rise to an irregular date for the Spring Festival.

Guānxi is a vital word to the Chinese. It varies in meaning depending on context, and regrettably it is not possible to encompass the scope of this term completely in English. **Guānxi** generally deals with relationships and connections, and here it appears in its simplest form (i.e., **yǒu guānxi** means to have connections with, or to have significance). Other specific nuances are explained as appropriate.

Bùtóng means dissimilar, not alike or unlike, or not the same. Another way of expressing difference would be **bù yíyàng** (*not one kind*).

6.2   HIGH DAYS AND HOLIDAYS

The Chinese tend not to observe anniversaries to the same extent as in the West. To start with, their perception of age is different. Traditionally, age counts from conception, and when the lunar calendar was dominant, all newborns became one year old at the Chinese New Year. Thus, although an infant's first birthday had some significance, its actual birth date was not of very great account. Consequently, even today, many Chinese consider themselves one year older than Westerners would. As for astrology and fortune-telling, the Chinese have their own signs of the Zodiac which represent certain years, rather than months. Thus someone born after February 17, 1988 (the Chinese New Year), and before February 6, 1989, would belong to the Year of the Dragon, which is followed by the Year of the Serpent. Although the Chinese do not set great store by birthday celebrations, the sixtieth birthday is considered significant, because a person has lived through a complete cycle of the Chinese calculations based on the lowest common multiple of the combinations of what they call the Ten Celestial Stems and Twelve Earthly Branches (represented by the Animals listed in the Zodiac).

While on the subject of longevity, the following expression, the equivalent of "Bless you" or "Gesundheit," is often used by the Chinese when someone sneezes!

Yìbǎisuì
a hundred years of age
May you live a hundred years.

R: **Zhèi xīngqī kě zhēn rènao.**
This week but truly lively.
This week really is a busy one.

Qiántiān shì wǒ shēngrì, kěshi zuì yàojǐn shì dà-hòutiān shì wǒ jiéhūn zhōunián jìniànrì.
Preceding-day be my birthday, but most important be big later-day be my wedding cycle-year commemoration-day.
The day before yesterday was my birthday, but what is most important is that two days after tomorrow is my wedding anniversary.

C: **Nǐmen jiéle hūn duó jiǔ-le?**
You tied nuptials how long ago?
How long have you been married?

R: **Wǒmen jiéle hūn yǒu èrshi nián-le.**
We tied nuptials have twenty years.
We've been married now for twenty years.

C: **Nà yídìng shi zhíde qìngzhù-de rìzi.**
That certainly be worthy celebrate-success-of day.
That's certainly a day worth celebrating.

Wó kěndìng lái zhùhè nǐmen.
I definitely come congratulate you.
I'll definitely come to congratulate you.

R: **Zhēn bù gǎndǎng. Wǒmen zhège zhōunián bìng bú xiàng Chūnjíe shì-de!**
Truly not deserved. Our this commemoration-day in-no-way resemble Spring Festival!
We don't deserve this. Our anniversary is certainly not like the Spring Festival!

C: **Nǐ tài kèqi-le.**
You too polite.
You're too modest.

In Chinese logic, Spring is naturally the first of the **Sìjì** (Four Seasons). These are:

Chūn	Spring
Xià	Summer
Qiū	Autumn
Dōng	Winter

Rarely do the names of the seasons take these mono-syllabic forms however; they usually occur as compounds, formed in one of the following ways. In spoken or colloquial language, the word **tiān** is added to the season stated, to give the sense of -time, i.e.:

chūntiān	the springtime
xiàtiān	the summertime
qiūtiān	the fall
dōngtiān	the wintertime

More formally, especially in writing, the word **jì** (season) is substituted for **tiān**.

VOCABULARY

zhēn	true, real; truly, indeed; unmistakably
rè	heat, hot; warm up; eager, popular
nào	noisy, make a noise; give vent to; suffer from
zuì	most (-est, i.e., adjective used to express superlatives)
jǐn	tight, pressing; extn.—urgent; stringent
hòu	behind, back, rear; extn.—after, later
jíe	tie, knot, knit; form, settle
hūn	to wed, marry; wedding, nuptials

zhōu	cycle, week; a surname
jì	discipline; to record, put in writing; epoch, era, period
niàn	to think of, miss; recite, read out loud; extn.—to study
duō	many, more; odd, any [amount]; (alt. pron. **duó**)
jiǔ	for a long time; long, ages
zhí	value, to be worth; on duty
kěn	to agree, consent, willing, ready to
dìng	calm, stable; extn.—fix, set, decide, to book, order
zhù	to wish, express good wishes; a surname
hè	congratulate; a surname
gǎn	to dare, make bold, venture
dāng	ought; proper, suitable; deserve; in the presence of
bìng	(before a negative) by no means
xiàng	appearance, image; extn.—resemble, like, take after
chūn	spring; life, vitality; a surname
kè	visitor, guest; extn.—traveller, passenger, customer
qì	gas, air; extn.—breath, atmosphere

RATIONALE AND INTERPRETATION

... **kě zhēn rènao**. Working backwards, **rènao** is a compound with a basic meaning of lively or bustling with activity, as one might expect of an active market place. This term also bears the nuance of excitement and fun, which is inherent to the meaning of this sentence. It is modified by **zhēn** (true); hence we have "a really active week." **Kě** is used to emphasize the words it precedes. Although **kě** has a number of uses, and is often used to form compounds, here it stands alone and expresses the idea of "nothing if not...." Thus the overall interpretation of this sentence is "This week will be nothing if not a lively one," or as presented in the dialogue.

Qiántiān stands for the day before yesterday. Figure 6.1.A indicates how days are labelled in succession. Notice also the variations that occur where the succession applies to different periods of time. Years and days are treated differently from months and weeks, as shown in subsequent paragraphs of the same dialogue.

Shēngrì means exactly the same as its English counterpart—birthday. **Shēng** is the same word used in **xiānsheng** (Mr.). As in English, date of birth is expressed a little differently, i.e., **chūshēng-rìqī**. Related to birthdays is the subject of age, or **suìshu**. This compound consists of the character **suì**, meaning basically year, but more commonly known for its extended meaning *year of age*; and the character **shù**, meaning number. When asking a person's age, use the QW **duó dà** (*how great?*). For example:

Qǐngwèn, nǐ duǒ dà suìshu?
Invite-query, you how great age-number?
May I ask your age?

The answer would normally be a figure, followed by the word **suì** (not **nián**!). For example:

Wǒ sānshilìù suìle
I thirty-six years.
I'm thirty-six years old.

Kěshi zuì yàojǐn... Again we encounter **kě**, this time as an equivalent of but or however, modifying **zuì yàojǐn**. The compound **yàojǐn** (*need urgency*) means important, essential or urgent, and **zuì** means most. Thus we get "the most important...."

Dà hòutiān. In Figure 6.1.A **hòutiān** stands for the day after tomorrow. In the case of one day further off, **dà** (great) may be placed before **hòutiān**. Time still further away calls for much the same treatment as in English, when one would probably resort to naming a specific day or date, or specifying a number of days.

Jiéhūn means to marry or to get married. Interestingly enough, the term means literally to tie the nuptials!

Zhōunián jìniànrì. **Zhōu**, meaning complete cycle, compounded with the word **nián** (year), means anniversary. To express the concept of anniversary fully in Chinese, however, the term **jìniànrì** (*record thought day*), meaning a commemoration day, should be added. Although in English this notion may be implicit in the word anniversary, in Chinese it is customary to say the whole expression.

Jiéle hūn. Note that **jiéhūn** may be split as shown here, because when there is a subordinate clause, as shown in the next paragraph, -**le** follows immediately after the verb it modifies.

Duó jiǔ-le means "how long ago?" **Duō** has the basic meaning of many. When pronounced in the second tone it acts as a QW, i.e., how many? In this expression **jiǔ** means ages or for a long time, thus **duó jiǔ**

(*how many ages*) can be seen to mean "how long for . . . ?" (Note also the previous use of **duó dà** as a QW.) The final feature of this construction is the **-le** at the end of this sentence. Although it is a particle, **-le** can also act as an auxiliary verb; occasionally it is seen to be movable—as in this instance. Here it serves to emphasize the duration of the marriage (**jiéhūn**), and therefore **-le** is placed after the question **duó jiǔ**.

. . . **yǒu èrshinián-le.** When **yǒu** is not conveying its basic meaning (to have), it is often used in the wider sense of *there is*, or *there are*. Taken a step further, when used in conjunction with figures—or, as here, a number of years—it has the essence of ". . . it's been twenty years now." The *now* comes from the final particle **-le**. While **-le** was used in connection with **jiéhūn**, to indicate *we have been married*, in this instance the placing of **le** at the end of the sentence serves to emphasize that twenty years will have elapsed by the time of the anniversary.

Zhíde qìngzhù-de rìzi means *a day worth celebrating*. **Rì** (*day*) rarely, if ever, stands alone in spoken Chinese. Here is one application where it is combined with the suffix **zi** to indicate a day in the general sense. **Rìzi** is modified by the compound **qìngzhù** (*congratulatory good wishes*) which, in turn, is modified by **zhíde**, meaning *worthwhile* or *deserving*, thus giving the overall meaning.

Wó kěndìng lái zhùhè nǐmen is an important sentence to remember.

Subject	—	Verb	—	Object
Wǒ		**zhùhè**		**nǐmen**
I		congratulate		you [plural]

The verb is modified simply enough with the auxiliary **lái** (*to come*), and **kěndìng**. The latter is similar to **yídìng—dìng** (*to fix*) being common to both terms. **Kěn** in this context means *willing*, and the compound it forms with **dìng** means *definitely*, in the sense of "You can depend on it." It is this essence of reliability which sets **kěndìng** off against **yídìng**, another compound meaning *certainly*, but not necessarily with quite the same degree of certainty. Note that in each case the adverb precedes the verb it modifies.

Bù gǎndāng is a conventional phrase used in reply to a compliment. Literally meaning *not daring to accept*, it implies "You are too kind," or "You do me too much honour."

. . . **bìng bù** is an expression used emphatically to indicate *in no way*, or *definitely not.* **Xiàng** means appearance or to resemble. Coupled with the preceding negative, it gives the nuance of "it isn't as if it was like. . . ." Note that the sentence ends with **shì-de** (to be of). This construction is often used in connection with **xiàng**, implying "to be of the kind . . . ," as well as "to be like . . ."

Chūnjié is the Spring Festival heralding the Chinese New Year which may be considered the traditional prime holiday of the lunar year. Usually a period of three days is set aside. Immediately prior to this event, a great flurry of activity occurs. The home is thoroughly cleaned and food prepared, since no cooking takes place on New Year's Day in case one's luck might be severed by a sharp instrument. Outstanding debts are settled after which business ceases. Families assemble and close friends may visit each other. Presents are exchanged and the children will be given Lucky Money in red envelopes.

Taì kèqi is also a courteous way of acknowledging a compliment or responding to flattery, meaning in essence too polite; conversely, it may signify unassuming, as it does here.

6.3   PERIODS OF TIME

The Chinese do not have nearly such an urgent sense of time as Westerners. That nearly everyone has a timepiece of some sort is a comparatively recent development. Previously, time was considered in relation to how long it took to achieve a certain purpose, such as the eating of a meal, the drinking of a cup of tea, or the smoking of a pipe. Rural folk often look to see where the sun sits overhead, for their day is divided into twelve periods, which partly accounts for their having two ways of referring to an hour. Punctuality may be expected of a foreigner who places much importance on it, but many Chinese consider such promptness almost demeaning. To arrive on time at a party could imply greed. Furthermore many guests of honour consider a late arrival enhances their prestige, since it implies that they have a great many priorities to consider. Thus a real VIP could be expected to be the last to arrive! However, the situation is slowly changing, and does not give the foreign visitor an excuse for being late; your guide may make this abundantly clear.

⌐○○⌐ R: **Xiànzài shénme shíhou?**
          Present-at what time-wait?
          What's the time now?

      C: **Zhěng shídiǎn-bàn-le.**
          Complete ten-o'clock-[and a] half.
          It's exactly half past ten.

          Nǐ máng shénme, tiān hái zǎo ne!
          You busy what, day still early eh!
          What's your hurry, it's still early!

      R: **Hái yǒu yíkèzhōng wǒmen yīngdāng chūfā. Liǎngge zhōngtóu kǒngpà dàobuliǎo.**
          Still have one-quarter-clock we ought go-start. Couple-[MW] clock-top fear reach-not-possible.
          In a quarter of an hour we ought to set out. I'm afraid we won't reach there in a couple of hours.

          Wǎnle, zěnme bàn?
          Late, how to do?
          What if we are late?

      C: **Búyào dānxīn. Yígebàn xiǎoshí zúgòu.**
          Not-want burden-mind. One piece-[and]-half small-time sufficient.
          Don't fret. An hour and a half is ample.

          Xiàwǔ yìdiǎnzhōng zǎo jiù dàole.
          Afternoon one o'clock early then reached.
          We will arrive well before 1 P.M.

VOCABULARY

xiàn	present, existing, current; extn.—appear; ready [money]
shí	time(s), days; opportunity; extn.—occasionally
hòu	to wait; enquire after; time; condition
zhěng	whole, entire, complete; tidy; mend
máng	busy, hurry

bàn	half, semi-; extn.—middle, halfway; partly
zǎo	early [morning]; long ago, in advance, beforehand
kè	to engrave; extn.—penetrating; a quarter [of an hour]
yīng	answer, reply; agree, accept; ought; a surname
chū	to come [or go] out; to produce; appear; surpass
fā	to issue, deliver; to start, raise, promote, become
zhōng	bell; clock
tóu	head; extn.—chief, first, top, end, [MW]
kǒng	fear, dread; to intimidate
pà	fear, dread, be afraid of
liǎo	to finish; extn.—to understand; solve (alt. pron. **le**)
wǎn	evening, night; extn.—late, later
bàn	to do, handle, attend to
dān	to carry on a yoke; extn.—to take on, undertake
xīn	heart; extn.—mind, feeling; centre, core
zú	foot; sufficient, enough; extn.—full, as much as
gòu	enough, adequate; extn.—reach; quite, rather
wǔ	noon, midday
diǎn	a drop, spot, dot, [decimal] point; extn.—a little; suffix indicating the comparative degree

RATIONALE AND INTERPRETATION

Xiànzài (*present exist*) means now, or at present. Figure 6.3.A illustrates the relativity of time.

Shíhou (*time wait*) is the compound used to indicate a point in time as shown by the clock. A lapse of time is signified by **shíjiān** (*time space*).

Zhěng shídiǎn-bàn. In this context, **zhěng** means precisely, or exactly. The half hour (**bàn**) logically follows the hour (**diǎn**), in the same way that the minutes do in these examples:

lìùdiǎn-èrshisān	six twenty-three
shiyīdiǎn-sìshibā	eleven forty-eight

Diǎn, however, also denotes a decimal point. Thus were it not obvious from the context that the subject was time, the unqualified expression of **lìùdiǎn-èrshisān** could be taken mathematically to be 6.23.

Nǐ máng shénme, an idiomatic expression, does not fit any standard pattern of construction. Meaning literally *You busy what [for]?*, it is a way of

FIGURE 6.3.A

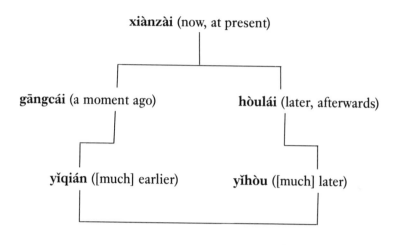

asking "Why are you in such a hurry?" or "What's your rush?" The word **máng** serves as an equational verb, while **shénme** is a standard QW.

   Tiān hái zǎo. Here **zǎo** ([to be] early), is used as an equational verb. Since **hái** means still, the sense here is "The day is early yet."

   Yíkèzhōng means a quarter of an hour. Although **kè** has several meanings, some of which have already been presented, here it is combined with **yī** (one) and **zhōng** (hour) to signify a quarter of an hour. (*Note*: **Kè** does not indicate a quarter in any other context.) To summarize, a one-hour time span can be divided into four parts:

   TOP OF THE HOUR
   [number] **diǎnzhōng**
   i.e., **Lìùdiǎnzhōng**   six o'clock

   A QUARTER PAST THE HOUR
   [number] **diǎn-yíkè**
   i.e., **Qīdiǎn-yíkè**   a quarter past seven
   or **Qīdiǎn-shiwǔ**   7:15

HALF PAST THE HOUR
[number] **diǎn-bàn**
i.e., **Sìdiǎn-bàn**   half past four
or **Sìdiǎn-sānshí**   4:30

A QUARTER TO THE HOUR
[number] **diǎn-sānkè**
i.e., **shídiǎn-sānkè**   a quarter to eleven.
or **Shídiǎn-sìshiwǔ**   10:45

The Chinese speak in terms of three quarters past the current hour rather than a quarter short of the next hour.

Yīngdāng means ought or should.

Chūfā means to set forth, or to start out. It is the compound of two verbs: **chū** which means to go out or to exit; and **fā**, in this instance meaning to start. This compound is best applied to trips or expeditions, or simply an outing, but it applies equally well in the sense of departure, as with bus or train timetables.

Liǎngge zhōngtóu—two hours. The means of differentiating between the appropriate uses of **èr** and **liǎng**, particularly with reference to a MW (such as **gè**) is explained in the Appendix, Section 4. **Zhōngtóu** is an alternative for **xiǎoshí** (*small time*), when referring to the hourly passage of time. When referring to an interval of sixty minutes, either **zhōngtóu** or **xiǎoshí** will do, although the preference nowadays is to use **xiǎoshí**. **Zhōngtóu** (*clock head*) refers to the time it takes for the minute hand to travel round the clock-face from the top, while **xiǎoshí** simply refers to any part of one of those twelve two-hour periods into which the day was divided. Hence, while Noon (**zhōngwǔ**) is when the sun appears to be at its highest point in the sky, the noon period (**wǔshí**) is from 11 A.M. till 1 P.M. Note that whereas the MW **gè** must be used with **zhōngtóu**, this is not essential with **xiǎoshí**, although its inclusion with the latter is permissible.

Kǒngpà. Despite this term being a combination of two words, both of which mean fear and dread, the compound is used rather as the conventional expression "I'm afraid..." is in English; that is, to signify afraid *that* (rather than afraid *of*), as for instance "I'm afraid it's too late!"

FIGURE 6.3.B

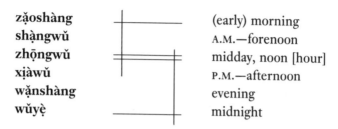

zǎoshàng	(early) morning
shàngwǔ	A.M.—forenoon
zhōngwǔ	midday, noon [hour]
xiàwǔ	P.M.—afternoon
wǎnshàng	evening
wǔyè	midnight

Dàobuliǎo (*arrive not complete*) conveys the idea of being unable to reach [a destination]. **Dào** means to arrive or to reach, while **bù** indicates the negative. **Liǎo** may not be familiar, but it is, in fact, the literary form of the particle -**le**, which indicates the completion of an action since **liǎo** is a verb meaning to complete. **Dàobuliǎo** is an example of a resultative compound verb, which is a fairly extensively used verb form in Chinese. In such compounds, the first element indicates the action, while the second shows the potential or actual result. The *potential* result is shown by inserting between the two verbs **dé**, meaning to obtain, if the result is positive, or **bù**, meaning not, if it is negative. An *actual* result is shown by simply adding the verb **liǎo**. Here, **dàobuliǎo** clearly indicates that the objective . . . cannot be reached [in time].

Wǎn is an equational verb meaning [to be] late.

Zěnme bàn. This is an idiomatic expression in common use. The QW **zěnme** (how) precedes the verb **bàn** (to do), giving the meaning "How shall [we] attend to it?" or "What shall [we] do?"

Búyào dānxīn means "Not to worry" or "Don't fret!" There are several expressions to allay concern or fear. This one is relatively mild, since **dānxīn** means to be concerned or to worry.

Xiǎoshí. Here is illustrated the difference between half an hour and an hour and a half. **Bànxiǎoshí** equates with the former, while the latter is expressed as **yígebàn xiǎoshí. Yíge** represents one whole unit.

Xiàwǔ refers to P.M., that half of the day which follows the moment of high noon. Logically, therefore, **shàngwǔ** refers to A.M., the period preceding noon. If there is a need to specify whether the time referred to is A.M. or P.M., this information is stated first, followed by the particular time of day, in accordance with the usual pattern of Chinese logic (from general to specific). Figure 6.3.B shows how the day is divided up in Chinese terms.

Báitiān (*white sky*) is an obvious allusion to the daylight hours; while **hēitiān** (*black sky*) clearly signifies the night, which may also be referred to as **yèlǐ** (in or at night).

Yìdiǎnzhōng means one o'clock. **Zhōng** is the word for clock, from which several compounds are formed. **Zhōngtóu**, for example, refers to a time lapse of one hour, while **diǎnzhōng** refers to the precise hour of the clock, i.e., o'clock. **Diǎn**, meaning dot or spot, here alludes to the spots or markings usually seen around the face of a clock or watch.

... **zǎo jiù dàole.** These three words complete the sentence. **Zǎo** (early) indicates earlier than or before the hour mentioned. **Jiù**, a word of many uses as indicated before, has the sense of then, while **dàole** means that the action of arriving or reaching the destination will have been accomplished.

6.4   MEAL TIMES

R: **Míngtiān zǎoshang jídiǎn yào qǐlái?**
Following-day early-on what-time require rise-come?
What time tomorrow morning do we need to get up?

C: **Liùdiǎn sānkè hǎo-buhǎo, yīnwei qīdiǎn-bàn chī zǎofàn.**
6 o'clock 3 quarters good not-good, because 7 o'clock-half eat early-food.
How about 6:45, because breakfast is at half-past seven.

R: **Nàme búbì tài zǎo. Chà wǔfēn qīdiǎn qǐlái jiù kéyǐ, yàoburán dàole wǎnshang jiù gǎnjué lèile.**
That not-need too early. Lack 5 minutes 7 o'clock rise then O.K., otherwise reach late-on then feel weary.
Then there's no need to be too early. Five minutes to seven will do to get up, otherwise we'll be feeling tired by the evening.

VOCABULARY

míng	bright, clear; extn.—following [in time]; a surname
shàng	top, to ascend; extn.—above, preceeding; on, up
jǐ	how many, [QW]; several
yīn	to follow; reason, extn.—because, as a result
wèi	for the sake of, because; (alt. pron. **wéi**—to serve as)
chī	eat; take; live on, absorb; incur
fàn	[cooked] rice; extn.—a meal
bì	certainly; surely; extn.—must, have to
chà	differ from, fall short of; extn.—lack, wanting
fēn	divide, separate; extn.—assign; branch, unit of currency (cent), length (cm.), time (min.) etc.
gǎn	feel, sense; feeling
jué	to sense, feel; extn.—become aware
lèi	tired, weary; extn.—toil, work hard

RATIONALE AND INTERPRETATION

Míngtiān zǎoshang jídiǎn—"What time tomorrow morning?" Apart from its basic sense of light or brilliance, **míng** possesses the added meaning of immediately following in time. Hence **míngtiān** (*following day*) is the term for next day or tomorrow, just as **míngnián** (*following year*) means next year. As shown in Figure 6.3.B, **zǎoshang** is the term for morning, which is close to its literal sense of *early on* [in the day]. Note again the logical sequence in the word order, with the larger concept preceding the smaller, in that the actual moment of time (the object of the question) comes at the end of the time clause. **Jǐ** means how many, while **diǎn** refers to a point on the clock-face; the two words thus combine to mean "what time?" The sentence construction illustrates the positioning of the time clause at the beginning of the sentence, which is a regular pattern in Chinese. **Zǎo** may also be used as an early morning greeting. **Zǎo'ān** may be loosely or poetically translated as "morning calm," but it is usual not to utter the second syllable, thus telescoping the expression into the single word **zǎo**, rather like the English greeting: "G'mornin'!" or "Morning."

...**yào qǐlái**. The word **yào** has a variety of uses. Here it acts as an auxiliary verb, indicating requirement or intention. **Qǐ** has the general meaning to rise. Compounded with the word **lái** (to come), it still means to rise, but in the specific sense of to get up or to get out of bed.

Yīnwei means because, on account of, or for [the reason that . . .].

Chī zǎofàn—to have breakfast. **Chī** means to eat, and **chīfàn** (*eat rice*) is simply a compound for to eat or, more specifically, to have a meal. It is possible to be still more explicit by modifying the word **fàn** so as to indicate a particular meal. Here **zǎo** (early) compounded with **fàn** indicates breakfast. The word **fàn** applies essentially to cooked rice, and by extension may refer to a meal. To specify which meal, it is necessary simply to prefix **fàn** with a modifying early, noon, or late, as follows:

zǎofàn	breakfast
wǔfàn	midday meal, lunch
wǎnfàn	evening meal, dinner, supper

The compound **mǐfàn** is also used to denote rice in its cooked form; uncooked it would be referred to as **dàmǐ** (*large rice*) or **báimǐ** (*white rice*), China's staple grain.

Búbì tài zǎo means "There is no necessity to be too early." If we analyze this phrase in reverse order, we see that **zǎo** here acts as an equational verb. **Tài** is used to indicate extremes; thus **tài zǎo** means too early. **Bì** means must, or have to. Combined with **bù** to give the negative form, it means, therefore, no necessity to or no need to.

Chà wǔfēn qīdiǎn. Chà means to lack or to be short of. **Fēn** is used as a unit of measure relating to time (minutes), money (cents), length, weight, and so on. The compound **fēnzhōng**, meaning a unit [of the] clock, is often used; otherwise **fēn** may be used on its own in terms of time. When nearing the top of the hour, as in this case, one can say:

liùdiǎn wǔshiwǔ	6:55
or	
chà wǔfēn qīdiǎn	five minutes to seven

. . . **qǐlái jiù kéyǐ**. This is the answer to the question asked in the first sentence of the dialogue. **Jiù kéyǐ** signifies that it will do [to] get up (**qǐlái**) at the time stated, i.e., five minutes to seven.

Yàoburán is useful as an adverb meaning otherwise, or else, or in which case.

Dàole wǎnshang means essentially [by the time] evening is reached.

By combining **zǎo** (early) or **wǎn** (late) with the suffix **-shàng** (on), we derive the general meaning for morning or evening respectively.

Gǎnjué lèile. By compounding **gǎn** (to sense or to feel) and **jué** (become aware), the meaning of perception or, simply, feeling is obtained. **Lèi** is basically the term for tired or weary, thus the whole expression means essentially [to be] feeling tired. It is not, however, essential to use the compound **gǎnjué**. It is sufficient simply to say, for instance:

Wǒ búlèi.	I'm not tired.
Nǐ lèi-bulèi?	Are you tired?
Tā hěn lèi.	She is very weary.

The presence of **-le** at the end of the phrase implies the result or end of a very long day. **Jiù** is used immediately before the phrase to emphasize the probability that the day will be quite long enough!

[OO] SUPPLEMENTARY VOCABULARY

jìsuàn	calculate, compute, count
gūjì	estimate, reckon
jiěshì	to explain; expound
jiéguǒ	result, outcome
jiāfa	addition
jiāhào	plus sign
jiǎn	subtract
chéng	multiply [by]
chúfa	division
nàozhōng	alarm clock
shùzi biǎo	digital watch
shóubiǎo	wrist-watch
yìmiǎo (zhōng)	a second (1/60)
miáobiǎo	stopwatch
rìjìběn	diary
jiàqī	holiday

jìniànpǐn	souvenir, momento
Yuándàn	New Year's Day (Gregorian)
Fùhuójié	Easter
Shēngdànjié	Christmas
hūnlǐrì	wedding day
ǒurán-de	occasionally
jīngcháng-de	regularly

SEVEN

MONEY MATTERS

"With money—a dragon; without money—a worm."

With the gradual return of private enterprise to the Chinese way of life, it is inevitable that the gentle art of bargaining (in which the Chinese delight and are highly expert) will return to trade and commerce. Not that the tourist is likely to get much exposure to this in the Friendship Stores, where prices are fixed and clearly marked; nevertheless, the simplified scenarios presented here should give some idea of the expressions commonly used in such transactions.

Ignoring for the moment travellers' cheques or credit cards, which are now more widely recognized, let us consider the merchandise as being paid for in local currency, which has been obtained over a bank or currency exchange counter. The casual visitor will receive **wàihuì-duìhuànquàn** or Foreign Exchange Certificates (FEC); only foreign residents and the Chinese themselves may deal in RMB, which stands for **Rénmínbì** (i.e., People's Currency). The denominations and exchange values of the FEC and RMB are identical; however, RMB may not be taken out of China. The standard breakdown is based on the **yuán** (dollar), which is subdivided into 10 **jiǎo** (dimes) and 100 **fēn** (cents). In terms of denominations, there are $1, $5, $10, $50 and $100 bills, as well as bills for 10 and 50 **fēn** (i.e., 10 cents and 50 cents).

It is rare for a foreign visitor to be shopping alone in China. It is usual for a group of visitors to be met at the point of entry into China by an experienced representative of the China International Travel Service (CITS) whose main duty is to act as a liaison between the group and all local points of contact, including the local guides. This national escort is known as the **quánpéi**, meaning literally overall attendant. One of his activities is to escort visitors on shopping expeditions. As they spend their FEC currency, he will gather it up from the shopkeeper, and return him an equal amount in RMB. Not only is this system effective as a check on the amount tourists spend while shopping, it also relieves the shopkeeper of the need to go to the bank for exchange purposes. (FEC are not negotiable for the Chinese under ordinary circumstances.) Such close control should also discourage any attempts to deal in black market or other illegal exchanges which either side might conceivably be tempted to negotiate. However, visitors may in fact receive RMB during their travels; there is nothing wrong with this unless an attempt is made to remove RMB from the country on departure.

7.1   MAKING A PURCHASE

R: **Zhèige dōngxi duōshao qián?**
This-piece thing much-little money?
How much is this thing?

C: **Shíkuài sānmáowǔ.**
10-dollars 3-dimes-5.
$10.35.

R: **Zěnme nàme guì a!**
How that expensive, eh!
How come it's that expensive!

Shǎo suàn yìdiǎr, xíng-buxíng?
Less calculate a-little, can not-can?
Couldn't you make it a little less?

C: **Zhème piányi hái yào jiǎngjià! Kǒngpà zhè kě-bùxíng.**
Such cheap still want discuss-price! Afraid this may not-able.
As cheap as this and you still want to bargain! I'm afraid this won't do.

Wǒmen-de língmài jiàgé dóu biāomíng dìngjià-de rénmínbì jiàqian.
Our retail price-structure all mark-clearly fixed-price- of people's-currency prices.
Our retail price tags all clearly indicate fixed RMB prices.

VOCABULARY

dōng	East; master
xī	West; extn.—occidental, western
zěn	how, why; MW
shǎo	few, little, less; extn.—to lack, missing
qián	copper coin, cash; extn.—money, funds
máo	hair, feather, wool; dime; a surname
suàn	calculate, compute, reckon; extn.—count, figure
biàn	convenient, plain; relief; (alt. pron. **pián**—cheap)
yí	suitable, appropriate; extn.—should, ought to
jiǎng	speak, say, tell; extn.—explain, negotiate, discuss
jià	price; extn.—value, worth
líng	zero; odd, fractional; extn.—no score, love [tennis]
mài	to sell
gé	squares, checks; extn.—divisions; pattern, structure
biāo	mark, sign; extn.—to label; bid
mín	the people, folk; civilian
bì	money, currency

RATIONALE AND INTERPRETATION

Dōngxi means thing. The compound is interesting because it is made up of the two words: east and west. In this connection, the most abstract concept in a Chinese mind is anything contained between the east and the west—hence **dōngxi**. Note that the second syllable is toneless in this compound. Were the second syllable to be stressed with its regular first tone, this would give the sense of East and West, the two opposing points of the compass, in either the literal or the cultural sense.

Duōshao qián? This useful expression deserves some explanation. **Qián** is the generic word for money, with **qiánbì** (*money currency*) denoting coin, while **qiánpiào** (*money note*) denotes paper money or bank notes. **Duōshao** is a standard expression used to ask either "How much?" or "How many?" Thus we have the essential question for use when shopping: "How much money?"—**duōshao qián**. While in English one might simply ask "How much?", in Chinese it pays to include the word **qián** (money); otherwise, the query could be mistaken to mean "How many?" A point to bear in mind is the slight change in meaning that occurs if the second syllable is toneless, as is sometimes the case in antithetical compounds. Just as **dōngxī** means East and West, while **dōngxi** means thing so **duōshǎo** means amount or quantity, while **duōshao** is a QW meaning "How much?"

When China became a republic in 1911, a new monetary system based on the decimal system was adopted. The term **yuán** (*round* or *circular*) is used to indicate a monetary unit (i.e., a dollar), which is equal to 10 **jiǎo** or 100 **fēn**. These are the terms or characters used on the currency; nevertheless, two terms in colloquial use are **kuài** and **máo**, indicating dollars and dimes respectively. Hence:

yíkuài (qián)	one dollar
yìmáo (qián)	a dime
yìfēn (qián)	one cent

An amount in excess of 9 cents is never given in any way other than in dimes and cents. For example, 12 cents is **yìmáo'èr** (one dime and two [cents]), and 25 cents is **èrmáowǔ** (two dimes and five [cents]), there being no equivalent of a quarter. Also, although one may see 50 **fēn** printed on a banknote, it is always spoken of as **wǔmáo**, (i.e., five dimes). When speaking in round figures, it is normal to add **qián** (e.g., **liùkuàiqián** for $6.00); similarly, **wǔkuài bāmáosān** will suffice for $5.83; but never does one say **bāshisān-fēn (qián)** for 83 cents. The word **qián** need only be added at the end of a sum of money if the context does not already make it clear that money is being referred to, for the words **kuài, máo,** and **fēn** do have other uses. If the context is clear, a concise expression such as

liùqiān wúbǎisì is readily understood to mean $6,540, and there is no need to add **-shíkuàiqián**. It would not be mistaken for simply 6,504, since that would be **liùqiānwúbǎilíngsì**. **Bàn**, meaning half, is used when talking of half dollars or 50 cents. For example, $6.50 may be expressed as **liùkuàibàn**, an alternative to **liùkuàiwǔ**.

Guì has been introduced as an honorific, but by extension it also is used to mean valued or valuable, precious, costly or expensive. **Nàme guì** here means "that dear," or "so expensive," and is an expression often used as an opening gambit should the intention be to start bargaining, or to begin *a price discussion* as the Chinese call it! The preceding **zěnme** is a QW, and thus the statement is at once an exclamation and a question, the equivalent of "How come it's that expensive!" or "Why is it so dear?"

Shǎo suàn yìdiǎr. This is a useful expression to use when bargaining, as it means to reckon on a little less. **Yìdiǎr** (a spot) means a little, a bit, or even a tad, being ever so little; hence the diminutive retroflex **r** attached to the word **diǎn**. This is one of a string of expressions used by the Chinese which start with the word **yī** (one). Moreover, to express a tiny bit, **yì-diándiǎn** (a spot [of a] spot) is the usual term used.

Piányi means inexpensive or cheap. The term **biàn** has an alternative pronunciation which is in use in this compound.

Jiǎngjià (*to discuss price*) is the compound for the verb to bargain or to haggle over a price.

Zhè kě-bùxíng means "This is not acceptable." Although in English the suffix -able is often added to a verb to convert it into an adjective, in Chinese a verb normally receives the prefix **kě** to serve the same purpose. What is significant, however, is the position of **kě** in relation to the negative **bù** in this instance, where **xíng** and **bùxing** are the V. not-V. alternatives. Since **bùxing** (not O.K.) is the option chosen, it is this term that **kě** must precede to indicate that bargaining is unacceptable.

Língmài means to sell retail, since **líng** here implies in odd amounts or in small quantities when compounded with **mài** (to sell).

Jiàgé is the term for price and, in this context, the price tag.

Biāomíng dìngjià—clearly marked fixed price(s). **Biāomíng** has the meaning of indicating clearly, while **dìngjià** is the compound for fixed prices.

Rénmínbì jiàqian means plainly enough Renminbi prices. Note that in **jiàqian** (*price money*) the second syllable is toneless, which helps to distinguish this compound, which is commonly used, from the term **jiàgé** (*price guide*). **Bì** has very limited application, as its only meaning is currency, in terms of money. **Rénmínbì** (RMB) refers to the people's currency. **Bì** is not used in connection with FEC, since these are not considered currency, but are certificates or scrip.

7.2   STRIKING A BARGAIN

The Chinese have a propensity for driving a hard bargain. Thrift is a necessity for survival in a society not affluent by western standards. Admittedly there is much in Chinese culture which is truly impressive in its opulence, but the visitor should not overlook at what cost to the masses this excellence was achieved. In China, a nation well acquainted with deprivation from natural and social causes, little ever goes to waste: for the majority of Chinese frugality is an essential part of daily life. It is no wonder then that every penny is made to count, since it was hard to come by in the first place. The skills of shrewd bargaining are developed early, but rarely should this skill be mistaken for avarice, or chicanery for its own sake. It cannot be denied that one can be taken advantage of, but—as in the West—it is up to the visitor to know how to protect his own interests. Bargaining is always a two-way process, and if the terms are considered harsh or unrealistic there is always the option to withdraw before a deal is done. "Buyer beware" has always been axiomatic in entrepreneurship the world over! The Chinese also are proudly determined to be as independent as possible. While they appreciate the necessity of outside assistance, which in turn generates an ever-increasing demand for foreign currency, they have no intention of accepting a further economic burden which, if not paid for readily, will ultimately put the nation in a perpetual state of dependence that may again render them vulnerable to foreign dictates. Self-sufficiency is a key aspect of their future planning; consequently the Chinese do not wish to be regarded as a vast potential market for exploitation. In effect, the moral intentions of the world outside their boundaries are being put to the test, which is why friendship is constantly being pleaded or cited. At the same time, standards of dealing must be defined positively, so that no one is drawn into situations which may mislead through misunderstanding or misinterpretation, thereby giving rise to disappointment, if not bitter acrimony.

For example, on the subject of tempting offers, Chinese rarely use loss-leaders as an incentive to buy, since the subsequent increase in the cost of the article would be considered suspicious. In dealing with the Chinese, it would be far better for the western businessman to make a gift to the customer as a gesture of friendship to encourage further trade or, by the same token to give a pointedly one-time only discount on what is plainly indicated as the regular price. Even this practice is debatable, for many a western businessman has been subsequently discomfited when a Chinese customer demands to know why such inducements cannot be repeated indefinitely. A large mark-up or profit margin is generally disapproved of, since the Chinese usually work on the principle of Small Profits and Quick Returns (SPQR). It is therefore up to the entrepreneur to know the extent of the competition when deciding on prices. As for the customer, he can either shop around looking for a better deal at sales, or become a regular client whose support may be recognized by an annual gift at, say, the New Year, as a personal friendly gesture. Such a gift should in no way be considered a bribe or misconstrued as an attempt to put one under any form of obligation. Should the recipient, say a Westerner with a different attitude towards such a gesture, feel uncomfortable about accepting a present, then let him respond in like manner with a present of his own—thereby squaring the account. To return the Chinese present out of hand would not be such a good idea, being a blunt gesture of rejection thus causing loss of face. A degree of circumspection is also advisable at most times before bringing up the subject of money. Not that the Chinese necessarily regard the mighty dollar as filthy lucre; however, Westerners are often considered indelicate by Chinese standards for the blunt way finances are introduced into a situation. There are as many Chinese euphemisms as there are English, when it comes to discussing payment for services rendered. One would no more discuss wages with a professional than an honorarium with a labourer. To do so might be considered inappropriate in either language, but to a Chinese, decorum would also be lacking.

The Chinese attitude toward nepotism should not be misunderstood either, for these pragmatic people consider that if one cannot trust one's own kith and kin, who can be trusted. Moreover, charity does begin at home. Chinese communities abroad are generally admired for the way in which they look after their own, and this characteristic reflects the essential difference between the opposing aspects on this subject.

R: **Qǐngwèn, nǐmen zhèige máobǐ yào jǐkuàiqián?**
      Invite query, you these hair-pens want how many pieces-money?
      Tell me, how much do you charge for these writing brushes?

C: **Zhè yào kàn ní xiǎng mái jǐge. Zhè yàng-de máobǐ mài sānkuàibàn yìzhī, kěshi mǎi yìdá zhǐ yào sānshiwǔ kuài.**
      This want look you consider buy how many. This kind-of hair-pen sells 3-dollars-half one stem; but buy one dozen only want 35-dollars.
      It depends on how many you want to buy. These brushes sell for $3.50 each, but bought by the dozen they are only $35.

R: **Wó mǎi sānzhī hǎole, géi nǐ shíkuàiqián!**
      I buy three stems alright, give you 10-dollars-money.
      I'd better buy three—I'll give you ten dollars.

C: **Yíjùhuà! Shíkuài-èrmáowǔ, hǎo-le?**
      One-MW-word! 10-dollars-2-dimes-5, good?
      [Just] one word! $10.25—that O.K.?

VOCABULARY

bǐ	pen, writing implement; extn.—calligraphy; stroke
xiǎng	to think, intend; consider; to miss (i.e., remember lovingly)
mǎi	to buy, purchase
zhī	to support; pay or draw money; branch, stem [MW]; a surname; (alt. pron. **zhǐ**—only, merely)
dá	dozen; (alt. pron. **dǎ**—to strike, break, etc.)
jù	clause, sentence; also MW for a sentence
huà	[spoken] word; extn.—language, speech

RATIONALE AND INTERPRETATION

Máobǐ. The word **bǐ** traditionally conjures up in a Chinese mind the picture of a brush, which even today may be the implement used for writing. A different picture is created, however, when the word is modified, as in:

fénbǐ (*powder pen*)	chalk
qiānbǐ (*lead pen*)	pencil
shuǐbǐ (*water pen*)	fountain pen

The last compound is an abbreviated rendering of the cumbersome former term **zìlái-mòshuǐbǐ** (*self-come ink-pen*).

The compound term for a Chinese writing brush is **máobǐ** (*hair pen*), held to be one of the Four Treasures (i.e., ink, paper, brush, and inkslab). The brush-pen is said to have been developed before 200 BC when the Chinese script was first standardized during the reign of the emperor Qin Shihuang. Conventionally the handle or barrel of the brush is made of a tube of bamboo; this is the origin of the MW **zhī** (a stem). This MW is applied to most writing implements, as they are long and tubular in shape. The tip of the brush is usually made of goat, wolf, fox, or even sable hairs, which are trimmed to a point. Brushes come in many sizes—up to two feet in length for sign-writing—and they serve equally well for art as they do for calligraphy.

Yào jǐkuàiqián? The use of **yào** in this context means to want. The term **jǐkuàiqián** is slightly ambiguous, since it could mean a few dollars or how many dollars. As a query, it is obvious that in this case **jǐ** is a QW, and is used here as an alternative to **duōshao**. While the two expressions may appear to be synonymous, and therefore interchangeable, in fact **jǐ** is used more for small amounts, say 10 or fewer items, while **duōshao** implies larger figures, as shown in the following examples:

Tā yóu jǐge háizi?	How many children has she?
Jiēshang yǒu duōshao rén?	How many people are on the street?

In Chinese, as in English, there are various ways of asking the price of something. For example:

Zhè *yào* **duōshao qián?**	How much is *wanted* for this [or these]?
Nǐ *yào* **duōshao qián?**	How much money do you *want*?
Nà *shì* **duōshao qián?**	How much *is* that?

Máobǐ *mài* **duōshao qián?** How much do brushes *sell* for?

Máobǐ duōshao? How much [for] brushes?

The reply in Chinese may be simply the statement of a sum of money, or a more complete response, such as:

Máobǐ sānkuàibàn yìzhī. Pens [are] $3.50 each.

Sānshiwǔkuài mǎi yìdá. $35 *buys* a dozen.

In order to highlight a tempting special offer, the price figure could be quoted first. In such cases, **mǎi** (to purchase) is used in the sense of will buy [you] or will get [for you] . . . and is followed by a quantity of the commodity.

Mǎi means to buy or to purchase, and is also compounded with **mài** (to sell) thus forming the term **mǎimai**. This means buying and selling or, in other words, business. Note that the second syllable of the compound is toneless. Be sure not to confuse the tones of these two antithetical words.

Zhè yào kàn has the direct meaning of it depends on, being literally "this requires looking [at]." What needs to be looked at is the number [of pens] wanted. In this case, rather than overwork **yào** (to want), the word **xiǎng** (to think, consider, or, by extension, to contemplate) is used instead.

Kěshi means but, as compared with **yàoshi** meaning if. While in English one can say "but if," in Chinese **kěshi** would suffice.

Yìdá means one dozen. This term is borrowed from **dǎ** (to knock or to strike) and in the second tone is used solely for this meaning. It should only be used in connection with objects. For instance, in English one can talk about a dozen people, but in Chinese the term is never associated with human beings.

Hǎole. As an exclamation, **hǎole** means "All right" or "O.K.," but here it implies that the purchase of three pens would be satisfactory.

Gěi is used here in the original sense of to give. As it follows from the previous sentence and the subject is still **wǒ** (I), there is no need to repeat what is obvious. Thus, **gěi** serves to indicate an offer, i.e., "[I will] give you $10."

Yíjùhuà—Obviously the bargaining process would take longer than it does in the micro-scenario presented here. However, sooner or later the bottom line is reached and the expression used at that point is **yíjùhuà**— "[Just] one word," (i.e., this is my final figure).

7.3   ACCOUNTS AND EXCHANGE

Money exchange is readily achieved in China. In fact, almost from time immemorial money-changers have made quite a lucrative living off travellers throughout the land. Nowadays all the major hotels have a counter in the Reception area, where a Bank of China teller will be available to effect the exchange. Whereas FEC is what is usually doled out to the visitor, this is not to say that RMB cannot be obtained as well. This makes it possible to buy things off the street-stalls or in the market-place, where either Chinese currency can be exchanged on a one-for-one basis. The main thing for visitors to remember is to retain not only the exchange receipt forms, but also the Customs declaration forms for incoming passengers. This is to avoid any clandestine disposal of valuables by visitors, as their holdings on departure from China will be compared with what was brought in! Converting Chinese currency back to hard currency is not difficult, since visitors are not allowed to take RMB with them when leaving China, and RMB is not negotiable outside the country. But exchange receipts should be kept handy.

R: **Wǒ yào huán zhàng. Qǐng géi wǒ kāi zhàngdān.**
I want repay account. Request for me open bill-form.
I want to settle my account. Please make out my bill for me.

C: **Zhàngdān dōu suàn hǎo-le. Zhè jiù shì.**
Bill-form all calculated complete. This then be.
Your bill has all been worked out. Here it is.

R: **Kǒngpà xiànqián búgòu. Yòng lǔxíng-zhīpiào kéyǐ ma?**
Afraid existing-money not enough. Use travel-cheque can, eh?
I'm afraid I don't have enough cash. Is it O.K. to use a travellers' cheque?

C: **Méi wèntí! Suí nǐ-de biàn.**
No question! Follow your convenience.
No problem! Please yourself.

R: **Wǒ zhèr yǒu Měiyuán lǚxíng-zhīpiào, kéyǐ géi wǒ duìhuàn ma?**
I here have U.S.-dollar travel-cheques, can give me exchange, eh?
I have here travellers' cheques in U.S. funds, can you exchange them for me?

C: **Dāngrán kéyǐ! Nǐ yào huàn duōshǎo?**
Naturally can! You want exchange how-much?
Certainly! How much do you want to exchange?

R: **Wó xiǎng sìbǎikuài zúgòule.**
I think 400-dollars sufficient-enough.
I think $400 should be adequate.

C: **Qǐng géi wó nǐ-de hùzhào kànyikàn; hǎi děi zhīpiào-shàng dāngmiàn fùshǔ-qiānmíng.**
Request give me your passport look-a-look; also require cheque-on in presence duplicate-signature sign-name.
Let me see your passport, please; you also need to countersign the cheques in front of me.

Zhèizhāng shēnbàodān yě yào qiān-shàng zì.
This sheet [MW] application-form also want sign-on letters.
This application form requires signing as well.

VOCABULARY

huán	to give back, repay (alt. pron. hái—still; also)
zhàng	curtain, canopy; account, debt
kāi	to open; extn.—begin, start, operate; to list
yòng	to use, employ, apply; extn.—usefulness, need
lǚ	travel, to stay away from home
zhī	to support; extn.—branch; pay or draw [funds]; a surname
piào	ticket; ballot; extn.—note, bill
tí	topic, title; problem; to describe
suí	follow; comply, go along with, extn.—let (i.e., up to you)
duì	to exchange, convert; to add [i.e., water, etc.]
huàn	to exchange, barter, trade; extn.—to change

měi	beautiful; extn.—good; term denoting U.S.A.
yuán	round, circular; extn.—monetary unit, i.e., dollar [$]
rán	right, correct; so; however; suddenly
hù	protect, guard, shield
zhào	shine, reflect; extn.—to photograph
miàn	face, extn.—reputation; prestige; surface, aspect
fù	deputy, vice-; extn.—auxiliary; duplicate; MW
shǔ	office; to arrange; to sign
qiān	to sign, autograph; label, sticker
zhāng	open, spread, display; [MW]; a surname
shēn	to declare, express, explain; a surname
bào	to report, announce, declare; extn.—respond
zì	character, word; name

RATIONALE AND INTERPRETATION

Huán zhàng (*repay account*) is the term meaning to pay, or to settle the bill. The word **huán** which also has another pronunciation **hái** meaning yet, here means to return (i.e., to come or go back) and, by extension to give back or to repay. **Zhàng** means account or debt.

Kāi zhàngdān means to make out a bill. **Kāi** has a wide range of meanings, all essentially to do with opening [up]. Both **kāizhàng[dān]** and **suànzhàng** mean to calculate or make out a bill, but each also has a secondary meaning which should be clear from the context in which it is used. **Kāizhàng** can also mean to settle or pay a bill, while **suànzhàng** has the added sense of settling an old score or getting even!

Zhàngdān dōu suàn hǎo-le shows how one can transpose the object to the subject's normal position in a sentence. Note the function of **hǎo-le**, with **hǎo** (good) being used to indicate satisfactory, completely, and, by extension, ready or finished, and **-le** being used to indicate that the action has been completed. Further emphasis is given by the presence of **dōu** (all). Thus, the sentence means "The bill's all ready!" (Similarly, in the next question, **kéyǐ** is transposed to the end of the sentence so as to emphasize the query; otherwise **kéyǐ yòng** is quite correct.)

Lǚxíng-zhīpiào. The term **lǚxíng** means travel. In this case it modifies the compound **zhīpiào**, meaning cheque, thus creating the compound for travellers' cheque[s]. Note the word order, whereby the modifying words or phrases precede the key word.

Xiànqián. **Qián,** the word for money or cash, when compounded with **xiàn,** means ready cash, since **xiàn** (present or current), by extension means ready in a monetary context. This term should not be confused with **língqián** (odd money), which signifies loose or small change.

Méi-[yǒu] wèntí! "No problem!" **Méi** is the elliptical form of **méiyǒu** (not have), just as No is the elliptical form of "There is no. . . ." **Wèntí,** depending upon the context, can mean quite simply a question. It could be misleading to simply say **Wó yǒu yíge wèntí,** since this could equally mean "I have a problem" or "I have a question (to ask)." If the latter were the case, it would be as well to say **Wó yǒu yíge wèntí xiǎng wèn,** which indicates clearly "I have a question I'd like to ask."

Suíbiàn is a most useful expression, particularly in social circumstances for putting someone at ease. It can be used as an equivalent for a number of English expressions, including: "Make yourself comfortable" or "Make yourself at home," "Suit yourself" or "Help yourself," and—closer to the literal sense—"at your convenience." **Suí** needs only the introduction given in the Vocabulary, but **biàn** can do with a little more explanation. The alternative pronunciation **pián** occurs in the compound **piányi** (cheap, inexpensive). The insertion of **nǐ-de** between **suí** and **biàn** simply emphasizes the permission given (e.g., "Do as you please").

Měiyuán stands for US dollars, with **yuán** being the word for dollar (round), and not only in terms of Chinese currency. While the basic meaning of **Měi** is beautiful, here the term represents in brief the USA, rather as **Huá** stands for China. It is doubtful whether the song "America the Beautiful" had much influence on the choice of the character **měi** to represent America, **měi** being the first significant syllable in the transliteration **Yā-měi-lì-jiā.** To differentiate between the main parts of the American continent, which—as a whole—is called **Měizhōu,** the Chinese refer to:

Béi Měi(zhōu)	North America
Zhōng Měi(zhōu)	Central America
Nán Měi(zhōu)	South America
Měiguó	United States of America

Note that the word **zhōu** (continent) may be omitted in the interests of brevity.

Duìhuàn means to exchange. It is a compound of two words, both of which have much the same import. **Duì** is not often used outside of this context; **huàn** however has a wider application, as shown in the Vocabulary.

Dāngrán. Here is an expression which—depending on the context—can mean certainly, without a doubt, of course, to be sure, as well as naturally, in the sense of as it should be.

Zúgòule means adequate or ample and generally can be applied in the same way as these words are in English to indicate a sufficiency.

Hùzhào is the compound for passport. It is essential for foreign visitors to carry their passports with them at all times. Apart from serving as identification, a passport is always necessary to conform with bureaucratic requirements when filling in application forms for exchange purposes and receiving exchange receipts with the money. Often the application form will be completed by the clerk and all you need do is sign it.

Dāngmiàn. Two distinct words make up this compound. **Dāng** has the meaning of "in the presence of," and **miàn** means face. These combine to mean in front of me or in my presence. The usual procedure when presenting a traveller's cheque is, of course, to countersign the cheque in the teller's presence.

Fùshǔ-qiānmíng is the term for countersignature. **Fùshǔ** (*duplicate sign*) and **qiānmíng** (*sign name*) combine to give this meaning, although they can be used separately as well. **Qiānmíng**, for example, is interchangeable with **qiānzì**, which occurs in the next sentence. By themselves, either of these two compounds can be used simply to mean to sign one's name.

Zhāng is used here as a MW. In conjunction with a number of nouns which imply a surface or spread, it may be considered synonymous with sheet, e.g., **yìzhāng zhǐ** (a sheet of paper). In Chinese this MW is also used with such items as pictures, maps, tables, or beds. Naturally a document such as an application form ranks as a sheet of paper.

Shēnbàodān is the term for an application form. It is, in effect, a compound within another. **Shēnbào** (*declare report*) means to report [to an authority], or to declare, as to a Customs officer. When changing currency, it is of course necessary to enter the particulars on a form, or **dān**, used here in the sense of a form or list. Other examples of the use of **dān** are:

dānzi	list, bill, form, schedule
càidān (*dish list*)	menu, bill of fare

jiémùdān (*division contents list*)	program, playbill
míngdān (*name list*)	nominal roll
wèntídān (*question list*)	questionnaire
zhàngdān (*account form*)	bill, check

-shàng. Note the use of this word, first with a noun, i.e., **zhīpiào-shàng** (on the cheque), and then with a verb, i.e., **qiān-shàng zì** (*sign on word*). **Qiānzì** means the same as **qiānmíng** (to sign or autograph). **Zì**, which basically means a character, by extension also means style of writing, and hence style of signature. In this context, the verb **qiān** with the suffix **-shàng** is used in the sense of affixing a signature on a form, or applying one's initials on a slip.

SUPPLEMENTARY VOCABULARY

zhīhuìbù	chequebook
dìngqián	deposit, down payment
zhékou	discount
duìhuànsuǒ	exchange office
duìhuànlǜ	exchange rate
lìqián	interest
dàiyù	remuneration
xīnshui	salary, pay
gōngqian	wages
bàozhǐ	newspaper
shóuzhǐ	toilet paper
bāozhuāngzhǐ	wrapping paper

EIGHT

GOING PLACES

"A wise man adapts himself to circumstances, as water shapes itself to the vessel that contains it."

Most Chinese cities have yet to develop a downtown as in the West. Nonetheless, western influence has had sufficient impact on the larger cities to create areas of commercial centralization, known as **shāngyèqū**. Many Chinese cities still retain their castellated walls and magnificent gateways, while others—like Beijing—have seen fit in the interest of modernization to demolish the walls which gave the word **chéng** (i.e., city) its original meaning. Within such confines were to be found areas containing concentrations of certain industries. Often streets are named after guilds, recognisable in such titles as Dengshikou (Lantern Market Entrance), or Xila Hutong (Pewter Lane), also places like the Meat Market (Roushi) or the Vegetable Market (Caishi). Such locales comprise what may be considered downtown areas in many municipalities, and are often referred to colloquially as **nàoshì** (busy markets). Chinese visitors abroad often use the expression **shìzhōngxīn** which is a direct translation of town center.

In many western cities, the area where Chinese businesses are concentrated is known as Chinatown. In Chinese this term is **Tángrénjiē**, which means the Streets of the Tang People. The Chinese have several ways of referring to themselves:

Zhōngguorén	the Chinese people
Láobǎixìng	Chinese term for their masses
Huáqiáo	Overseas Chinese

Hànrén	Han people
Tángrén	Tang people

Most Overseas Chinese are originally from South China. While the term **Zhōngguorén** refers to a Chinese citizen of any ethnic origin, **Hànrén** excludes the minority tribes which co-exist in China. It alludes to the Han Dynasties (206 BC-24 AD, and 25-219 AD), which followed on from the Qin Dynasty (246-207 BC), which were periods of the nation's greatest historical development and grandeur. In South China the Tang Dynasty (618-906 AD) is considered to be of greater significance, and the one to which the Southerners relate themselves more closely. Overseas Chinese were prone to refer to themselves as Tang people, regardless of their place of origin.

Note that the second syllable in **Zhōngguorén** is toneless. When **guó** appears as the last syllable of any country's name, it is given its full tone value. However, when it is used in an adjectival role, the tone is not stressed, for example:

Yīngguo yǔyán	the English language
wàiguorén	foreigner(s)
Fǎguo fànguǎn	French restaurant

8.1 PLACES DOWNTOWN

R: **Wó xiǎng qù kànyikàn chéngshì-shāngyèqū.**
I think go look-a-look town-business-district.
I'm thinking of looking around downtown.

C: **Ní yǒu shénme tèbié dìfang yào qù kàn ma?**
You have what special place want go look eh?
Have you any special place[s] you want to go and see?

R: **Wó xiǎng zhīdao nár zhǎo yínháng, lǔxíngshè, yóuzhèngjú, bǎihuòdiàn, zhè zhǒng dìfang.**
I contemplate know where find bank, travel agency, post office, department store, this type place.
I'd like to know where to find the bank[s], a travel agency, post office, department stores, places like these.

C: **Zhèxiē dìfang dōu háo zhǎo, yīnwei wǒmen zhèige lǚguǎn lí nàr chàbuduō dōu hěn jìn.**

This lot places all good find, because we this hotel separate there nearly all very close.

These places are all easy to find, because nearly all of them are very close to our hotel.

VOCABULARY

qù	to go [away], leave, to do away with
chéng	city wall, wall; extn.—city, town
shāng	to discuss; extn.—business, trade; a surname
qū	area, district; division, extn.—to classify
tè	special; specially; unusual
bié	to leave; other; don't; (abbrev. of **búyào**)
zhī	to know, realize, be aware of; inform
dào	road, way, path; method; extn.—principle
zhǎo	to seek, look for, find; extn.—ask for, call on
yín	silver—relating also to money or coin
háng	business firm, trade, profession (alt. pron. **xíng**)
shè	organized body; extn.—agency, society
yóu	mail, post, postal
jú	chessboard; extn.—game, innings; office, bureau
bǎi	hundred; extn.—numerous, all kinds of
huò	goods, commodity; money, extn.—to sell
diàn	shop, store
xiē	a few, some
guǎn	inn, hostelry; office; hall, pavilion
lí	part from, leave, away, from; extn.—without
nàr	that place, those places; there
jìn	near, close, extn.—recent

RATIONALE AND INTERPRETATION

Qù. This word means to go, in the sense of movement, but essentially it indicates a movement away from one's present location. This is especially apparent when the word is used as an auxiliary to an active verb. In this particular usage, the meaning is simply that of going to another place for a specific purpose.

Kànyikàn means to take a look at. Duplication of the verb renders the meaning less formal or specific, and at the same time implies for a while, thus protracting the action of looking, to yield looking around. The presence of the **yī** is not essential, except to make the expression mandatory, thus **Nǐ kànyikàn** equals "You have a look," whereas **kànkan zhèige** implies "Look at this!"

Chéngshì is the compound for city or town, and is used as those words are in English to denote sizeable urban communities. This compound is the combination of two characters denoting a walled municipality.

Shāngyèqū is the term used for the business or commercial district in a city; **shāngyè** means business, trade or commerce, while **qū** denotes an area or region.

Tèbié means special or especially.

Zhīdao means to know. The two components of this compound are interesting, insofar as **zhī** has to do with knowledge and awareness, and **dào** is considered very much in the same manner as way is in English. The latter character is used to represent both the Way referred to in the Holy Bible and Taoism, despite the slight change in romanized spelling, i.e., from Tao to Dao.

Yínháng, literally a business house dealing in silver (in the sense of coin or currency), is the compound word for a bank. As part of an official designation it follows the bank's name. Thus **Zhōngguó Yínháng** is Chinese for the Bank of China.

Lǚxíngshè. This compound means a travel agency or tourist bureau. There is little differentiation between these terms in the Chinese mind, since all such offices in mainland China are enveloped by the monolithic state-owned China International Travel Service. The CITS is usually referred to simply as the **Lǚxíngshè. Lǚxíng** by itself means travel (noun or verb). When **shè** is added to a compound, it denotes an organized staff or body dealing with that compound's subject matter.

Yóujú is an abbreviated form of **yóuzhèngjú. Yóuzhèng** refers to the postal service or administration, and the compound created by adding **jú** indicates the local offices where postal services are rendered.

Bǎihuòdiàn is an abbreviated compound used for a department store, and is the combination of **bǎihuò**, meaning general merchandise, and **shāngdiàn**, which means store or shop.

Zhè zhǒng dìfang means this sort of place.

Háo zhǎo means easy to find. **Hǎo** (whose tone has been modified here, as it precedes a third tone word) has a wide variety of uses; here it indicates easy [to do] or convenient. After all, what could be more good—the basic meaning of **hǎo**!

Lǚguǎn is the modern term used for hotel. However, a traditional term still in common use is **fàndiàn** (*food inn*), signifying an establishment providing food as well as accommodation. Many hotels use the term **fàndiàn** in their titles (e.g., **Běijīng Fàndiàn** = Peking Hotel, **Jīnlíng Fàndiàn** = the Jinling Hotel [Nanking's finest], or **Bái Tiān'é Fàndiàn** = the White Swan Hotel in **Guǎngzhōu** [i.e., Canton]). Such hotels include restaurant facilities for nonresident visitors. These facilities are not necessarily to be found in other establishments such as hostels or guesthouses. **Fàndiàn** is not to be confused with **fànguǎn**, which is the appropriate term for a restaurant.

Lí nàr indicates from there, i.e., [away] from those [places just mentioned]. **Lí**—despite its use as a verb meaning to separate—is very frequently used as an equivalent of the preposition from. **Nàr** is a contracted form, commonly heard in Beijing, of the formal **nàlǐ** (*therein*) implying in that place.

Chàbuduō (*lack not much*) means nearly or almost. This useful compound is used in about the same way as its English equivalent.

Dōu hěn jìn means all very near. Whereas the visitor wants to establish the location of a number of places downtown in relation to the hotel, the receptionist naturally bases her outlook on the location of the hotel in relation to those places. Hence the discrepancy between the English dialogue and the Chinese version which actually states "... because this hotel of ours is very close to nearly all of them."

8.2   IDENTIFYING BUILDINGS

R: **Qǐngwèn, wǒ zhèr xiě-de dìzhǐ lí zhèr yuǎn buyuǎn?**
Invite-query, I here write-of place-location separate here far not-far?
Excuse me, is the address which I have written [down] far from here?

C: **Ní zhǎo Guójì Shūdiàn! Zhèr jiù kuài dàole; nèige dìfang zhèng zài zhèitiáo dàjiē-shàng. Yí guò qiánbiar nèige lùkǒu, nǐ yídìng kàndejiàn.**

You seek international bookshop. Here just soon reach; that one place precisely at this length [MW] big-street-on. Once cross front-side that street-mouth, you certainly look-able see.

You're looking for the International Bookstore! You're nearly there; that place is right on this avenue. As soon as you cross the intersection ahead, you're bound to see it.

R: **Nàme, zhè shì shénme dìfang?**

Then, this be what place?

So what place is this?

C: **Zhè shì Guójì Lǚxíngshè bànshìchù.**

This be international travel agency office.

This is the [China] International Travel Service office.

R: **Nèige dà lóu ne?**

That one big building then?

[And] that large building?

C: **Nà shì yíge zhǎnlánguǎn.**

That be one piece display hall.

That is an Exhibition Centre.

R: **Duìbuqǐ máfan nǐ!**

Facing-not-rise trouble you!

Sorry to trouble you!

C: **Búyào kèqi! Yìdiǎr ye bù-máfan!**

Not-need courtesy! A little even not-trouble!

No trouble at all!

VOCABULARY

xiě	to write; extn.—to compose; describe
zhǐ	location, site

yuǎn	far, distant, remote
jì	border, boundary; extn.—between, inter-
shū	to write, writing style; extn.—book, document
kuài	fast, quick; extn.—soon; hurry [up]; sharp; pleased
zhèng	straight, upright; main; correct, precisely
tiáo	twig; a long narrow piece or slip, [MW]; extn.—item
jiē	street
biān	side, edge; border; extn.—limit; a surname
lù	road, way; extn.—journey, route; surname
kǒu	mouth; extn.—opening, entrance; port; [MW]; hole
dé	to obtain, gain; result in; -able; (alt. pron. děi)
chù	place; extn.—office; (alt. pron. chǔ—to manage)
lóu	a storied building
zhǎn	to unfold; exhibit; extn.—to extend; a surname
lǎn	to look at, view, see
má	hemp, flax; coarse, pitted; a surname
fán	to be vexed, irritated; extn.—tired of, trouble

RATIONALE AND INTERPRETATION

Xiě-de dìzhǐ means "the address which is written [down]" and contains a relative clause utilizing the particle -de. There are several ways of using this important little particle. These are summarized in the Appendix,

When the British refer to their Royal Air Force or other armed services whose titles include the word Royal, it is considered tautological to refer to nationality. In other words, they would never refer to the British Royal Air Force. Similarly, when the China International Travel Service is referred to in Chinese, it is considered superfluous to use the word China as part of its title.

It should also be borne in mind that when the Chinese refer to their own language, internal affairs, and so on, they assume that people will understand that they are talking about themselves unless they indicate otherwise. For example, **guóyǔ**—meaning national language—refers to the Chinese national language (as spoken in, say, Taiwan); and **guónèi** alludes to [affairs] within [their own] country.

Section 13. In the case in hand, -de serves to introduce a modifying clause. In essence, it is used as a relative pronoun; hence its English equivalent may be which, that, who or whom. The particle -de is usually placed after the modifier which precedes the object under reference. In this case, the modifier is **xiě** (to write) and the noun is **dìzhǐ** (*place location*), meaning address. Chinese consistently work from the general to the specific. For example an address in Chinese would be written as follows:

1. People's Republic of China
2. Harbin, 150010, Heilongjiang Province
3. Harbin Educational Committee, 133 Shitoudao
4. Zhen Peide, Director of Foreign Affairs Dept.

Remember that the individuals' names begin with the surname, with the title coming last.

Lí zhèr means from here, and is used in the same way as **lí nàr**.

Yuǎn is an equational verb meaning [to be] far, and is the opposite of **jìn** (near). The questions have been phrased in a V. not-V. manner; the reply, however, is given in the affirmative without reference to the verbal choice.

Guójì Shūdiàn is the International Bookstore, **guójì** being the compound for international, while **shūdiàn** means bookshop or bookstore.

Zhèr jiù kuài dàole. To analyze this, let us work back from the end of the sentence. **Dào** here means to arrive, and the suffix **le** indicates the completion of an action. **Kuài** here has the meaning of soon or almost, so that **kuài dàole** means almost arrived. **Jiù** has an active role in Chinese syntax which is not necessarily duplicated in English. When **zhèr** and **jiù** are combined, the essence of the two words is *here then*, so that virtually the sentence means "Here then [you have] almost arrived," i.e., "You're nearly there."

Zhèng zài often means *in the process of*, but here the expression more closely approximates the meaning of precisely at or right on.

Zhèi tiáo dàjiē-shàng means on this avenue. Whereas **jiē** means simply street, **dàjiē** refers to a main street or avenue, though not necessarily one which runs east and west (as in Canada). This calls for the use of a MW, i.e., **tiáo**, thus **zhèi tiáo dàjiē** means this avenue. **Shàng** serves as the preposition on in this instance.

Yí guò here means "as soon as you cross." **Yī** is the word for one, while **guò** means—among other things—to pass or cross over; hence the sense of *once you have crossed over*.

Lùkǒu (*road mouth*) means street corner, road junction, or intersection.

Yídìng is the term used to mean definitely or certainly.

Kàndejiàn. The word **-de** (sometimes pronounced **děi**), means to obtain or to gain. (It is not the same as the particle in the term **xiě-de**.) Here, it is the equivalent of the English verbal suffix -able. In this instance, it is used to affirm that by looking (**kàn**) it will be possible to see or to encounter (**jiàn**).

Bànshìchù means literally the *handling affairs place*, that is to say an office, in the broadest sense of the word. If the office referred to is the room in which one works, the expression **bàngōngshì**—i.e., *handle business room*—is more appropriate. The general office, where the typing or bookkeeping takes place, and where the clerks or secretaries work, is called the **shìwùsuǒ**—the *general affairs room*. Overall, however, **bànshìchù** will suffice.

Dà lóu. Since any building of two or more floors in height is referred to by the word **lóu**, **dà lóu** (i.e., big building) simply refers to a large structure or a high-rise.

Zhánlǎn is a compound meaning to exhibit. When the word **guǎn** is added, the term becomes a display or exhibition centre (*exhibit view hall*).

Máfan nǐ is an expression used to apologize for causing any inconvenience, since **máfan** means trouble or bother.

Búyào kèqi is an expression which is used to put a person at ease. The compound **kèqi** on its own means polite or courteous and, by extension, modest. Therefore the whole expression, often used in Chinese, conveys the assurance that there is "no need for courtesy" or "no need to stand on ceremony." In the appropriate context, it may simply mean "Relax!"

Yě (also), placed before a verb to stress a point, means even, and is interchangeable with **dōu** (all); either word, when used with **yìdiǎr** and a negative verb, expresses the meaning not at all. Chinese people tend to make less use of the stereotypical expressions Westerners consider adequate for the sake of courtesy. This is not to say that it is out of place to say simply "Hello," or "Thank you," "Goodbye" or "Sorry." That there are Chinese equivalents for such expressions is already apparent; but the

Chinese have a wide range of other expressions which they are more prone to use. Hence, instead of the prosaic form of thanks being given, a more typical Chinese expression is offered.

⊙⊙ SUPPLEMENTARY VOCABULARY

měishùguǎn	art gallery
lǐfàdiàn	barbershop, hairdresser
cānguǎn	cafe
diànyǐngyuàn	cinema
lǐngshìguǎn	consulate
bīnguǎn	guesthouse, hotel
túshūguǎn	library
jiǔlóu	licensed restaurant
bówùguǎn	museum
zhàoxiàngguǎn	photo studio
yóulǎn	sightseeing
cháguǎn	teahouse
fēngjǐng	view
xīcān-guǎnzi	western cuisine restaurant
dòngwùyuán	zoo

NINE

GETTING
DIRECTIONS

"Don't look for a phoenix in a
hen's nest."

One place in China most foreigners will visit is the capital, Beijing. An old adage states that "China is a sea which salts all waters flowing into it." Similarly Beijing, arising from the historical township of Yanjing, has blended the culture and pageantry of centuries of dynastic rulers who moulded this great nation. In particular the Manchu emperor, Qianlong, of the Qing Dynasty, made the greatest visual impact on the city until recent times. Despite the demolition of the city wall with its magnificent gateways, much of the majesty of the imperial days is still to be seen along its main streets running north/south and east/west as in many modern cities of today. In consequence it is not difficult to get around when sightseeing or shopping.

The Palace Museum, formerly referred to as the Forbidden City, may justly be considered the focal point for sightseers to Beijing. To the west are the three man-made lakes of what were referred to as the Sea Palaces (dating back to the twelfth century), and the earth from further excavations was piled up to create Prospect Hill (**Jǐngshān**) to the north of the Palace walls. On this hill (originally known as the Coal Hill) are five pavilions, or gazebos, which offer splendid views of the capital, extending as far west as the Western Hills when visibility permits. To the south can be seen the roof of one of the best known and most beautiful temples in China. The Temple of Heaven—as it is referred to in foreign guide books—is known as the Altar of Heaven (**Tiāntán**) to the Chinese. (Else-

Heart of Beijing
Běijīng Zhōngxīn Huàtú

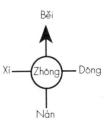

Běi
Xī — Zhōng — Dòng
Nán

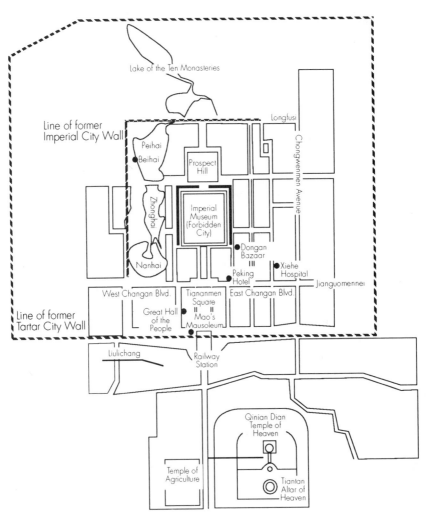

Lake of the Ten Monasteries

Longfusi

Line of former
Imperial City Wall

Peihai

Beihai

Prospect
Hill

Chongwenmen Avenue

Zhonghai

Imperial
Museum
(Forbidden
City)

Dongan
Bazaar

Xiehe
Hospital

Nanhai

Peking
Hotel

West Changan Blvd.

Tiananmen
Square

East Changan Blvd.

Jianguomennei

Line of former
Tartar City Wall

Great Hall
of the
People

Mao's
Mausoleum

Liulichang

Railway
Station

Qinian Dian
Temple of
Heaven

Temple of
Agriculture

Tiantan
Altar of
Heaven

where in Beijing are to be found the Altar of the Earth and the Altar of the Sun). It is situated in a walled park, about three and a half miles in circumference. Dating back to 1420 AD, it is of great historical importance. The altar is made of white marble in three circular terraces, ranging from 90 feet in diameter at the top to 210 feet in diameter at the base. To the north of the great altar is a circular walled enclosure (which boasts a remarkable echo) situated with an octagonal building that was used for ceremonial purposes at the time of the annual sacrifices to the imperial ancestry in accordance with Confucian doctrine. Still further north, on a magnificent marble terrace, stands a circular edifice—90 feet high, with a beautifully proportioned triple-tiered blue-tiled roof. This is the Hall for Harvest Prayers (**Qínián Diàn**) where the Emperor—the Son of Heaven—prayed before his ancestral tablets once each year, asking his forebears to intercede for an abundant harvest. The building is in a splendid state of preservation, being less than a century old. The original structure was completely destroyed by lightning in 1899 and took ten years to rebuild. It was the ceremony of sacrifice at the altar that was significant. As the most important of State observances, it took place on the day of the Winter Solstice and was performed by the Emperor in person, in order to ensure good harvests for the ensuing year.

9.1   ASKING THE WAY

R.   **Qǐngwèn, Béihǎi lí zhèr hén yuǎn ma?**
      Invite-query, North-Sea separate here very far, eh?
      Tell me, is the Winter Palace far from here?

C: **Gòu yuǎn. Cóng zhèr děi wàng xībéi zǒu.**
      Sufficient far. From here need towards west-north walk.
      Far enough. From here you'll need to walk to the Northwest.

R: **Háo zhǎo ma?**
      Easy find, eh?
      Is it easy to find?

C: **Hǎo zhǎo, yīnwei zhèng zài Jǐngshān-gōngyuán xībiar.**
Easy find, because precisely at View-Hill-Park west-side.
Very easy, as it is just west of Prospect Hill Park.

R: **Zuǒbiar nèige dàlóu shì shénme dìfang?**
Left-side that big-building be what place?
What is that big building on the left?

C: **Nà jiù shì Běijīng Fàndiàn.**
That just be Beijing Hotel.
That's the Peking Hotel.

R: **Zài wàng nán qù yǒu shénme tèbié-de dìfang ma?**
Again towards south go have what special place, eh?
Are there any places of note further to the south?

C: **Yàoshi dào nánbiar qù jiù kéyi kànkan Tiāntán.**
Suppose reach southside go then can look-look Heaven Altar.
If you go south you can visit the Temple of Heaven.

The four cardinal points of the compass are named:

dōng	east
nán	south
xī	west
běi	north

Since western navigators use the North Pole or North Star as a point of reference from which to measure direction, the tendency is to work round the compass from North to South, and East to West. The Chinese, have a different—but equally logical—approach to direction-finding. Since the Sun appears daily in the East, this is used as the cardinal datum point. As the Sun appears to move in a clockwise direction, the Chinese refer to the cardinal points of the compass in that same sequence, East—South—West—North. Although the compass needle is subject to the magnetic north, the Chinese—ever since they began using the lodestone compass over 2000 years ago—refer to it as the south-indicating needle (**zhǐnánzhēn**).

In addition, the Chinese use a fifth main point of reference on the compass card, that is

zhōng   center

The rationale here is obvious when one considers that one's present position is the datum point from which the direction is being assessed. The sub-cardinal points, also referred to in a clockwise sequence, are as follows:

dōngnán (east [of] south)   southeast
xīnán (west [of] south)   southwest
xībĕi (west [of] north)   northwest
dōngbĕi (east [of] north)   northeast

VOCABULARY

hăi	sea, large lake; extn.—great capacity; a surname
cóng	from, through; ext.—comply with
dĕi	need, must, have to (alt. pron. **dé**)
wàng	to, toward
zŏu	to walk; to go [away]; to escape, leak out
jĭng	view, scenery; extn.—situation, condition, a surname
shān	hill, mountain; a surname
yuán	area for growing plants; recreation ground
zuŏ	left side; different, contrary; a surname
jīng	capital [of a country]; extn.—abbreviation for **Bĕijīng**
zài	a second time, again, once more
kĕ	to approve; extn.—may; however; (preceding a verb)-able

RATIONALE AND INTERPRETATION

Béihăi, alludes to what is generally known as the Winter Palace, which—apart from its many other attractions—is well known for its landmark of the White Dagoba. This is the northernmost of the Sea Palaces, hence the name of the North Sea for this lake. (The so-called Summer Palace is in the western suburbs of the city.) The other two lakes, **Zhōnghăi** and **Nánhăi** (Central and South Seas respectively) are currently not open to the public, providing as they do secluded residences set in beautiful surroundings for the government leaders. The water supply for the lakes springs from the Jade Fountain, which is located in the Western Hills near the Summer Palace. **Běi** occurs in numerous Chinese titles. Of course the best known is Beijing, which stands for Northern Capital. By the same token, Nanjing refers to what was the southern capital in the early Ming Dynasty, as well as just before World War II. Similarly, one will hear North China referred to as Huabei. The term **běifāng** is often used to denote the northern part of a country, and where China is concerned this alludes to the area north of the Yellow River (Huanghe). Thus Northerners are known as **běifāngrén**, just as Southerners are called **nánfāngrén**.

Lí zhèr hén yuǎn—Lí zhèr means [away] from here and **hén yuǎn** means very far. The clause **lí zhèr hén yuǎn** becomes interrogative by placing the particle **ma** at the end.

Gòu yuǎn. On its own, **gòu** means sufficient or, by extension, to reach, and thereby [to be] really or [to be] rather. In this instance, therefore, the full expression means quite far or rather far away, since **yuǎn** means distant or far.

Děi is the alternative pronunciation for **dé**. Used in the third tone, it has the meaning of necessity or requirement.

Wàng may also be pronounced in the third tone, but in either tone the word has much the same meaning, i.e., to or toward. In Chinese syntax this word is essential for indicating direction of movement.

Xīběi. Should one be situated somewhere to the east of the Palace Museum in Beijing, to reach the Winter Palace would necessitate heading westward and to the north—hence the Chinese rendering of **xīběi** (*west north*) for northwest in a clockwise sequence.

Zǒu has the primary sense of to walk, and therefore, by extension, means to move or to go away. It is obvious from the context what the subject is, therefore there is no need to specify it. The logic of this sentence construction is based on the verb "to go." As the sentence has no object, the verb is the last word, and since **zǒu** has the basic meaning of walking, it implies going on foot. Had the original question come up in a vehicle, the appropriate verb would most likely have been **qù** (to go). **Děi** is used as an auxiliary verb, hence the meaning of need to walk. The modifying phrase *to the northwest* precedes the main verb and indicates the direction to go, while **cóng zhèr** (*from here*) is at the head of the sentence, indicating the starting point from which the movement takes place.

Gōngyuán is the compound word for a park. By its composition, it indicates that the park is open to the public, and is an area used mainly for recreation or for horticultural purposes. Thus, when **gōngyuán** is combined with **jǐngshān**, we have the name Prospect Hill Park.

Zuǒbiar means the left-hand side or simply the left. **Biān** is often written or spoken with the retroflex **r** (i.e., **biār**). This is not the only word for side, but it is commonly used as a generic term in a similar fashion to **miàn** (face). Also, to refer to the compass points only **biān** (or **biār**) is ever used.

Zài wàng nán qù—Since **zài** has the meaning of again, by extension it also has the sense of further or still [more]; therefore this clause means to go further south.

Yàoshi is a compound meaning if. In reply to the preceding question is the statement "Should you want to . . . ," or "If you go [further to the] south, it will be possible (**kéyǐ**) to take a look at the Altar of Heaven." Note the duplication of the verb **kàn**.

Dào . . . qù, like **wàng . . . qù**, is a useful phrase for indicating direction. The difference is that while **wàng** indicates a general direction to proceed towards, **dào** implies arrival at a given place.

9.2   STREET IDENTIFICATION

Actual parts of Beijing are used in this dialogue. Two main streets in the East City are referred to, and as the sketch map shows, the eastern end of Chang'an Avenue intersects Chongwenmen, which runs north and south. The compound **jiēdào** is used as a generic term for streets. Off the main streets are lanes or alleys, that is to say smaller roads which, though they may be paved, do not have sidewalks such as larger sidestreets may have. Such lesser roads are called **hútòng**. **Jiē** or **dàjiē** generally follows the particular names given to thoroughfares, many are named after the imposing gateways (**mén**) which once straddled them. Several main avenues and streets also carry East or West before their names to indicate the section of the district they traverse through.

Not only are compass points included in numerous street names, two other words often occur at the end, namely **nèi** and **wài**. **Nèi** stands for inner or within, while **wài** means the opposite. For example, in Beijing there is a long street—Jianguomennei and Jianguomenwai—which is an extension of Chang'an Avenue going eastward. To include the word for street would make the name unwieldy, but the words **nèi** and **wài** respectively indicate that the street runs from *inside* the gate and extends eastward a considerable distance beyond or *outside* the gate (i.e., into the suburbs on that side of the city).

R: **Zhèi tiáo dàjiē jiào shénme?**
This strip [MW] main-street call what?
What is this avenue called?

C: **Zhè jiùshi Chóngwénmén Dàjiē.**
This simply Sublime Learning Gate main-street.
This is Chongwenmen Avenue.

Nǐ yào dào nǎr qù a?
You want arrive where go, eh?
Where do you want to get to?

R: **Dǒng Cháng'ānjiē zài nánbiar ma?**
East Long-Peace-Street at south-side, eh?
Is Chang'an Avenue East south of here?

C: **Duìle. Yí dào nánbiar nèige lùkǒu wàng yòu zǒu, nǐ jiù zài Cháng'ānjiē-shàngle.**
Correct. Once reach south-side that street-mouth towards right walk, you then at Long-Peace-Street on.
Correct. As soon as you reach that intersection to the south and go right, you'll be on Chang'an Avenue.

VOCABULARY

chóng	lofty, sublime; extn.—to esteem; a surname
wén	writing; language; extn.—culture, learning
mén	gate, door, entrance; a switch; a surname

cháng	long, length; extn.—strong suit; (alt. pron. **zhǎng**)
ān	calm, peaceful, quiet, secure; a surname
nán	South; a surname
yòu	right side

RATIONALE AND INTERPRETATION

Chóngwénmén (Gateway of Sublime Learning) is the new name of what was once a gate known as Hatamen in the old city wall. Since the wall was demolished, the gateway has also vanished.

Dào nǎr qù a? With the QW **nǎr** (where), the question is self-evident. The **a** is an exclamatory particle used to emphasize the query.

Dōng Cháng'ānjiē (*East Long Peace Street*). This is probably the best known avenue in Beijing, running east/west past the Forbidden City's south entrance, which is called **Tiānānmén** (Gate of Heavenly Peace). This structure is about as well known a national symbol as Big Ben in London or the Statue of Liberty in New York. Chang'an was the original name of the city now known as Xi'an (Western Peace), when it was the capital during the Qin, Han and—500 years later—the Tang dynasties.

Duìle. This is a standard expression of agreement, translating into "Correct," or "That's right!" Said with sufficient emphasis, it would be equivalent to "Right on!"

Yí dào. With **yī** meaning one, it is only a short step to its meaning once, and this use of the word is very common. Hence **yí dào** (note the change of tone) is used here to mean once arrived at or as soon as [you] arrive. . . .

Wàng yòu zǒu—Since **zǒu** means to walk or to go, and is modified by **wàng yòu** meaning towards [the] right, the whole phrase means ". . . go to your right."

Zài Cháng'ānjiē-shàngle. Apart from the street name, consider the term **jiē-shàng**. This means on the street. Since **zài** here means at or on, it requires a PW by way of an object—hence street. The particle **-le** is used to indicate the completion of the action.

9.3   INDOOR DIRECTIONS

Traditionally, multi-storied buildings were rare in China, but this is so no
longer. In China, as in North America, the ground floor constitutes the
first floor, so that—taking the example of the following situation—the
third floor, or storey, is two above the ground floor. When asking for a
particular floor in an elevator, there is no need to use the word **céng**: simply state the floor number, followed by the word **lóu**.

R: **Wó yǒu yíwèi péngyou zài zhèr zhù. Tā xìng Chǒng. Qǐng
gàosu wǒ tā zhù něicéng lóu?**
*I have one [MW] friend at here live. He surname[d] Chong. Invite inform
me he live which tier storey?*
I have a friend living here by the name of Chong. Tell me, please,
which floor does he live on?

C: **Chóng Xiānsheng zhù zài sān lóu. Wǒ kéyi gàosu tā nǐ láile.**
Chong Mr. lives on three tier. I can tell him you come.
Mr. Chong lives on the third floor. I'll tell him you're here.

R: **Wǒ bú shànglóu qù zhǎo tā, yīnwei wǒmen zhè jiù yào yíkuàr
chūqù. Wǒ zhèr děng tā hǎo-buhǎo?**
*I not ascend building go find him, because we directly want together go out.
I here await him good not-good?*
I won't go upstairs to see him as we are going out together shortly.
I'll wait here for him, if that's all right?

[After a brief house-phone conversation]

C: **Chǒng Xiānsheng qǐng nǐ zuò yìhuěr. Tā lìkě xiàlóu lái
huānyíng nǐ.**
*Chong Mr. invites you sit awhile. He immediately descend building come
welcome you.*
Mr. Chong invites you to take a seat for a moment. He's coming
down at once to welcome you.

VOCABULARY

zhù	to reside, live, stay; extn.—stop [at]
céng	layer, tier, stratum; extn.—storey, floor
děng	class, grade; equal; to compare; wait
zuò	to sit, take a seat; extn.—to travel
huì	to meet, assemble; extn.—association, meeting; be able to [through acquired skill]; opportunity
lì	to stand, set up, establish, erect; vertical; immediate
huān	joyful, jubilant, merry; extn.—vigorously
yíng	go to meet, greet, welcome, receive

RATIONALE AND INTERPRETATION

Tā zhù něicéng lóu? **Něicéng** in effect means which floor, with **lóu** used to reinforce the idea of a multi-storied building. Thus, the question asked is "Which floor does he live on?"

Wǒ bú shànglóu qù. The word **shàng** means not only to ascend or to climb, but in conjunction with the verb to go (**qù**) it has the sense to go up. This indicates that the subject is at a lower level and is initiating the action; otherwise Mr. Chong—being upstairs—would be inviting him to come up (**shànglái**). Verbs of action of this sort in Chinese usually indicate quite specifically the direction of the action in relation to the speaker. Therefore this sentence has the meaning "I won't go upstairs," since **shànglóu** (*ascend building*) gives the sense of going up—by stairs or by elevator being irrelevant. Conversely, the expression **xiàlóu qù** (to go downstairs) indicates that the subject is at a higher level and initiating the action; or **xiàlóu lái** would be used if the speaker were downstairs and inviting someone to come down.

Wǒmen zhè jiù yáo yíkuàr chūqù. The basic part of this sentence is **wǒmen chūqù**, which means "we go out . . . ," using a compound verb of movement meaning literally *to exit go*. By insertion of the verb **yào** (to want), the intent to act is indicated; **yíkuàr** (*one piece*) is used to mean together. The expression **zhè jiù** essentially means now, directly, very soon after, or shortly.

Wǒ zhèr děng tā, hǎo-buhǎo? The main force of the sentence is "I await him" (**wó děng tā**). Note that the PW **zhèr** (here) comes before the relevant verb. The sense of **hǎo** is a good [idea] or a good [thing to do], and hence, by extension, "it would be best" or "I'd better..." The V. not-V. construction at the end of the sentence, indicates a question in the form of a suggestion, implying "...shall I?"

Zuò yìhuěr means to sit down [for] a moment.

Lìkè means at once or immediately, and therefore it is more precise or urgent than **zhè jiù**.

Lái huānyíng nǐ—here the verb to come (**lái**) is primarily tied to **xiàlóu** in the expression **xiàlóu lái** (to come downstairs), but it is also linked with the object of the action, which is "...to welcome you" (**huānyíng nǐ**).

SUPPLEMENTARY VOCABULARY

shìnèi	indoor
hùwài, lùtiān	outdoor, open-air
zài shìlǐ	indoors
wàimiàn	outdoors
lǐmiàn-de	inner
-wài	outer
zài lǐmian	inside
zài wàibiar	outside
nèibù	interior
wàimian, wàibiar	exterior
neìbù-de	internal
zài wàimian	external
zài shàngmian	on top of (above)
zài dǐxia	below (underneath)
dìxià	underground
zài nèi	within, included
chú...yǐwài	excluding (apart from)
shuāngmùjìng	binoculars
luópán	compass
dìtú	map

xiāngxià	countryside
shōucheng	crop, harvest
nóngchǎng	farm
tiándì	farmland, fields
shuǐdàotián	rice fields, paddy
cūnzhuāng	village

TEN

TRAVEL
ARRANGEMENTS

"The farmer prays for rain, the traveller for fair weather."

Visitors or delegations to China under the aegis of a particular State Commission, Bureau, Department, or Trade Corporation are assigned to the related **dānwèi**. To many this might appear autocratic, or at least an infringement of one's personal freedom. Tourists, transient as they may be, come under the umbrella of the CITS, and the **quánpéi** (national guide) will unobtrusively ensure that these visitors are suitably provided for through his **dānwèi**. There is no doubt that foreign visitors need to be able to fit into the system somehow if their Chinese counterparts are to feel comfortable with them.

Customs and security procedures abound in China as in any other part of the world, but they are not as aggravating as in many other places. As long as the stipulated proscriptions are observed, and the required documentation and receipts are to hand, the process is rarely very irksome. Chinese officialdom as a rule no more wants embarrassment in either direction than does any other walk of life in China. No toiletries of an aerosol nature should be carried, for these may be confiscated out of hand. Also any certification for valuables already in your possession, as well as for curios—and especially antiques—bought in China should be kept handy. It is admissible to keep films separate and, if desired, in lead packages, for protection from X-ray equipment at the security barrier.

In China aviation, like the railways system, is nationalized. The Civil Aviation Administration of China (CAAC) controls the nation's airline, known as Air China. As an international carrier competing on world routes, there is room for refinement in terms of service, at least by western standards. However, changes are taking place which enable Air China to please foreign travellers as well as their own nationals. Of course domestic flights are a different matter; since CAAC is a state monopoly, there is no competition to consider. Humorous as well as horrendous stories abound, but in all fairness tourists do arrive at their destinations—eventually! Probably because of obsolete equipment more than for any other reason, flights are frequently subject to delays, and to diversions due to weather. Seating arrangements also leave room for improvement. While bulk allocations of seats are usually provided for tour parties, it is not always possible to get the precise seating expected. Your airline ticket may lead you to expect due delivery to your destination; but much of the sophistication one might expect to get on the ground, concerning luggage handling, documentation, or the hotel accommodation, has yet to be achieved.

The trains in China provide a reasonable standard of speed and comfort. They run dependably on schedule and they do not take a lot longer than aircraft to get to destinations on shorter routes. They also provide cheaper travel. While there is no class differentiation, there is a discrepancy of comfort provided by hard or soft accommodation. Hard seat or sleeper is not recommended for long-distance travel, nor is this usually arranged for visitors or tourists unless specified for economic reasons. Whenever it is necessary to travel by train, express service is most likely to supply what is required. To many tourists, particularly steam locomotive buffs, Chinese trains provide a touch of nostalgia, since diesel or electric train travel is only now being developed to any great extent. Interior furnishings, such as lace curtains, antimacassars, and brass fittings, are reminiscent of a past era. As for the plumbing arrangements, they are at the end of the carriages, extremely basic, and can be deplorable.

Highways are being improved considerably in the vicinity of the larger cities along the tourist routes, and coaches provided for touring parties are of a good standard. Rental cars are not yet a feasible alternative to other modes of transportation because of the lack of service stations. Bicycle touring is possible, but hitch-hiking is not to be contemplated. Chinese conservatism has not yet yielded that much ground to western emancipation, and the language barrier is only one of the many obstacles still to be overcome.

While naturally limited in its application, boat travel is one of the most enchanting ways of viewing China wherever the opportunity presents itself. Three boat tours recommended are the Grand Canal in the province of Jiangsu which takes one to Suzhou, the Venice of the East and the centre of China's fabulous silk industry; the awesome gorges on the Yangzi Jiang; and the unique limestone pinnacles of the karst mountains through which the Li River winds its way past Guilin.

When travelling in China, as in any of the world's other larger countries, remember the size and scope of the country. Choose carefully your mode of transportation based on the amount of time you have and where you want to go. The slower pace of the boat or coach enables one to see so much more of a small part of the country than does the train, while the aircraft provides more opportunities for sight-seeing in different parts of the country. In terms of local mobility, one can usually rely on the taxi service, if not the bus or auto-trishaw (a three-wheeled power-driven version of the pedicab and its precursor, the rickshaw). To get around locally, however, walking in comfortable shoes is still as good a way to go as any.

10.1   TRAVEL INFORMATION

R: **Wǒ gāng chákàn wǒ-de qīngdān.**
        I just examine-look my distinct-list.
        I've just been looking over my checklist.

C: **Qīngdān shì guānyu shénme?**
        Distinct-list is about what?
        What's your checklist about?

R: **Dōu shì kǎolǜ qù Zhōngguó-de qíngxing. Wó bǎ dānzi fēnchéngle sānge bùfen.**
        All be investigate-ponder go China-of condition-contrast. I take list divide-become three [MW] section-divisions.
        It is for considering all the circumstances of going to China. I have divided the list into three parts.

Dìyì bùfen dōu shì lǚxíng-zhǔnbèi; dà bùfen kéyi jiào lǚxíngshè géi wǒ ānpai.

First section all be travel-preparation, big portion can call travel-agency give me arrange.

The first part is all the travel arrangements; the majority I can get the CITS to arrange for me.

C: **Duìle, yīnwei tāmen kéyi bǎ fēijīpiào, huǒchēpiào, zhāodài-shèbèi, lǚxíng-jìhuà yíqiè dōu tì nǐ guánlǐ.**

Right, because they can take airplane-tickets, train tickets, hospitality-facilities, travel-plans everything all for you manage.

That's right, because they can supervise everything on your behalf regarding airline tickets, train tickets, accommodation and the itinerary.

Zhè shì hǎo zhúyi. Hái yǒu shénme?

This be good idea. Still have what?

This is a good idea. Anything else?

R: **Dì'èr bùfen wó xiǎng shēnqǐng wàishìbàn zhǐjiào; bǐfang shuō: wǒ-de hùzhào, qiānzhèng, wèishēng-tiáojiàn, huòzhě shénme tèbié xúkězhèng huò biéde wénjiàn.**

Second section I consider request external-matters-office to direct; instance say, my passport, visa, hygiene-conditions, or what special permit-certificates or other documents.

For the second part I am thinking of applying to the External Affairs Office for advice; say for example: my passport, visa[s], health requirements, or any particular permits or other documents.

C: **Dāngrán-le! Bìngqiě tāmen zhènghǎo géi nǐ tuījiàn tuǒdàng-de dānwei bāng nǐ-de máng.**

Naturally! Besides they just-good give you recommendation proper-of units help your business.

Of course! What's more, they're just right for recommending the appropriate units to help you.

Dānzi-shàng dìsānge bùfen ne?
List-on third part eh?
What about the third section on your list?

R: **Nà wó děi gēn yínháng qù bàn, yīnwei dōu shì guānyu wǒ-de cáiwù-xūyào, zhǔyào shì lǚxíng-zhīpiào lián qí tā suóyǒu-de xìnyòngzhèng guīze.**
That I need with bank go do, because all be about my money-matters must-want, main-want be travel-cheques including other what have-of trust-use-permit rules.
That I will have to deal with through the bank, since it all concerns my financial needs, especially travellers' cheques and all the Letter of Credit regulations besides.

C: **Zhù nǐ shùnlì!**
Wish you success!
I wish you luck!

VOCABULARY

gāng	firm, strong; barely; extn.—just, a short while ago
chá	to check, examine, investigate; extn.—consult, look up
qīng	clear, distinct; to clean up, settle up; Manchu Dynasty
kǎo	to give or take an exam; extn.—inspect, investigate
lù	to consider, ponder
chéng	to become, to succeed; extn.—achievement; able; O.K.
bù	ministry, department; section, part
qíng	feeling, sentiment; extn.—passion; favour; situation
xíng	form, shape; extn.—entity; to appear; contrast
bǎ	to hold, grasp; extn.—control; [MW]
dì	rank, order; extn.—ordinal numbers prefix
zhǔn	to allow, grant, permit; extn.—accurate, definite
bèi	to be equipped with; extn.—prepare; equipment
pái	to arrange, put in order; extn.—line, row; eject, push
chē	vehicle; extn.—machine; a surname

zhāo	to beckon, attract; extn.—enrol
dài	to deal with; extn.—entertain; (alt. pron. **daī**—to stay)
shè	to establish, set up, facilitate; extn.—design
jì	to count, calculate; extn.—plan, idea; a surname
huà	differentiate; transfer, assign; extn.—plan, mark
qiè	correspond to; (alt. pron. **qiē**—to cut or slice)
tì	take the place of, replace; extn.—on behalf of
guǎn	tube, pipe; manage, be in charge of; mind, concerning
lǐ	to arrange, regulate, manage; principle, reason, acknowledge
yì	meaning, idea; wish; intention; extn.—anticipate, expect
zhǐ	finger, digit; extn.—to point, indicate; depend on
bǐ	to compare
zhèng	to demonstrate; evidence; extn.—certificate, [I.D.] card
wèi	to defend, protect, guard
huò	perhaps, maybe; extn.—or; someone, something
zhě	suffix used with verbs or adjectives to denote some*body*
xǔ	to promise; permit, allow; perhaps, maybe; a surname
bìng	to combine, merge; extn.—together, and; simultaneously
qiě	temporarily, while, even
tuī	to push, grind; extn.—promote, advance; postpone, elect
jiàn	to recommend
tuǒ	appropriate, proper; settled, finished
bāng	to help, assist; clique, gang
cái	wealth, money
wù	affair, business
xū	need, want, require; extn.—necessaries, needs
lián	link, connect; extn.—including; even; a surname
qí	his, hers, their; that, such; other, else
xìn	true, trust, faith; extn.—believe; signal; letter, message
guī	compasses, dividers; extn.—to plan, regulations
zé	standard, criterion; regulation
shùn	in the same direction as, with, along; extn.—put in order
lì	sharp, favourable, benefit; extn.—profit, interest

RATIONALE AND INTERPRETATION

Wǒ gāng chákàn . . . **Gāng**, immediately preceding the verb it modifies, means essentially *a short time ago*, thus indicating an immediate past action. Here it precedes **chákàn** (*examine look*), meaning to look over, where the object of the action is **qīngdān**—a detailed list or checklist.

Guānyu. This compound consists of **guān**, meaning to comment or to be concerned with, and **yú**, which is a general-purpose preposition found in numerous compounds; therefore this compound means concerning, about or with regard to.

Kǎolǜ means to think over or to consider and by extension, to take into account, or to go into [thoroughly].

Qíngxing may seem less obvious a compound, considering its literal meaning (*situation contrast*). Nevertheless, circumstances—as the Chinese conceive of them—are the result of a *contrast* or balance in the conditions surrounding any given *situation*.

Wó bǎ dānzi fēnchéngle sānge bùfen. This sentence deserves a detailed analysis, because it introduces a new element: **bǎ**. With its basic meaning of to take or to hold, **bǎ** is a particularly useful word. It allows the object of a sentence, which usually comes after the verb, to be transposed to a position between the subject and the verb. The net effect of this is to lend emphasis to the object. Thus **bǎ** may be considered as a coverb. Although in essence it expresses the idea that "one takes (or took) something [with the intention of . . .]," for practical purposes there is no need to translate the coverb itself. Should it be necessary to physically take or take hold of something, the verb **ná** is used. Bear in mind that both **bǎ** and **ná** can appear in the same sentence. For instance:

Tā bǎ qìchē kāizǒule.   She [took] the car [and] drove away.

as compared with:

Tā yào ná wǒ-de qìchē.   She wants to take my car.

A possible combination might be as follows:

Tā yào ná wǒ-de qìchē,   She wanted to take my
suóyǐ wó bǎ yàoshi gěi   car, so I gave her the
tā-le.   keys.

Here are some further samples of how sentences using the **bǎ** construction are formed:

Subject —	bǎ—Object	—	Verb —	Complement
Wó	bǎ wǒ-de míngpiàn		gěi	tā le.
I	*my card*		*gave*	*him.*
Tā	bǎ shóubiǎo		mài	gěi tā le.
He	*[the] watch*		*sold*	*to her.*
Nǐ péngyou	bǎ tā-de shū		dài	zǒu le.
Your friend	*his books*		*carried*	*away.*
Wǒ	bǎ dānzi		fēnchéngle	sānge bùfen.
I	*the list*		*divided*	*three sections.*

Lǚxíng-zhǔnbèi refers to travel arrangements. **Lǚxíng** should now be a familiar term, but **zhǔnbèi** is new. It is useful for signifying preparations in a general sense, or to prepare.

Dà bùfen is one term for majority, indicating the larger portion or greater part. Conversely, **xiǎo bùfen** can be used to mean the smaller part or minority. There are also other words for majority and minority.

Jiào . . . ānpai. Jiào was introduced as meaning to call. It also has a further meaning of to cause, and is used here in the sense of *causing* [something] *to be done* or *getting* [something] *done*. Complementing **jiào** is the term **ānpai**, a new compound meaning to arrange, to plan, or to fix up. The use of **jiào** results in a passive construction. Had **bǎ** been used, the result would have been an active construction. **Jiào** is explained in the Appendix, Section 17, in conjunction with **ràng** (to allow, or to make). As an example of the way **jiào** can be used in contrast with the **bǎ** construction, and how **jiào**, like **ràng**, can create a passive construction, consider the following:

Wó bǎ fàn gěi tā chīle.   I gave the food for him to eat.

Tā bǎ fàn dōu chīle.   He ate all the food.

Fàn dōu jiào tā gěi chīle.   The food was all eaten by him.

Fēijīpiào is an airline ticket. **Piào** means, among other things, a ticket. When used in this sense, **piào** needs to be modified; the purpose for which the ticket is intended must be stated.

Huǒchēpiào. The term for a railway ticket is formed by the same process. **Huǒchē** (*fire vehicle*) is the term for a train, and is not to be confused with the term for a fire engine, which is **mièhuǒchē** (*extinguish fire vehicle*). Incidentally, a locomotive, regardless of its motive power, is generally referred to as a **huǒchētóu** (*fire vehicle head*).

Zhāodài-shèbèi. Zhāodài may mean hospitality or to entertain, and to serve or to wait on [as customers]; however, it is also used as a general term for accommodation, particularly when it appears in conjunction with shèbèi. Shèbèi is made up of shè (to establish), and bèi as in zhǔnbèi (preparation). Together these two compounds form zhāodài-shèbèi (*hospitality facilities*), which stands for accommodation.

Jìhuà means plan or program. When coupled with lǚxíng (travel) it yields the compound for itinerary.

Yíqiè (one whole) is the term for everything or all.

Tì indicates *on behalf of*, or *as a substitute for* in the sense of in the place of. . . . It may be used also to mean for, but should not be confused with gěi. Compare these two examples:

> **Tā géi wǒ zuòfàn.** She is cooking *for* me.
> [i.e., for my benefit]

but

> **Tā tì wǒ zuòfàn.** She is cooking *for* me.
> [i.e., in my stead]

Guánlǐ (in charge of arrangements) is the compound for manage, run, or supervise. Thus the phrase . . . **yíqiè dōu tì nǐ guánlǐ** means ". . . to supervise everything on your behalf." It can be seen that the use of tì is a moot point since the words gěi and tì are virtually interchangeable.

Hǎo zhúyi means a good idea. The compound zhúyi consists of zhú, the secondary meaning of which is to manage or to direct, and yī, meaning wish or intention. Together they mean essentially to think about or to plan—hence idea.

Shēnqǐng. The compound, composed of shēn (to express) and qǐng (to invite, request), means to apply for or, more formally, to submit an application.

Wàishìbàn—the literal and free translations of this term are virtually the same, i.e., External Affairs Office. The foreign service which one meets in Chinese embassies around the world is known as the wàijiāobù. Wàishìbàn is the office which controls the movements of foreign visitors while they are in China.

Zhǐjiào (*indicate instruct*) is a polite term to use in formal circumstances when seeking advice or direction with regard to procedure.

Bǐfang means analogy or simile, and is used to say for example. Here **bǐfang shuō** is to cite as an example, or for instance.

Qiānzhèng is a visa. **Qiān** means to sign or a signature, and **zhèng** means a certificate or a permit; thus **qiānzhèng** alludes to the official government representative's signature or stamp in one's passport.

Wèishēng-tiáojiàn. **Wèishēng** varies in meaning from health to hygiene or sanitation, according to context. It is a combination of **wèi** (guard, protect) and **shēng** (life). **Tiáojiàn**, the term for requirements, terms, or conditions is a compound made up of **tiáo** (item), and **jiàn**, which can mean document.

Huòzhě means either, perhaps, or maybe.

Xúkězhèng. By itself, **xǔ** means to allow or to permit, while **kě** means to approve. Combined with **zhèng** they form the compound indicating a document serving as a permit or authorization.

Biéde wénjiàn refers to other documents. The compound **biéde** made up of **bié** coupled with the particle **-de**, means of another or simply other. **Wénjiàn** is a general term used for documents or papers, **jiàn** being as in **tiáojiàn** above.

Bìngqiě. This compound means besides, moreover, or what is more.

Zhènghǎo, in this context, means just right.

Tuījiàn is a compound meaning to recommend.

Tuǒdàng (*proper to bear*) is a compound whose meaning is determined mainly by its first portion. It means essentially suitable, proper or appropriate.

Bāngmáng means to help [out], to lend a hand or even to do a good turn. The term may be split, as it is in this instance, since **bāng** has the primary meaning of to help or to assist, and **máng** means [to be] busy. Consider these examples:

Qǐng *géi* **wǒ** *bāng* **yìdiǎr** *máng*.	Could you *give* me a little *help*, please?
Wǒ lái *bāng* **nǐ-de** *máng*, **hǎo-buhǎo**?	How about my coming to *lend* you a *hand*?
Tā qù jiào rén *bāngmáng*.	He's gone to call for *assistance*.

Bāngmáng is only appropriate for the use indicated. It is not a suitable term for help in the sense of rescue, aid or succour, although sometimes in colloquial usage the dividing line may seem fine indeed. The Chinese equivalent for the expression of "The blind leading the blind" is amusing. They say:

Xiāzi bāngmáng,	When a blind man lends a hand,
yuè bāng yuè máng!	the more he helps, the more busy you get!

Cáiwù-xūyào. Cáiwù refers to financial matters or finance, while **xūyào** (*must want*) means needs or necessities.

Zhǔyào is a compound of **zhǔ** (main, primary) and **yào** (to want), meaning principally, especially or most importantly.

Lián qí tā suóyǒu-de . . . This is an idiomatic phrase, which may be broken down as follows:

lián (*to link*)	and, or including
qí tā (*such [as] it*)	besides
suóyǒu-de (*what-have of*)	all

Xìnyòngzhèng-guīzé. Xìnyòngzhèng (*trust use certificate*) means a letter of credit (L/C). **Xìn** serves to indicate two sets of meanings. The first set is trust or faith, and to believe. By extension, it also takes the meaning sign or signal, from which is derived the sense of credentials, letters, and mail. The latter meanings may seem far removed from the former, nonetheless, it is met in current use far more frequently. Oddly enough, a full circle is formed when dealing with terms such as certification, credit, and confidence. **Guīzé** (*rules duty*) is the term for regulations.

Zhù nǐ shùnlì (*wish you success*) can be used as an expression of sincere good wishes (i.e., "I wish you luck"); or simply "Good luck!" in an ironic sense. In this context it can be taken either way, considering all the bureaucracy and time-consuming effort likely to be involved.

10.2   LUGGAGE HANDLING

 R: **Wǒ méiyǒu xíngli biāoqiār.**
I not-have luggage labels.
I have no luggage labels.

Wǒ ná jǐtiáo, xíng-buxíng?
I take several [MW], can not-can?
May I take a few?

C: **Wǒ kéyi géi nǐ jìshàng.**
I able give you fasten-on.
I'll stick them on for you.

Nǐ nàr yóu jǐ jiàn xíngli?
You there have how-many items [MW] luggage?
How many pieces of luggage have you got there?

R: **Yígòng sānjiàn; liǎngjiàn shì shǒutíxiāng, háiyou wǒ zhèige pibāo.**
One-altogether three-[MW]; two-items [MW] be hand-carry-boxes, still-have my this [MW] hide-bag.
All together three pieces; two are suitcases, and there is this travel-bag of mine, too.

C: **Gōngshìbāo, zhàoxiàngjī, yǔyī shénmede dōu néng shàng fēijī-de shíhou zìjǐ xiédài.**
Official-duties-satchel, reflect-likeness-machine, rain-clothes, what-of all can ascend flying-machine of time self-personal carry-take.
Briefcase, camera, raincoat and so forth can all be carried on by yourself when you board the aircraft.

Lìngwài liǎngjiàn tíxiāng dōu bú-guòzhòng; hǎiguān gēn ānquán shǒuxù bànhǎole jiù lìkè zhuāng fēijī-shàng.
Other-out couple [MW] carry-boxes all not pass-weight; sea-control with safety-completion handy-extend attend-well then immediately pack flying-machine on.
Neither of the other two suitcases are over-weight; when the Customs and Security formalities have been dealt with they'll be loaded straight on to the aircraft.

Dēngjīzhèng-shàng yǒu nǐ-de zuòwèi hàomǎ, háiyou nǐ-de xínglipiào tiē zāi fēijīpiào-shàngle.

Mount-machine-certificate on have your seat-place number, still-have your luggage-ticket stick at flying-machine-ticket on.

Your seat number is on your boarding card, and your baggage checks are attached to your airline ticket also.

VOCABULARY

jì	to tie; extn.—to fasten, button up
jiàn	MW for garments, documents, luggage, and matters or things in general, translatable as an item;
gòng	common, general; altogether, in all, all told
tí	to carry; lift; extn.—raise, put forward; mention, refer to
xiáng	case, trunk, box, case
pí	skin; hide, leather
bāo	to wrap; extn.—bundle, package; swelling; a surname
xiàng	resemblance; extn.—photograph (alt. pron. **xiāng**—mutually)
jī	machine, engine; opportunity
yǔ	rain
yī	clothes, clothing, garment; extn.—covering, coating
néng	to be able, can [i.e., have the physical capacity]; skill
fēi	to fly; flutter; extn.—swiftly; unexpected
zì	self, oneself; from, since
jǐ	oneself; one's own, personal
xié	to carry, take along; extn.—take or hold by the hand
dài	belt; ribbon; tire; area, zone; take, carry, bring; raise
lìng	other, another, separate; besides
zhòng	weight; important (alt. pron. **chóng**)
quán	complete, total, whole; extn—to complete; a surname
shǒu	hand, extn.—skilled "hand"
xù	continuous, successive; to extend; extn.—to join on
zhuāng	attire; clothing; extn.—pretend; to load, pack
dēng	to ascend; to record; to step on, tread, extn.—to pedal
tiē	to paste, stick; glue

Xíngli biāoqiār. **Xíng** and **lǐ** form a compound which means luggage or baggage. (Note that the second syllable is toneless.) **Biāo** (mark) and **qiān** (to sign, also a label) are compounded to give the term for label or tag. Since the tags are only small, the diminutive r is added to the word **qiān**, making the compound **biāoqiār**.

Ná jǐtiáo means to take a few [MW]. **Ná** is used here in its basic meaning to take or to hold. **Jǐ**, when used as a QW, signifies how many (as in **jǐge**); otherwise it means a few or several. **Tiáo**, the MW meaning a strip has been substituted for the general MW **gè**. Note the following comparison:

Wǒ ná jǐ tiáo?   How many shall I take?

but

Wǒ ná jǐtiáo, xíng-buxíng?   May I take a few?

In the first question **jǐ** is used as a QW, while in the second question its significance is altered by the presence of **xíng-buxíng**, which asks the question "Will it be O.K. if . . . ?" or, as presented, "May I . . .": hence, **jǐtiáo** is used here to mean a few.

Wǒ kéyi géi nǐ . . . [verb]. This is a useful phrase to know when offering to assist someone. It should precede the main verb, which would indicate the service being offered (e.g., an introduction or a favour). **Géi nǐ** means for you, while **wǒ kéyi** means I can or I will.

Jìshang. Jì means to tie, and thus by extension to fasten or even to stick on. It is a particularly appropriate word since luggage labels can be tied on with string, or stuck on as in the case of air travel luggage where the numbered destination tag is looped around the handle.

Jǐ jiàn. Here **jǐ** is used as a QW, with **jiàn** as a MW for luggage, so the query is "How many pieces [of luggage] . . . ?"

Yígòng (*one common*) is a compound meaning total in terms of numbers or amounts of money.

Shǒutíxiāng is the term for a suitcase (*hand carry box*). **Shǒu** is not essential to this compound, so that often suitcases are referred to simply as **tíxiāng**.

Píbāo is a term relating loosely to any type of bag, ranging from a handbag to a flight or travel bag. **Pí** (skin or hide) can be applied to either leather or plastic covering, while **bāo** (parcel or wrapping) implies a small carrying bag. Generally speaking **bāo** (package) refers to smaller and lighter bags, while **xiāng** (box) is used for larger luggage receptacles.

Gōngshìbāo (*official duties satchel*) means a briefcase. **Gōngshì**, a term applied to one's official business or public matters, by extension thus refers to the documents and papers one normally carries around in the course of work. **Bāo**, the term applicable to an item carried under one's arm is appropriate for a briefcase, hence **gōngshìbāo**.

Zhàoxiàngjī is a camera. This is another term which sometimes discards its first syllable. Hence a camera may just be called a **xiàngjī**. However, the compound **zhàoxiàng** means to take a photograph, while **jī** refers to the machine which does it.

Yǔyī (*rainclothes*) refers to any form of waterproof clothing.

Shénmede. While not the proper term for et cetera, it serves the same purpose, in the sense of *what have* you, *and so* forth, and *customary* extras.

Néng in essence means can or to be able to . . . , indicating that one has the physical capacity to perform an action. This word may sometimes be substituted for **kéyi**.

Shàng fēijī-de shíhou. **Shíhou**, immediately preceded by the particle **-de**, modifies an action earlier in the sentence. The combination **-de shíhou**, virtually *[at the] time of*, may always be interpreted as when. **Fēijī** (*flying machine*) is an aircraft, and this term combined with **shàng** (to ascend) indicates when going on board a plane.

Zìjǐ xiédài. **Zìjǐ** means oneself or own. **Xiédài** has the meaning of to carry, or to take along, and thus indicates portability.

Lìngwài means other or besides. Here the term modifies **liǎngjiàn tíxiāng** (two [MW] suitcases), giving the meaning of the other two suitcases.

Dōu bú-guòzhòng . . . This phrase calls for a little explanation. **Dōu** can perform slightly differing roles. Basically it means all, but when applied to two subjects, it may be interpreted as both. In the negative, however, all becomes none and, as here, both may become neither. **Guòzhòng** means overweight, as the character **chóng** (duplicate, etc.) may also be pronounced **zhòng**, when it is used to mean weight or heavy.

Hǎiguān. The component parts of this new compound are already known, particularly the term **guān** (barrier) which here indicates Customs. **Hǎi** (sea) reinforces that meaning, possibly being the earliest national barrier at which inspection and taxation were enforced. Nowadays, whether the country is entered by land, sea, or air, the Chinese term for Customs is **hǎiguān**. The expression for going through Customs is **tōngguò hǎiguān**.

Ānquán. The principal character, **ān**, means peaceful or serene, while **quán** reinforces it with the implication of totality. **Ānquán**, then, is the compound for security or safety in the broad sense.

Shǒuxù (*hand extension*) is the term for procedures or formalities, particularly those relating to, say, **hǎiguān** and **ānquán**.

Bànhǎole means to have been dealt with [satisfactorily]. **Hǎo** gives the nuance of satisfactory to the verb **bàn** (to attend to, deal with), while **-le** indicates completion of the action.

Jiù lìkè zhuāng fēijī-shàng. **Jiù** and **lìkè** reinforce each other, to emphasize the immediacy of the action. **Zhuāng-shāng** means to load up or, in this case, to load onto.

Dēngjīzhèng (*mount aircraft certificate*) is a boarding card.

Zuòwèi means a seat. **Zuò** (to sit) is compounded with **wèi** (MW for people), which is used here with its primary meaning of place or location. Hence, the compound's meaning is a seating place, or simply a seat—as at a table, for instance. Apart from its primary meaning to sit, **zuò**—by extension—also implies to travel, since so much travel is done in the sitting position. Types of travel include:

zuò chuán	go by boat
zuò fēijī	go by air

One can also say **zuò chē** to indicate in general terms travelling by vehicle, which in turn is better amplified as follows:

zuò chūzū-qìchē	go by taxi
zuò gōnggòng-qìchē	go by bus
zuò huǒchē	go by train

Xínglipiào is the term for baggage checks. **Piào** has the generic sense of ticket, therefore the compound **xínglipiào** refers to the numbered tickets which travelers are given for the purpose of identifying their luggage. **Qǔ xíngli** is the expression used for collecting or claiming luggage.

Tiē zài fēijīpiào-shangle. The only new word here is **tiē**, meaning to stick on or to adhere. By extension it could even be used to mean stapled together, as in the case of baggage checks and airline tickets (**fēijīpiào**). Note the difference between **tiē**, which has the definite sense of sticking papers together, and **jì**, which implies tying things together.

SUPPLEMENTARY VOCABULARY

chuánpiào	boat ticket
chēpiào	bus ticket
diànyǐngpiào	cinema ticket
yuètáipiào	platform ticket
láihuípiào	return/round trip ticket
dìngqīpiào	season ticket
dānchéngpiào	single ticket
xìpiào	theatre ticket
tōngpiào	through ticket
shòupiàochù	ticket office
shíkèbiǎo	timetable/schedule
zhèngshí	confirmation
hángbān	flight number
xìndài	credit
xìnrèn, xìnxīn	confidence
xìntuō gōngsī	trust company
xìnyòng	trustworthiness
yǐngxiǎng	effect, influence
jīngyàn	experience
shìshí	fact(s)
chéngxù	procedure
jiéguǒ	results, outcome
qīngxiàng	tendency, inclination
yīshang	clothes
màozi	hat, headgear

wàzi	hosiery, stockings
xié, xiélèi	shoes, footwear
shūxǐ-yòngjù	toiletries
yúsǎn	umbrella
chènyī	underwear

ELEVEN

HOTEL
ARRANGEMENTS

"The bird chooses the tree, not the tree the bird."

Few hotels in China are much more than 75 years old, and since the late 1970s many hotels have been built to cater to the tourist trade. Most are built according to western standards, but some vary considerably. There is no shortage of hotel staff and they aim to please the foreign visitor. However, should irregularities occur, it is advisable to let the CITS guide deal with the situation. The guide is responsible for your safety and satisfaction, and will know how to handle any crisis.

Officially, tipping is not countenanced, however remuneration of some kind never goes amiss. More and more a tip is expected—and even demanded, sometimes in advance—to ensure good service. Gifts in kind such as lapel pins or light English reading material, especially magazines, are seldom declined. While tips are very acceptable, a personal touch is much more distinctive; obviously a combination of both is a good solution.

11.1 BOOKING IN

  R: **Wǒ méiyǒu yùdìng fángjiān. Yǒu kōngfáng méiyǒu?**
I not have schedule room. Have empty-room not-have?
I do not have a reservation. Do you have any rooms available?

C: **Jiù yóu nǐ yíwèi ma?**
    Only have you one [MW] eh?
    Is it just for yourself?

R: **Duìle, zhí wǒ yígerén.**
    Correct, only me one [MW] person.
    Right, only myself.

C: **Nǐ zhù jǐ tiān a?**
    You stay how many days?
    How many days are you staying?

R: **Wǒ hái búyidìng, kěnéng yíge xīngqī ba; kěshi zuì sháo děi sìwǔ tiān.**
    I still not-certain, possible one [MW] week; but most few must be four-five days.
    I'm not sure yet, possible for a week; but at least it'll be four to five days.

C: **Qíng nǐ dēngjì.**
    Request you enter-record.
    Please sign the register.

R: **Fángjiān dài yùshì ma?**
    Room attach bathroom eh?
    Does the room have a bathroom?

C: **Dāngrán ne, quánbù xiàndàihuà shèbèi dōu yǒu.**
    Naturally-eh, complete modernized installations all have.
    Of course, there are all the modern conveniences.

R: **Fángfèi duōshao?**
    Room-fee how much?
    How much do you charge?

C: **Dānzi-shàng yǒu shuōmíng.**
Form-on have explanation.
It is set out on the form.

R: **Huǒshifèi zàinèi ma?**
Meal-fees at-within eh?
Are meals included?

C: **Chúle zǎofàn, nà shì lìngwài suàn-de.**
Exclude breakfast, that be besides calculate-of.
Apart from breakfast, meals are charged separately.

Note that the basic word for a house is **fáng**, and a number of compounds stem from this word, more especially from its extended meaning of a room. Since **jiān**, a MW, refers essentially to the dividers or inner walls of a house which define the chambers, the compound **fángjiān** clearly means a room. There are several synonyms for **fángjiān** in Chinese, as there are for room in English, but the main alternative is **tīng** (hall), which is applied to the public or reception rooms, i.e., the living room or lounge (**kètīng**), and the dining room (**fàntīng**). **Kètīng**, however, is not to be confused with **kèfáng**, which is the guest bedroom. This stems from the layout of a traditional Chinese single-storied house with buildings surrounding three, or all four sides of a central courtyard. The main and more imposing parts would be south-facing, forming the halls, while the private dwelling and functional parts such as the kitchen, would be found on the east or west side of a house. The practical aspect of this arrangement becomes apparent when you consider that the public areas joining the main part of the house are used for housing other branches or generations of the family in residence. Another common alternative for room is **wūzi**, particularly in Northern China. In the South, **wū** tends to mean a house, and indeed **fángwū** is a compound meaning houses or buildings. A room may be referred to as **yìjiān wūzi**, with **jiān** used as a MW. Finally, another alternative word, **shì** (a slightly more literary word for room), is met in such terms as **yùshì** (bathroom) in place of **xǐzǎofáng**, a more colloquial term in Northern China, and **bàngōngshì**, meaning an office.

VOCABULARY

yù	beforehand, in advance
fáng	house; extn.—room; a surname
jiān	between; room, [MW]
zhǐ	only, merely
a	final particle
ba	suggestive particle—how about, let's
jì	to remember, memorize; to record; notes
yù	bath, to bathe
shì	room
huà	to change, transform; a suffix indicating -ize
fèi	fees, dues, charges; extn.—cost, expenses; wasteful
huǒ	meals, board; partnership, mate; extn.—combine
shí	to eat; extn.—food, meal; edible
chú	to remove, eliminate; extn.—besides; to divide

RATIONALE AND INTERPRETATION

Yùdìng (*advance fix*) is a compound meaning to predetermine, to schedule or, in this context, to make a reservation. The fact that it is preceded by **méiyǒu** indicates that no reservation has been made. **Yù** (beforehand), combines with **dìng** (to fix or to book) to give the meaning indicated.

Kōngfáng (*empty room*) is obviously a reference to unoccupied rooms available to guests. Note the split V. not-V. manner in which the question is asked.

Zhǐ wǒ yígerén means just myself. **Zhǐ** means only, while **wǒ yígerén** (*I one person*) is a means of referring to oneself.

Wǒ hái bùyidìng simply means "I'm still not sure."

Kěnéng yíge xīngqī ba. The suggestive particle **ba** at the end of this phrase reinforces the possibility (**kěnéng**) of a week's stay. **Kě** has been presented in a number of compounds and is known as an indication of contingency. Since **néng** means ability, the compound **kěnéng** can mean either probable or possible, according to context. In Chinese, the difference between the two is academic.

. . . zuì sháo děi sìwǔ tiān. Here is the likelihood of a guest needing a room for at least four to five days. **Zuì shǎo** means the least or, as here, at least. Where a couple of figures are used in succession to indicate an approximation, it is unnecessary in Chinese to use *or* or *to* between them; hence the use of **sìwǔ tiān** to indicate four [to] five days. It has been explained that **děi** (sometimes pronounced **dé**) means to need or to require.

Dēngjì (*enter record*) signifies to enter one's name in the register or to check in.

... **dài yùshì**. **Dài** as part of the compound **xiédài**, meaning to carry, is used on its own and means to take or to bring; thus, by extension, it implies availability. Here, **dài** may be interpreted as meaning to have. The compound **yùshì** means bathroom.

Quánbù xiàndàihuà shèbèi, means all modern amenities when applied to hotels or guesthouses, etc. **Quánbù** (*entire portion*) means complete, total or whole. **Xiàndài** (*present generation*) is the term for contemporary or modern. Add to this term the word **huà** which is used as a suffix, the equivalent of -ize in English, and we get the term for modernize (**xiàndàihuà**). When applied to **shèbèi** (installations), **xiàndàihuà** implies that all the house facilities have been modernized to the latest standards. **Dōu yǒu** at the end of the sentence reinforces the inclusive **quánbù** at the beginning.

Fángfèi (*room charge*) is the appropriate term for accommodation rates. **Fèi** is used as a suffix to a number of terms to indicate charges or cost. **Fèi** is an easy word to remember, approximating as it does, in sound as well as in sense, the English word fee. The compound **fèiyòng** (*expense use*) means expenditure, as does **huāfèi** (*spend cost*). Other examples of **fèi** are:

chēfèi	bus fare or train fare
chuánfèi	boat fare
lùfèi	travelling expenses
xuéfèi	school fees

By extension, **fèi** also has the meaning of wastefulness or to squander. Thus, we have:

làngfèi	squander; waste, extravagance
fèi gōngfu	time consuming
fèi qián	costly
fèi shì	give or take a lot of trouble

Shuōmíng (*speak clear*) can mean anything from explanation to directions, according to context. It can equally well be used to denote a caption, to illustrate or to show clearly, and even be a synopsis as a form of description.

Huǒshifèi refers to the cost of meals. **Huǒshi** is a compound created from **huǒ**, meaning meals or board, and **shí**, also meaning meals as well as to eat. Thus the compound indicates board, or fare. Note that here the second syllable **shi** is toneless.

Zàinèi (*exist within*) means inclusive or included; thus **bú zàinèi** means not inclusive or not included.

Chúle means except or apart from. If the conditional phrase is a long one, it may be closed by the term **yǐwài**, which also means outside of or other than. In this case, however, it would be considered tautological to do so. Hence, "Except [for] breakfast..." is rendered simply by **chúle zǎofàn**.

Lìngwài (*separate outside*) has a similar meaning to **yǐwài** but is used differently. It is linked not with the term **chúle**, but with **nà** (that), referring to **huǒshifèi**. It means not only besides but, more effectively, in addition to or separately.

11.2   HOTEL SERVICES

R: **Láojià, zhèige lěngqì zěnme kāi?**
   Excuse me, this cold-air how to run?
   Excuse me, how does this air-conditioning operate?

C: **Méi shénme! Yǐjīng géi nǐ bōhǎole.**
   Not whatever! Already for you dialed.
   Nothing to it! It's already set up for you.

R: **Zhèr yǒu xǐyīfáng méiyǒu?**
   Here have laundry not-have?
   Is there a laundry here?

C: **Yǒudeshì. Yàoshi bādiǎn yǐqián bǎ zāng yīfu jiāogei wǒ, jīntiān wǎnshang liùdiǎnzhōng jiù kéyi sònghuílái.**

*Have existing. If 8 o'clock before take dirty clothes hand me, today evening
6 o'clock then can send-return-come.*
Sure there is. If you give your dirty clothes to me before 8 o'clock,
they can be returned by 6 o'clock this evening.

Gǎnxǐ-de yīfu míngtiān cái dé.
Dry-wash clothing tomorrow then ready.
Dry cleaning won't be ready till the following day.

VOCABULARY

láo	work, labor; extn.—fatigue, toil; service; a surname
jià	harness; extn.—to drive, to pilot
lěng	cold, cool off; storage; rare
jīng	to manage, engage or deal in; extn.—as a result of
bō	to turn, stir; extn.—to dial
xǐ	to wash, bathe; extn.—develop [film]
zāng	dirty, filthy, soiled; (alt. pron. **zàng**—internal organs)
fú	clothes, dress; serve, obey
jiāo	hand over; deal with; intersect; relationship, friendship
sòng	to carry, deliver; extn.—to present, give; see someone out
huí	to return; answer; time[s], [MW] turn; chapter [book]
gān	dry; (alt. pron. **gàn**—to do, work, manage; business)
cái	ability, talent; just now, only then

RATIONALE AND INTERPRETATION

Láojià is an archaic expression which still endures in polite usage, meaning in essence *to trouble your chariot.* As an apology, it stands for "Excuse
me," in the sense of "Please make way" or "Forgive my intrusion," and it
is a good substitute for **duìbuqǐ**. This expression is more commonly used
in North China in the neighbourhood of Beijing when one is about to ask
a favour, meaning "May I trouble you . . . ," and thus could be a suitable
alternative to **qǐngwèn**, with which you should now be quite familiar. To
complement the use of **láojià**, the expression **fèixīn**, signifying "You have
been most kind!", is the equivalent of "Thank you [for all your trouble]"
to acknowledge some favour or service by a peer or superior, when a
simple **xièxie** would be inadequate.

Lĕngqì (*cold air*) is the term for air conditioning. Lĕng is the opposite of rè (hot). However, rèqì is not the term for central heating, since it means steam or heat. The appropriate term would be nuănqì (*warm air*). The opposite of nuăn is liáng, meaning cool.

Kāi is about as overworked as a Chinese word can be. It indicates to open, but it has many more meanings. One of these is to operate, to activate, or to run, in reference to most equipment, mechanical or electrical. In much the same fashion as zuò (to sit) is used to indicate travelling, kāi takes on the meaning of to drive. For example:

kāi chē	to drive a vehicle
kāi chuán	to sail a boat, navigate a vessel
kāi fēijī	to pilot an aircraft

The essence of to open is retained in the sense of to drive, since the starting of any machine usually requires the application of an electrical circuit, an action described as kāi diànmén (*open switch*) despite the western concept of closing a circuit. One of the terms for a switch is diànmén (*electric door*). Needless to say, kāimén means to open a door. The same essence is retained in the use of kāi to convey the idea of to start in the following compounds:

kāi dòng	to start, set in motion; move
kāi gōng	to go into operation; start work
kāi huì	to hold a meeting
kāi mù	to inaugurate
kāi qiú	to kick off, start a ball game
kāi yăn	to perform (theatre)

Kāi also has its application in the kitchen. For example,

kāi fàn	to serve a meal
kāi guō	to boil (in a wok)
kāi shuĭ	boiled water

A few further random samples of the use of kāi follow:

kāi dāo	to perform or have an operation
kāi huā	to blossom, bloom, flower
kāi qiāng	to fire a gun
kāi shĭ	to commence; beginning, outset
kāi wánxiào	to crack a joke

Yǐjīng géi nǐ bōhǎole means "already set up for you." **Bō** (to dial) is useful in this context since most controls for this sort of equipment are of the dial type.

Xǐyīfáng (*wash clothes house*) refers to the laundry.

Yǒudeshì. This is an idiomatic expression indicating "There are [plenty] to be had," or "[Of course] we have."

Bādiǎn yǐqián bǎ zāng yīfu jiāogei wǒ . . . The time factor is generally stated at the beginning of the sentence; thus, here we have *before 8 o'clock*. The phrase **bǎ zāng yīfu** (*take dirty clothes*) is another example of the use of **bǎ.** **Jiāo** means to deliver or to hand over, with **gěi** (to give) reinforcing this meaning.

Jīntiān wǎnshang. Note the use of **jīntiān** (today) in conjunction with **wǎnshang** (evening). Whereas in English one says "this evening," in Chinese it is necessary to say "today evening." There is no problem relating to tomorrow since the Chinese and English treatment is the same, i.e., **míngtiān zǎoshang** is tomorrow morning. In signifying weekdays, English and Chinese constructions are also alike. For example,

zhèi xīngqīwǔ	this Friday
xià xīngqīliù	next Saturday

Sònghuílái. Both **sòng** and **huí** are words which, when compounded, mean to send back, or to return [something]. You may recall previous references to resultative compound verbs. In this connection these have distinctive functional endings which may be divided into two main categories: resultative and directional. Remember also what was said regarding direction of movement in relation to the subject or speaker. In this instance **lái** (to come) is added to the compound **sònghuí**, to give the meaning of *bring* back, which is more specific than to return, which on its own could imply to *send* back. The Chinese rendering in that case would be **sònghuíqù**, since **qù** (to go) is the opposite of **lái**. More on the subject of resultative verbs may be found in the Appendix, Section 9.4.

Gānxǐ-de yīfu refers to clothing for dry cleaning. **Gān** (first tone) indicates dry or clean; **gàn** (fourth tone), means to do. **Xǐ** means to bathe or, in this case, to wash. **Gānxǐ** (*dry wash*) is the term for dry-cleaning. This term should not be confused with **gānjìng** (*dry clean*), which means clean and tidy. Many parts of China—particularly in the North—are very dusty indeed, a situation that calls for frequent wiping or dusting to keep things jìng (clean), the opposite of zāng (dirty). Unlike Westerners who believe "If it's wet, it's clean," the Chinese consider it easier to keep things clean if they are dry, i.e., gān. Even if the tone is not spoken quite correctly, the compound in which this word is involved helps to make the meaning clear. Compare the following two sets of examples:

gān bēi (*dry glass*)	"Bottoms up!"
gān guǒ (*dry fruit*)	dried fruits (and nuts)

gànbù (*work command*)	cadre, functionary
gànhuó (*do work*)	to work, work on a job

. . . cái de. Cái, meaning only or then, may also signify not until. Dé, with its basic meaning of *result in*, implies completion. Note, however, the slight change of emphasis in the Chinese construction. Whereas in English one says "It will not be ready *until* the next day," the Chinese construction comes out as "It will be ready *by* tomorrow." What is important in each case is not the state of readiness, but the time frame.

11.3 PROTECTION OF VALUABLES

R: **Qǐngwèn, wó bǎ zhèxiē guìzhòng-wùpǐn jiāogei nǐmen bǎocún, xíng-buxíng?**
Please, I take this-lot valuables hand you to safeguard, can not-can?
May I give you these valuables for safekeeping?

C: **Dāngrán kéyi fàng zài wǒmen báoxiǎnguì-lǐ.**
Of course can place at our safety-cupboard in.
Of course, you can keep them in our safe.

Qǐng nín xiān kāiliè qīngdān suóliú-de wùjiàn, wó hǎo jiāogei nín shōutiáo.
Please you first list-inventory leaving-of articles, I handy give to you receipt.
Please first make out a list of all the items you are leaving, so that I can give you a receipt.

VOCABULARY

wù	thing, matter; extn.—substance, content
pǐn	article, product; grade, class; extn.—quality; character
bǎo	to protect, defend; keep, maintain; extn.—ensure, guarantee
cún	to accumulate, collect, store
xiǎn	place of difficult access, defile, pass; extn.—danger, risk
guì	cupboard, cabinet
lǐ	inside; in; lining
liè	to arrange, line up; extn.—row, file; to list; [MW]
suǒ	place; what, whom, where; [MW]
liú	to remain, stay; extn.—to reserve, keep; leave
shōu	to receive, accept; extn.—take in, harvest; put away

RATIONALE AND INTERPRETATION

Guìzhòng-wùpǐn refers to valuables. **Guì** (costly) and **zhòng** (important) are two of its components, in conjunction with **wùpǐn**, a term for articles or goods in general, being a more sophisticated alternative for **dōngxi** (things).

Bǎocún means to protect or safeguard, being the combination of **bǎo** (to defend or protect) and **cún** (to store or harbour).

Báoxiǎnguì is a safe [deposit]. **Bǎo** combined with **xiǎn** (risk) gives **baóxiǎn**, the term for insurance and, by extension, safety as well as to preserve, to maintain, or to defend and to protect. Adding to this compound the word **xiāng** (trunk, case or box) yields the term **báoxiǎnxiāng**, meaning safety deposit-box, implying something small or light, if not actually portable—like a cash box. Substitute the word **guì** (cupboard) to get the term **báoxiǎnguì**, which implies a large heavy safe protected by a combination lock.

Kāiliè qīngdān means to make out a list or to make an inventory. **Kāi** (to open) with **liè** (to line up) means to make a **qīngdān**, the term for a detailed or itemized list.

Suǒliú-de wùjiàn refers to *the items being left* [for safekeeping]. **Suǒ** is used here in conjunction with **liú** (to leave), and serves to indicate that which or those which. In this case the reference is to *those which are being left*. **Wùjiàn** is another general term for articles, and may be substituted for **wùpǐn**.

Shōutiáo (*receive strip*) is the compound for a receipt.

⊙⊙ SUPPLEMENTARY VOCABULARY

wòfáng	bedroom
fángwū	buildings, house
chēfáng	car garage
kèfáng	guest room
shūfáng	a study
ménfáng	gatehouse
fángzi	a house
lóufáng	multi-storied building
píngfáng	single-storied building, bungalow
chuángdān	bed sheet
tǎnzi	blanket
yǐzi	chair
diànlú	electric heater
rèshuǐdài	hot water bottle
zhěntou	pillow
féizào	soap
máojīn	towel
liángkuai	cool, cool down
nuǎnhuo	warm
lěngdòngjī	freezer
bīngxiāng	icebox, refrigerator
huǒlú	stove
nuǎnpíng	thermos flask
báoxiǎndài	safety belt
báoxiǎndāo	safety razor
báoxiǎn gōngsī	insurance company
báoxiǎndān	insurance policy
báoxiǎnfèi	insurance premium

TWELVE

ON
COMMUNICATIONS

"The blind have the best ears,
and the deaf the sharpest eyes."

By western standards, telephone communication facilities in China are still rather behind the times. There is still a considerable language barrier to overcome, so hotels prefer that their telephones should be operated by manned exchanges. Moreover, this enables a high degree of monitoring, which is considered to be necessary. Generally speaking, local calls are free and the Chinese love to chat endlessly over the phone. A lot of the equipment is obsolete, so conversations are frequently conducted at the level of a shout. Such obsolescence also accounts for conversation being punctuated frequently with **wéi, wèi** or **wài** which substitutes for our "Hello!" Telephone booths and directories are found rarely, and you need to know Chinese well to use them, because the directories are printed in characters.

Postal facilities are generally dependable, and the stamps will delight most discerning philatelists. However, incoming foreign mail is often subject to crude censorship, and pilfering is not unknown. Should the telegraph service be a serious requirement, it would be as well to get help from a knowledgeable Chinese friend. Meanwhile, though not yet commonplace, Telex and Fax facilities are readily available at government offices and other organizations dealing with overseas interests.

12.1   OPERATOR-ASSISTED PHONE CALLS

R: **Wèi, zǒngjī ma?**
Hello, general-machine eh?
Hello, is that the switchboard?

C: **Duì! Ní dǎ nèixiàn háishi dǎ wàixiàn?**
Correct! You make inside-wire or make outside-wire?
Yes! Do you want an inside or an outside line?

R: **Wǒ kéyi zhíjiē bō waìxiàn ma?**
I can direct dial outside-wire eh?
Can I dial directly to an outside number?

C: **Kéyi, kěshi děi xiān bō jiǔ hào cái bō dāngdì hàomǎ.**
Can, but must first dial 9 number then dial local number.
Sure, but you must first dial 9 before dialing a local number.

Yàoshi xiáng dǎ chángtú-diànhuà wǒ jiù tì ní dǎ.
If considering make long-distance telephone I then replace you make.
Should you wish to make a long distance call, I will make it for you.

R: **Dǎ wánle yǐhòu, kéyi tōngzhī wǒ diànhuàfèi duōshǎo ma?**
Make finish after, can notify me telephone-fee amount eh?
After I've finished the call, can you give me the cost of it?

C: **Xíng, zhè dào hǎo bàn!**
O.K., this reach easy to do!
Sure, that'll be simple!

VOCABULARY

wèi	hey, hello; to feed
zǒng	assemble, sum up; extn.—chief, overall, head, general; always, invariably, inevitably
dǎ	to hit, knock, strike; extn.—break, fight; also general purpose verb of action, i.e., make, create, etc.

nèi	inner, inside, within
xiàn	thread; wire; extn.—line; route; boundary
zhí	straight, directly; vertical; extn.—upright, frank
jiē	come into contact, connect; extn.—take hold of, meet with
tú	way, road, route
diàn	electricity, electric
wán	intact, whole; use up; extn.—finish, complete
tōng	open, through, lead to, go to; extn.—connect, notify

RATIONALE & INTERPRETATION

Wèi. Despite the other meaning of this word, *to feed*, it is frequently used over the phone, as the equivalent of "Hello." The Chinese use the word avidly, since it also serves the purpose of "I say" and "You know," or "Listen to me" in the attempt to rivet attention. (Perhaps it might be better described as an exclamation; if you don't quite get the point yet, you soon will!)

Zǒngjī—(*main machine*) is a compound meaning a telephone exchange. **Zǒng** has varying connotations, according to context; here it means chief or main. The two words together mean, in this context, the switchboard.

Dǎ is an active verb with many uses. In this instance, **dǎ** is the operative part of the expression **dǎ diànhuà**, meaning to make a phone call. **Dǎ** is the only character of this configuration uttered in the third tone. Its basic meaning is to beat or to strike; nevertheless in many dictionaries three or four pages are needed to cover the whole scope of its use (e.g., from breaking to sneezing, and belching to whispering). Its use here has been confined to telephoning and to associated matters such as dialing numbers or making inquiries (see the selection of terms using **dǎ** listed in the Supplementary Vocabulary).

Nèixiàn (*inside wire*) refers to an internal telephone line, or extension.

Wàixiàn (*outside wire*), in contrast to the preceding term, means an external line or outside number.

Zhíjiē (*straight join*) means direct[ly] or immediate[ly].

Bō. Since the primary meaning of this word is to turn or to stir, it is easy to see its connection with dialing a telephone number.

Cái. Although this word is often used in compounds in its primary sense of talent or ability, it may be used on its own with **cái** deriving its meaning *then* from the previous words **děi xiān** (*must first*).

Dāngdì. Here **dāng** means to serve as, and **dì** means place. Thus we get the term for local or in the locality. The full expression **dāngdì hàomǎ** means local number.

Chángtú (*long route*), when applied to **diànhuà** (a [telephone] call), is the term for long distance. **Cháng** (long) is compounded with **tú** (route) to supply this meaning. The character for **cháng/zhǎng** may be pronounced either way. Its use should be obvious from the context; in fact, **cháng** is the more common pronunciation. The reasons for the pronunciation **zhǎng** are explained as appropriate when they occur. **Cháng** is widely known for its use in some famous geographical names, for example:

> **Cháng'ān** (*long peace*) refers to Xi'an which is the present name for this city.
>
> **Chángchéng** (*long wall*) signifies the Great Wall of China. This is the abbreviation for the full title of Wanli Changcheng (*10000 li long wall*).
>
> **Chángjiāng** (*long river*) alludes to the Yangtse River, formerly shown in atlases as the Yangtsekiang. While the traditional spelling of Yangtse still prevails on most maps printed in English, Yangzi Jiang is the correct presentation.

Although the appropriate translation for **cháng** is long, the more poetic interpretation of great continues in popular usage. Thus occasionally the Yangzi is referred to as the Great River, thanks to its Chinese name, Changjiang. This is, in fact, the name given to the whole water course, extending from the high hinterland in Western China to the East China Sea nearly 4000 miles away. The name Yangzi River applies generally to the navigable portion. The upper reaches are known as Jinsha (Golden Sands, attributable to the alluvial matter colouring the water), or by the various other names of the lesser tributaries which feed the main flow.

Diànhuà (*electric speech*) refers to the telephone in a general sense. The specific term for the instrument is **diànhuàjī** (*electric speech machine*). A number of compounds have **diàn** as their first syllable, denoting the use of electricity.

Wǒ jiù tì ní dǎ. The use of **tì** meaning on behalf of has been explained; here is a second example of **tì** being used in this sense. **Dǎ** refers
briefly to the whole process of putting through the long distance call, signifying the same as to make in English.

Wán, in this context, means to finish or complete; consequently, **dǎ
wánle yǐhòu** is a phrase meaning "after the call has been completed."

Tōngzhī is a compound meaning to notify or to inform, **tōng** (to notify) being coupled with **zhī** (to know, inform).

Diànhuàfèi refers to the charge for a telephone call.

Xíng, zhè dào hǎo bàn. Although **kéyi,** signifying "[Will you] be able
to . . . ," was used as a QW in the request, the response using **xíng,** indicating O.K., is idiomatically acceptable. It implies that the operator is not
only capable of rendering this service, but also perfectly willing to do so.
The use of **dào** to complement **hǎo bàn** (*easy to do*) creates an idiomatic
expression, the equivalent of "That's easily done!"

12.2   LEAVING A MESSAGE

R: **Wèi, ní nǎr?**
Hello, you where?
Hello, who's there?

C: **Zhōngguó Yínháng; zhǎo shéi shuōhuà?**
China Bank, seek whom to speak?
Bank of China; whom do you want to speak to?

R: **Qǐng Lǐú jīnglǐ tīng diànhuà.**
Invite Liu manager to listen telephone.
Have Manager Liu take a call, please.

C: **Duìbuqǐ, Lǐú Xiānsheng bú zài. Fù-jīnglǐ xíng-buxíng?**
Sorry, Liu Mr. not at. Assistant manager do not-do?
Sorry, but Mr. Liu is not in. Would the assistant manager do?

R: **Xíng, kěshi búbì máfan rénjia. Wǒ gēn mìshū liú huà jiù déle.**
Can, but not need trouble people. I with secretary leave word then satisfactory.
O.K., but there is no need to trouble anybody. I can just leave a message with the secretary.

C: **Hǎo, wǒ géi nǐ jiēxìàn.**
Good, I give you connection.
Right, I'll put you through.

VOCABULARY

shuō	to speak, to talk, to say; to explain; to scold
tīng	to listen; extn.—hear; heed, obey
mì	secret, keep secret; extn.—secretary
liú	to remain, stay; extn.—to reserve, keep; leave

RATIONALE AND INTERPRETATION

Wèi, ní nǎr? This is a standard phrase with which to begin a telephone conversation in Chinese. It is usually said by the caller, as soon as the other party answers. There are obviously variations on this theme, but identification usually runs along the following lines.

Zhǎo shéi shuōhuà? This, and **Ní zhǎo shéi a?** are two of the most common ways of asking "Whom do you wish to speak to?" **Shuōhuà** (*say words*) means to speak.

Jīnglǐ is the term generally used to denote a manager, and occurs in expressions dealing with management.

. . . tīng diànhuà. In general, this expression means *. . . to take a phone call.* Although **tīng** means to listen, it need not be taken literally; it implies essentially *put me through to . . .*

Bú zài means literally *not at [a place]* or *not in*; in other words to be out or not available.

Fù-jīnglǐ. The term **fù** indicating auxiliary or vice-, when used in conjunction with **jīnglǐ**, forms the compound for deputy-manager or assistant manager.

Rénjia (*person family*). The elements of this compound should be familiar, even if the compound itself is a new one. It refers to people in general or, simply, anyone. Note that the second syllable is toneless. If the second syllable were stressed, the word **rénjiā** would mean household or family.

Mìshū (*secret book*) is a compound meaning secretary, implying a person entrusted with confidential matters.

Liú huà means simply to leave word or to leave a message.

Jiù déle. Dé (all right) implies a satisfactory conclusion. Thus, this idiomatic expression means essentially "That will do," "That's fine," or simply "It is O.K."

Jiēxiàn (*connect wire*) is no more or less than to make a connection. In the context of telephone calls, the meaning is therefore to put [the call] through.

12.3 POST OFFICE FACILITIES

R: **Qǐngwèn, zhèi fēng xìn jì dào Déguó děi duócháng shíjiān cái dào?**
Invite-query, this [MW] letter send arrive Germany need how-long time then reach?
May I ask how long it would take for this letter to reach Germany?

C: **Kōngyóu háishi píngyóu?**
Space-post or level-post.
Air mail or surface mail?

R: **Jì hángkōng.**
Send aviation.
By air.

C: **Zuì duō wǔliù tiān jiù kéyi dào.**
Most many five-six days then can arrive.
At the most five or six days.

R: **Guówài yóufèi duōshao qián?**
    Country-outside postage how much money?
    How much is the postage for overseas?

C: **Kōngyóu děi yíkuàiwǔ. Xǐhuan jìniàn-yóupiào ma? Nǐ zìjǐ tiāoxuǎn jǐzhāng, hǎo-ma?**
    Space-post require 1 dollar 5[0]. Like commemorative stamps eh? You yourself select few [MW], O.K.?
    For air mail that'll be $1.50. Would you like commemorative stamps? How about selecting a few yourself?

R: **Nǐmen zhèr yǒu-meiyǒu yònghù-diànbào kéyi jièyòng?**
    You here have not-have consumer-telegraph can borrow?
    Do you have a telex here [one] could borrow?

C: **Āiyā! Kǒngpà wǒmen méiyǒu zhè zhǒng shèbèi. Zuì hǎo dào yóudiànjú qù dǎge diànbào.**
    Oh! Fear we not-have this type equipment. Best good reach postal-telegraphic-office go send telegram.
    Oh dear! I'm afraid we don't have this sort of facility. It would be best to send a cable from the Telegraph Office.

Note that the telegraph office is often separate from the post office, and is known as **diànbàojú**. A post office which also has telegraph services is known as **yóudiànjú**—a term generally used for main post offices that offer all services. While telegrams can be readily transmitted in the Roman alphabet in clear language or in cipher, it is obvious that texts in Chinese characters require different treatment. There exists what is known as the Chinese Commercial Code (CCC) which is transmitted in four-figure numerical groups. The characters are arranged in the stroke order they would be given in a dictionary, with a specific number allocated to each character. For example, China—i.e., **Zhōngguó**—would be transmitted as 0022/0948. This procedure naturally requires the text to be encoded before transmission, and decoded again for the recipient to read it. However, with the rapid development nowadays of facsimile transmission and other electronic communication techniques, the CCC method is becoming obsolete since the text can be relayed more and more as is.

fēng	seal; extn.—envelope, MW [for letters]
jì	send, to mail; entrust, deposit
dé	virtue; kindness; abbreviation denoting Germany
kōng	empty, hollow, void; extn.—sky, air, (alt. pron. **kòng**)
píng	flat, level; extn.—equal; tie, draw; peaceful; a surname
háng	boat, ship; extn.—navigate
xǐ	joy; pleased; extn.—to like, be inclined to
tiāo	to choose, to pick
xuǎn	select, choose, extn.—elect
hù	door; extn.—household; [bank] account
jiè	borrow; lend; extn.—make use of

RATIONALE AND INTERPRETATION

Zhèi fēng xìn means this letter and introduces the MW—**fēng**. With its basic meaning of to seal, this word is used in expressions indicating not only a letter, but also an envelope. It derives its use as a MW from the latter meaning. Note the placement of the word in these two examples:

Yì fēng xìn	a letter (i.e., item of mail)
Yíge xìnfēng	an envelope

Fēng, while not a very commonly used character in Chinese, is interesting in its particular connotations. In bygone days, the voice of authority was considered to be as efficacious as any lock and chain when it came to security. Consequently, buildings or boxes, for instance, were sealed by a strip of paper (**fēngtiáo**). On it would be inscribed a brief proscription with the impression of an official seal of authority. This paper pasted over the access was considered to be effective as a deterrent against all but the most lawless elements. An infringement might be easy, but the consequences would be dire! When used in a compound, **fēng** requires the addition of the general MW **gè**, as shown in the second example above. The same requirement applies to a few other MW to distinguish between, for example, a teacup and a cup of tea, or a ricebowl and a bowl of rice. With regard to the word **xìn**, here are a few compounds that are useful in the context of the postal service (**yóuzhèng**):

huíxìn	return mail
xìnjiàn	mail, letters
xìntǒng, xìnxiāng	mailbox
xìnzhǐ	note paper

Jì in this context means to send by post or to mail. **Dào** is used to emphasize the point of reaching the destination or arrival.

Déguó is the commonly used name for Germany, as it was before the East/West division in 1945. **Dé** is the abbreviation for **Déyìzhì** (i.e., the German word Deutsch). West Germany (FRG) was called **Xīdé**, just as East Germany (GDR) was known as **Dōngdé** or alternatively **Míndé** (*People's Germany*). Since reunification, **Déguó** is, of course, the term once more in current use.

Kōng appears in the compounds **kōngyóu** and **hángkōng**, both of which have virtually the same meaning; that is, air mail. In the first instance, **kōngyóu** (*air post*) is used to establish the contrast with **píngyóu** (*level post*). **Hángkōng** (*navigate air*) is the term for aviation and is the more common term used on all airmail stationery.

Píng, meaning level or flat, alludes to the horizon. Thus the compound **píngyóu** refers to surface mail and, like its equivalent in English, disregards the specific means of transportation.

Zuì duō (*most many*) means the most or, as here, at most.

Guówài yóufèi. **Guówài** means abroad, and **yóufèi** (*mail cost*) is the term for postage.

Xǐhuan (*like joyful*) means to like or, to be fond of, or to be keen on. The primary meaning of **xǐ** is joy or happiness; by extension it also means to enjoy. **Huān** (*joyous*) occurs not only in **xǐhuan**, but also in the compound **huānyíng** (to welcome). The compound **xǐhuan** can vary in its depth of meaning. It may mean simply to like, or may indicate a more intense partiality or enthusiasm, depending on the context in which it occurs. Generally, it signifies enjoyment rather than mere preference. **Xǐ** is one of the popular characters in the scheme of felicity. Apart from the trio **Fú Lǔ Shòu** (representing Prosperity, Happiness, and Longevity), **Xǐ** is the character for Joy and it is often portrayed in dual form, indicating Double Joy and representing connubial bliss (Figure 12.3).

FIGURE 12.3

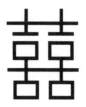

Stylized presentation
of the character
referred to as **shuāngxǐ**,
meaning doubled joy.

Xǐ is represented also by the colour red, which is the colour denoting festive occasions—such as weddings—often referred to as **hóngshì** or **xǐshì** (*joyful matters*). By contrast, white denotes mourning. **Báishì**, for example, signifies obsequies or funeral rites.

Jìniàn-yóupiào are commemorative stamps. **Jìniàn** means to commemorate or commemoration, and **yóupiào** (*mail ticket*) is the compound for stamps. Although small in size, stamps rate **zhāng** as a MW since they come in sheets.

Tiāoxuǎn. Both elements of this compound mean to choose or to select. **Tiāo** is often used on its own to mean to pick out. **Xuǎn** is more frequently encountered in compounds, designating a variety of concepts (e.g., a selection, or to elect in the political sense).

Yònghù-diànbào is the term for telex. **Diànbào** (*electric report*) is the compound for telegram or telegraph, and here it is combined with the compound **yònghù**, meaning consumer or user, to give the term for telex. Another shorter term, **diànchuán** (*electric transmit*), is also used to denote telex. Fax machines are called **chuánzhēn** (*transmit truly*), possibly preceded by **túxiàng**, meaning image.

Jièyòng. On its own, **jiè** can mean to borrow or to lend. Although the word **jiè** can be used for either of its antithetical meanings, it is not hard to determine which is the intended meaning. The context here is not of primary importance, as the sentence construction should make the meaning clear. In general, **jiè** is taken to mean to borrow when used in conjunction with **yòng** (to use), and to lend when used with **gěi** (to give). Compare the four sentences below:

Wó bǎ shuíbǐ jiègěile wǒ péngyou.	I lent my pen to my friend.
Wó gěi tā jièle bùshǎo dōngxi.	I lent her quite a few things.

**Tāmen cháng jièyòng wǒde
     qìchē.**   They often borrow my car.

Qǐng jiè yíxià nǐde shuíbǐ.   Please [let me] borrow your pen a
                                        moment.

Note that in the last example it matters very little whether you mean to say
"May I borrow your pen for a moment?" or "Please lend me your pen for
a moment." Should you wish to be quite precise, however, consider these
two final examples:

Wǒ gēn nǐ jiè shíkuàiqián,   Would it be O.K. to borrow
     xíng-buxíng? $10 from you?

Nǐ jiègei wǒ shíkuàiqián   How would you like to lend me
     hǎo ma? $10?

Āiyā is a common exclamation which can mean anything from "Oh
dear!" to "Heck!," with "Gosh!" or "Good Lord!" in between. It is in no
way profane or obscene.

SUPPLEMENTARY VOCABULARY

dǎ tōng	to get through on the phone
dǎ zhékòu	to give a discount
dǎ máoyī	to knit [woolen garments]
dǎ jiāodao	to make contact/have dealings
dǎ zhàng	to make war
dǎ pái	to play cards
dǎ májiàng	to play mahjong
dǎ guānsi	to take legal action
dǎ zì	to type
dǎzìjī	typewriter
fùyìn	to photocopy
diànzǐ jìsuànjī	computer
wénzì chúlǐqì	word processor
diànbiǎo	any type of electric meter
diànchē	tram, streetcar, trolleybus
diànqì	electrical equipment
diànlì	electricity

diàndēng	electric light
diàntī	elevator
diàntǒng	flashlight, [electric] torch
diànxiàn	[electric] wire, lead
diàndēngpào	light bulb
shǎnguāngdēng	photoflash
diàntái	radio station
guǎnggaò	advertisement
guǎngbō	broadcast
xīnwén	news

THIRTEEN
ON CHINESE FOOD

"Fatty did not get that way on one mouthful."

The Chinese have endeared themselves to much of the world with their culinary skills. Many visitors to China will have tasted Chinese food already, but for the few who have not, a visit to a local Chinese restaurant is recommended. The visitor should be prepared for a major change in diet, and a familiarity with Chinese foods and cooking methods before arriving in China will make it easier because most food provided in China will be Chinese rather than western.

In China, rice is analogous to the Westerner's bread and potatoes. The Chinese refer to the **wúgǔ** (*five grains*), i.e., rice, wheat, millet, barley and maize. Grain is an essential ingredient in their diet, while rice is the main crop of the cereals the Chinese cultivate. **Fàn**, referring to cooked rice, is the generic term for food or a meal. **Cài**, meaning vegetable, is the word generally used to denote a course or a dish and applies to everything— including meat or fish—which is eaten with the staple grain. Due to the climate distribution rice is grown mainly in South China—south of the Yangzi River—while most of the other grains are cultivated in North China. This is where the farinaceous foods were developed so prolifically. It is claimed that Marco Polo, after his sojourn under the Great Khan of the Yuan Dynasty seven centuries ago, introduced Chinese recipes to Europe. Whether or not the claim is valid, the similarity of **miàn** (noodles) to spaghetti, or **jiǎozi** (meat dumplings) to ravioli is striking.

A meal in China would not be complete without tea. The tea ceremony figures rather less prominently in China than it does in Japan; nonetheless tea is the main beverage enjoyed by the Chinese. While relatively few people can afford to indulge in wine, everyone can now afford some tea. **Chá**, the word for tea, refers to the beverage in its ready-to-drink state. **Cháyè** (*tea leaves*) alludes to the dry goods purchased from a grocer, and not to the dregs in the bottom of the teacup, or the teapot. Generally a teapot is placed on the table as soon as one sits down in a restaurant. There are many popular brands (some more expensive than others), but generally it is what is known as **hóng** (red) **chá** which is brewed lightly in a teapot. **Qīngchá** (*green tea*) is drunk in a tall glass with a cover, to which boiling water may be added from time to time. This is drunk especially during the hot weather, and is not accompanied by anything to nibble, whereas a pot of tea is usually partnered with a dishful of something—if only salted melon seeds. When the teapot needs replenishing, simply tilt the lid, and the waiter will know what to do. In official circles, a polite hint to a visitor that his time has run out, or that the interview should be terminated, is for a fresh pot of tea to be ordered. This should be declined with thanks and followed up with a dignified exit.

Westerners believe there are only two kinds of Chinese cuisine, Northern and Southern, otherwise often known as Peking and Cantonese, respectively. This simply is not accurate. Because many Chinese restaurants abroad cater to southern tastes, since the vast majority of overseas Chinese are from South China, it was inevitable that Westerners were first treated to the Cantonese style of cooking.

A small but popular part of the great variety of Cantonese cuisine is known as Dimsum (in Putonghua **diǎnxīn**, meaning literally *to dot the heart*). Although sometimes referred to as a Chinese smorgasbord, this description is misleading. Dimsum actually consist of small helpings of a variety of dishes. A selection is presented to the customers' tables on something resembling scaled-down hors d'oeuvres trolleys. A comprehensive assortment is available throughout the meal, and this is a favourite repast in the middle of the day. You should be aware, however, that Dimsum is known by Cantonese speakers as Yamcha (*drink tea*). Nonetheless, it is easy to tell that this meal has more to do with than just tea. What Westerners often see as well is a form of the Chinese banquet with its many courses, but the Chinese themselves only enjoy this style on great occasions. You should therefore be aware of the difference between

yànhuì, the sumptuous banquet with its endless variety of dishes, and the much simpler fare of a typical home meal (**jiāfàn**).

China, the second largest country in the world, with her twenty-two provinces and five autonomous regions containing a fifth of the people on Earth, has a history of over three millennia of the past half million years of early population. One is inevitably aware of a vast and varied culture. One facet of such a culture is manifested in its gastronomy. It is hardly surprising, considering its size, that China has such a wide variety of cuisine. To some extent the variety corresponds to the simplified breakdown of the linguistic groups in China reflecting the North, Central and Southern regions.

(a) *Northern China* includes the regions of the Far North, i.e., Inner Mongolia and Northwest China. The Far North originated the barbecue style of cooking, well suited to the nomadic lifestyle of a man in the saddle or a shepherd. The meat grilled is largely mutton, since oxen are too valuable as draught animals to be slaughtered young. Other than in the heat of summer, many restaurants in the North serve these rather heavy meals with sesame seed buns, marinading the meat in a variety of sauces according to individual taste. The lack of green vegetables in the regular diet is compensated for by drinking koumiss (fermented milk).

The style of cooking of the Far North differs somewhat from that of the North region, where **jīngcài** (*Capital dishes*) cuisine figures largely. Beijing, or the North Capital, the seat of government centered round the emperor's court, received from officials and administrators a vast array of what their areas had to offer to delight the emperor's palate. These offerings had to be submitted at their best, consequently the kitchens were said to be an accurate indication of the excellence of administration, and of the speed and security of transportation and communication. Refrigeration—then as now—depended on natural ice, so far more emphasis was put on fresh food. Even today live fare is seldom killed before it is actually needed in the kitchen. It is still claimed that many of the best of all Chinese feasts abound in this region.

(b) *Central China.* Shanghai, the center of the East region, also claims to serve some of the best food in China. This is debatable, particularly among the Chinese, and especially among those in the

South, who consider Shanghai dishes to be over-flavored, because of the liberal use of soy sauces, pickles, and salted vegetables. The region is a large area extending inland to the province of Hubei and embracing the Yangzi River basin where the Wu dialects predominate. Historically, credit for this particular cuisine belongs mainly to Yangzhou, near Nanking. However, Yangzhou's stir-fry style of cooking has been adopted in China's culinary art to such an extent that it has become a national rather than a regional feature.

(c) *Southern China*, may be sub-divided into two parts. The West region is best known for its spicy food, as anyone who has tasted Sichuan dishes will realize. However history shows that Hunan Province—east of Sichuan—was the original source of Chinese peppers and other pungent seasonings well over 2300 years ago. Only about three centuries ago did the West region develop the culinary technique so widely popularized nowadays. It is probable that the original Chinese pepper was the forerunner of the herbs which gave rise to the spice trade, first between East and West, and subsequently around the globe. The best known Chinese cuisine is undoubtedly Cantonese cooking from the South-East region which covers two provinces, Fujian and Guangdong. The variety of dishes they produce is prodigious, and Westerners have only themselves to blame if they have experienced no more than chopsuey, or sweet and sour dishes.

Despite the variety of fare to be obtained in different parts of the country, the meals of the average family (**jiāfàn**) are, of necessity, fairly simple. Indeed, all kitchen-related activities are rather basic. In addition to the staple dish of rice, one or two large dishes of sweet potatoes or other choices depending on family means, will be placed in the middle of the table. The family can help themselves from these to flavour the staple dish. Often these will be a simple vegetable dish (**cài**), such as the ubiquitous cabbage in a soup if the family is poor, or a soybean product such as **dòufù**, a curd most Westerners know as Tofu. The soya bean is probably China's richest source of protein, and supplies most of what might otherwise be lacking in terms of balanced nutrition. Many Chinese are considered to be vegetarian by choice due to the influence of Buddhism, but it is possibly the budget which exercises the greater influence. Taoism too enjoins them to cook lightly, although it may well be the cruel force of grinding poverty which prevents them from obtaining a greater variety of food and the fuel to cook it with. Should a family be able to afford better ingredients, then fish or poultry may be included in the diet. Pork is the most popular meat, except among Muslims. Mutton is eaten mainly north of the Yangzi, while beef is a luxury reserved for special occasions.

Traditionally a dining-table was square, seating two to a side. The menu, based on the principle of one course per person, generally consisted therefore of eight main courses (not counting appetizers or fillers). Nowadays a round table seating ten to twelve people is favoured. Regardless of the shape or size of the table, it is usual to urge the guests of honour to sit at the top, that is to say in the East, facing the center of the proceedings. An earlier practice was for the host to seat himself with his back to the door, a tradition that is said to date from the time of the Tartars. These marauders placed themselves near the entrance of the room (formerly the tent) so as to defend their guests from attack, this being a point of honour with them. Consequently, it is recommended that a western host should bear such points in mind, rather than install himself at the head of his table—at least in public places. Home habits are another matter altogether.

At a restaurant, a waiter is likely to ask **nín yào shénme yǐnliào?** ("What beverage do you want?"). A plain question such as **ní xiǎng hē shénme?** ("What do you want to drink?"), would be considered somewhat familiar, if not abrupt. **Yǐnliào** (*drink material*) pertains to all types of drink, hot or cold, alcoholic or not, and may therefore be translated as beverages. While the guests are eating, it is the host's duty to see that their wine cups are replenished. It is considered less than courteous to leave this important duty to a waiter! If not the host, then friends or relatives seated with the guests around the banquet table will attend to the needs of the visitors and ensure their satisfaction. A high-grade **Shàoxīng** wine is called **huādiāo** (after the ornate jars it is stored in), and one can generally imbibe this without too much trepidation! Such wines as **máotáijiǔ**, **méiguilù**, or **báigār** (also known as **báijiǔ**) are universally acknowledged as potent, and should be indulged in lightly. If you do not want any more to drink, you need only put your hand over your glass, since it is not considered good manners to make anyone drink against their will. **Chībǎo hēzú** is a four-character expression a host might use to urge his party to have their fill. It means to "Eat and drink till satisfied." At the end of a banquet, when you are feeling replete, an appropriate response is: **Jiǔzú fànbǎo**, meaning "Adequate wine and a surfeit of food"; in other words—"No more, thank you. I'm full!"

13.1   EATING OUT

C: **Jīntiān wǎnshang wǒ dài nǐ qù Dōngláishùn, qíng nǐ chī yídùn biànfàn, hǎo ma?**
Today evening I take you go Donglaishun invite you eat a [MW] simple-meal, good eh?
How would you like me to take you out to Donglaishun this evening for a simple meal?

R: **Nà hǎojíle! Wǒ tīngshuō zhè shì Běijīng yíge zùi yǒumíng-de Huíjiào fànguǎnzi.**
That good-extremely! I hear-tell this is Beijing one most famous-of Moslem restaurants.
That's marvelous! I hear that it is a very famous Beijing Moslem restaurant.

C: **Duìle. Tāmen-de shuàn-yángròu shì fēicháng hǎochī-de. Nǐ chángguo méiyou?**
Right. Their dipped mutton is particularly delicious. You taste-past not-have?
Right. Their dipped mutton is particularly delicious. Have you ever tasted it?

R: **Zhè búshi yòng huǒguō zuò-de cài ma? Wǒ shìguo yìhuí; búguò kǒngpà bǐbushàng zhèr.**
This not-be use fire-pot make-of dish, eh? I try-past one-time; only fear compare-not-on here.
Isn't that what they cook in a hot-pot? I've tried it once; however I dare say it doesn't compare with here.

C: **Nàme wǒmen shìshi-kàn ba. Jīntiān diǎn-de jiǔ-cài kěndìng wánquán shì zhēnzhèng-de běifāng shǒuyi.**
Then we try-try-see let's. Today mark wine-food definitely entirely be genuine-of north-side handiwork.
Let's try it then. The food and drink I've ordered today is certainly all authentic Northern style [of cuisine].

[On entering the restaurant]

C: **Nǐmen zhèr yǒu kòng wèizi méiyǒu? Wǒmen yígòng wǔge rén. Zhǎo yìzhāng hǎo zhuōzi gěi wàiguo kèren, hǎo ma?**
You here have empty places not-have? We altogether five [MW] persons. Find one [MW] good table for foreign guests, good eh?
Have you any places available? There are five of us altogether. Would you find a nice table for our foreign visitors?

Waiter: **Lǐbiar hái yǒu kòngr, kěshi fàntái hái méi cā-wǎn. Qǐng nǐmen děng yìhuěr; gǎnkuài jiù bái-hǎole.**
Inside still have space, but food-table still not [have] wipe-finish. Request you wait a moment, quickly then arrange well.
There's still room inside, but the table has not been cleared yet. Please wait a moment; it will soon be laid.

[After a short interval]

Waiter: **Duìbuqǐ jiào gèwèi děngzhe. Xiànzài dōu yùbèi hǎole, qǐng gēn wǒ lǐbiar qù ba.**
Excuse cause everyone waiting. Now all prepare well, invite follow me inside go let's.
Sorry to have kept you waiting. All is ready now, please follow me inside.

Dōngláishùn is an old established restaurant in the heart of the city, specializing in the hot-pot. This is often served in Chinese restaurants abroad as one of a number of courses in a meal, and often listed—rather erroneously or misleadingly—as Mongolian rather than Moslem. It is usually served in North China as a whole meal in itself. It may be preceded by a cold dish appetizer, and while this is being eaten the waiter will set up the meal. First of all the glowing charcoal is placed in the funnel of the hot-pot, while the kitchen staff get the ingredients ready. Apart from the thinly sliced mutton (some lean, and some half lean and half fat), sliced liver and kidney will be served. There will also be plates of cabbage—both raw and pickled—and vermicelli, but there are two further ingredients which make this meal special. First is the stock in which the food is dipped, and second is the trayful of condiments known as **zuò-liàor**, which virtually means *the makings*! This trayful may contain at least a dozen small bowls of condiments such as sesame oil, soya sauce, vinegar, curry oil—to name but a few of the best known. The guests mix these ingredients in their own bowls to taste, or the host may undertake the task for the uninitiated. Having retrieved from the steaming stock whatever was dipped into it (the trick is not to allow the food to cook too long), the morsel is then lightly dipped into one's own bowl of condiment mixture for flavouring. If you find fondue fun, you should try this Oriental version! From time to time the waiter may add further stock to the pot as it steams away, and finally a marvelous soup results with which to wash down the meal. The Chinese rarely use soup to initiate a meal. In a banquet they prefer to use two or more soups in the course of a meal in order to separate the flavour of one main course, say pork, from that of another—possibly fish.

VOCABULARY

dùn	pause; MW for a meal
jí	very, extremely, exceedingly, utmost point; extn.—Pole
shuàn	dip; to scald thin sliced meat, fish, or vegetables
yáng	sheep; a surname
ròu	meat, flesh
fēi	wrong, evildoing; not, no; have got to, simply must
cháng	common, normal; frequently, often, usually; a surname
cháng	to taste, try the flavour of
huǒ	fire; extn.—urgent; anger
guō	[cooking] pot, pan [wok], cauldron; boiler
jiǔ	wine; any alcoholic drink
cài	vegetable, greens; [nonstaple] food; extn.—courses, dishes

shì	to try, test; extn.—examination
yì	skill, art
zhuō	table, desk
tái	platform, stage; terrace; table; radio station; MW
cā	to rub, wipe, polish; spread on; brush, scrape
gǎn	to catch up, overtake; extn.—hurry; drive
bǎi	to place, put, arrange; assume [attitude]
gè	each, every, various
zhe	toneless suffix indicating current action; e.g., -ing; (alt. pron. zháo—to touch, feel, reach)

RATIONALE AND INTERPRETATION

Chī yídùn biànfàn appears to be a straightforward suggestion to partake of a simple meal. However, this is rather a deceptive invitation, since modesty dictates a degree of understatement on the part of the host. The host may insist that the repast is quite inadequate and poorly prepared— even though it is patently just the opposite. Although the host is in no way guilty of fishing for compliments, much less of putting down his wife's or family's skills in the kitchen, the guests—naturally enough—will be lavish in their praise of the fine meal they have helped to put away. This form of etiquette applies whether the host entertains at home or in a restaurant, and everybody should know the form.

Hǎo jíle means extremely good, marvelous, or even terrific. While **hén hǎo** (very good) is praise enough, the use of **jí** (extremely) makes the superlative far more enthusiastic. Notice that the adverb follows the adjective, rather than preceding it as it would in English.

Tīngshuō (*hear say*) means to hear tell, or simply to hear.

Yíge zuì yǒumíng-de Huíjiào fànguǎnzi means a most famous Muslim restaurant. **Zuì** is also a means of expressing the superlative. **Yǒumíng** (*have name*) means famous, celebrated, or well-known. The addition of **-de** defines the expression as adjectival. **Huíjiào** refers to the Islamic religion, and **fànguǎnzi** is an eating house or restaurant. **Yíge** is equivalent to the article a; to omit it would suggest that the restaurant was "*the* most famous restaurant."

Shuàn-yángròu (*dipped mutton*) is another way of referring to the hot-pot meal already described, but is more specific. **Shuàn** is a somewhat esoteric word equating with fondue. **Yángròu** (*sheep meat*) is the term for mutton. A lamb is **xiǎoyáng** (**xiǎo** being little), so its flesh would be **xiǎo yángròu**. It is not usual Chinese practice to slaughter livestock for food before the animals reach their prime. The purpose of adding the term **ròu** after the creature's name is to refer to its flesh.

Fēicháng hǎochī means particularly delicious. The term **fēicháng** means uncommonly or unusually, and provides yet another form for expressing a superlative, though not quite as enthusiastic a superlative as the previous two. **Hǎochī** (*good to eat*) is the word for delicious or tasty. **Hǎo** can be applied to a number of verbs relating to one's senses or feelings in this manner. For example:

hǎokàn (*good to look at*)	pretty, attractive, nice
hǎoshòu (*good to bear*)	comfortable
hǎoshuō (*good to say*)	complimentary
hǎotīng (*good to hear*)	tuneful, easy on the ear
hǎowár (*good to play*)	fun, amusing, interesting
hǎowén (*good to smell*)	fragrant
hǎozuò (*good to do*)	easy [to do]

Nǐ chángguo méiyou? The word **guò** not only means to cross or to pass but also, by extension, past. It can also be used as shown here to indicate past action. **Cháng** means to taste, hence **nǐ chángguo méiyou** means "Have you ever tasted it?"

Huǒguō (*fire pot*) is often translated as a chafing dish. However, the heaters used in connection with dipped mutton are not to be confused with the small heaters often used to keep food warm in Chinese restaurants abroad. Such heaters are in fact not often seen in China, since the courses are usually served in rotation, fresh out of the kitchen so that each successive dish is eaten hot before the next arrives. Nevertheless, tourists on the move are served virtually all the food at once, since this is the way the foreigner is believed to prefer, and it facilitates a quicker turnaround.

The hot-pot is a cone-shaped utensil, usually made of brass. It comprises a funnel containing glowing charcoal, the heat source, and about halfway up the cone, a bowl welded around it to contain the stock for cooking the meal. The whole thing is set in the middle of a round table so that everyone can reach it. **Guō** is the term for any cooking pot the Chinese use. This may or may not have a short handle to one side, and is shaped like a partial hemisphere made of iron, which disperses the heat evenly and economically. This is the utensil more readily known to most Westerners by its Cantonese name, wok.

Wǒ shìguo yìhuí means "I have tried [it] once." The term **shì** means to try [something out], while **guò** is used to indicate a past action. **Yìhúi** alludes to one occasion, or once.

Búguò as used here means however. It may also be used to signify notwithstanding or only, but and not more than.

Fig. 13.1. A Chinese hot-pot.

Bǐbushàng means cannot be compared with. Here is a further example of the use of resultative verbs—in this case a negative. The positive form is **bǐdeshàng** (i.e., comparable); **dé** (to obtain) changes to **bù** for the opposite sense.

Nàme wǒmen shìshi-kàn ba. The repetition of **shì** (to try, test), implying *to try [a] try*, in combination with **kàn** (to look), gives an approximate equivalent of the English expression to try and see. Therefore, in idiomatic English, **shìshi-kàn** can be translated simply as to try. The suggestive particle **ba** provides the sense of let's. **Nàme** which begins the sentence indicates in *that* case, or simply *then*.

Diǎn...cài means to order from a menu. It was customary for a waiter to place before a host a list of courses available that day. The host, brush in hand, would place a dot beside each dish of his choice, hence **diǎn** (dot), which in this instance takes on the role of a verb (*to make a dot*) and implies selecting dishes for a meal. The combination **jiǔ-cài** (*wine dishes*) may be translated as the food and drink, or the wine to go with the food, since the Chinese seldom drink wine except with a meal.

Wánquán zhēnzhèng-de means entirely authentic. The compound **wánquán** (*finish complete*) means complete, whole or all. The second compound, **zhēnzhèng** (*truly upright*) conveys the idea of genuine or authentic.

Běifāng shǒuyì means literally *northern workmanship*. **Shǒuyì** (*hand skill*) is a compound consisting of **shǒu** (hand), and **yì**, meaning skill or art. Since Chinese cuisine at its best may rightly be considered an art form, the use of **shǒuyì** is justifiable in this context, particularly when one considers the importance the Chinese place on the presentation of a special dish.

Wèizi means place or seat or, by implication in this context, a table. It serves the same function as **zuòwèi** (*sitting place*), since it implies a place [at a table].

Zhǎo . . . hǎo ma? Zhǎo means to look for, or to find. **Hǎo ma** is an idiomatic expression which, at the end of a sentence, has the nuance of "how would you like to . . ." or simply would you [please], **hǎo** being the operative part of a good idea "if you wouldn't mind [carrying out a suggestion]." It may be considered as an alternative for **hǎo-buhǎo**.

Yìzhāng zhuōzi, incorporating the MW **zhāng**, means a table. **Hǎo zhuōzi** (*good table*) simply implies a well-situated table, such as a table conveniently placed so as to give maximum exposure to the ambience or comforts of the establishment.

Lǐbiar hái yǒu kòngr. Lǐbiar (*inner side*) is a compound referring to the interior or inside, specifically the enclosed space (see Appendix, Section 8, Figure 2). **Hái yǒu** is straightforward, meaning still have. **Kòngr** is the same character as **kōng** (empty, void). When pronounced in the fourth tone (with or without the retroflex **r**, popular in Beijing), it refers specifically to a vacant or unoccupied space (or period of time, in context).

Fàntái. Fàn is the general term used for food. While **zhuōzi** is explicitly a table, **tái** only assumes this meaning when compounded with another word; otherwise it means something more like a platform, or possibly a counter. However, for a dining-table, either **fàntái** or **fànzhuō** will do.

. . . **hái méi cā-wán. Hái méi** presents nothing new, but you are reminded that **méi** is the abbreviation for **méiyǒu** (*not have*). **Cā** (*to wipe*) in this context, means to clean up, or to clear away. **Wán** (*to finish*) is an auxiliary verb annexed to an action verb to indicate that the action has been completed or finished.

. . . **gǎnkuài jiù bái-hǎole. Gǎnkuài** (*overtake hurry*) means quickly or at once. **Bǎi** (*to place*) means, in this instance, to arrange the table. As explained before, -**hǎole** after a verb indicates a satisfactory conclusion or completion of the action. Thus the phrase here may be translated as ". . . will soon be laid [or ready]."

Duìbuqǐ jiào gèwèi děngzhe. You are familiar with the term of apology **duìbuqǐ**, and **jiào** is used in the sense of to cause. The suffix -**zhe** added to the word **děng** (*to wait*) indicates that the action lasted some time. In this case, then, the action is wait*ing*, providing the sense of "Sorry to have kept each [of you] waiting." **Gè** in this instance means each, and the compound **gèwèi** is a polite reference to everyone present, since **wèi** is a formal MW.

Xiànzài dōu yùbèi-hǎole means "Everything is now ready." **Yùbèi** has the specific meaning of to prepare being the combination of **yù** (beforehand) and **bèi** (to prepare). It can be seen that **bái-hǎole** and **yùbèi-hǎole** mean virtually the same in this context.

13.2   EATING AT HOME

The Chinese set great store on celebrating an occasion with a feast, and a good meal nearly always figures as a focal point in their festivities. How well they know how to rise to a special occasion! The menu is chosen so that each successive course is a complement or introduction in flavour or texture to the next. There is in effect a ritual to be observed in the selection of the courses for a banquet.

To be invited to a Chinese home to partake of **jiāfàn** (home cooking) in the form of a **jiǎozi**-fest is quite a compliment, since, generally speaking, foreigners are usually entertained in restaurants. This is an occasion when family and friends alike not only eat dumplings, but get together in the final preparation of them. The expression **bāo jiǎozi** (*wrap dumplings*) emphasizes the preparation aspect. People gather round the table to wrap the filling (**xiàr**) with the dough skins (**píer**), thus making bite-size crescent-shaped dumplings. These are called **shuǐjiǎor** (*water dumplings*), because they are cooked by boiling or steaming. A variety particularly popular in the south is known as **guōtiēr** (*pot-stickers*); they are lightly pan-fried before serving.

C: **Yàoshi zhōumò méi shì, yào-buyào dào wǒmen jiā lái bāo jiǎozi?**
If weekend not [have] business, want not-want arrive our home come to make dumplings?
If you've nothing on at the weekend, would you care to come to our place for dumplings?

R: **Nǐ tài kèqi! Zhēn búyào géi nǐmen zhǎo máfan.**
You too polite! Truly not-want give you find bother.
You're too kind! I really don't want to put you to any trouble.

C: **Méi nèi huíshì. Wǒ rènwéi wǒmen-de zuòfǎ bǐ nǐmen wàiguórén-de jiǎndǎn-de duō.**
Not [have] that [MW]-matter. I consider our methods compare you foreigners' simple-of much.
Not at all. I reckon our ways [of doing things] are much simpler than those of you foreigners.

Shǒuxiān, chúfáng yòng-de jiāhuo bìng bù duō. Qí tā, jiāli-de cānjù lián cíqì yé bǐjiào shǎo.
First, kitchen use-of utensils certainly not many. Besides, home-in tableware link crockery also comparatively few.
In the first place, there aren't nearly as many implements used in the kitchen. Besides there are somewhat fewer table utensils and chinaware in the home.

Chúle fànwǎn, cháwǎn, diézi, jiǔbēi, kuàizi, gēngchí shénmede, fànzhuōzi-shàng biéde dōngxi shì búbìyào-de.

Besides rice-bowls, tea-bowls, dishes, winecups, chopsticks, ladles what-ever, food table-on other things be not-essential-want-of.

Apart from bowls, teacups, dishes, winecups, chopsticks, spoons and so on, anything else on the dining table is unnecessary.

R:　**Hǎole, wǒ bù gēn nǐ biànlùn. Wó wǎnshang lái bàifǎng nǐmen. Késhi ànzhao wàiguo xíguàn wó kěndìng dàilái liǎng píngzi Shàoxīngjiǔ.**

Good, I not with you argue. I evening come call on you. But according to foreign custom I surely bring-come two bottles Shaoxing wine.

Right, I won't argue with you. I'll come and visit you this evening. But in keeping with foreign custom, I'll definitely bring a couple of bottles of Shaoxing wine.

C:　**Nà wó děi xièxie nǐ-de hǎoxīn. Zhè shì zuìhǎo-de jiǔ! Wǒmen liùdiǎnzhōng kāifàn hǎo ma?**

Then I must thank your good-heart. This be most good-of wine! We six o'clock start-food good-eh?

Then I'd be much obliged to you. This is the best of wines! Shall we say a six o'clock start [for supper]?

R:　**Hǎo, huítóu jiàn.**

Good, turn-head meet.

Right, see you later.

VOCABULARY

jiǎo	stuffed dumpling
fǎ	law; method, mode; extn.—standard model
jiǎn	simple, simplified, brief; to select, choose
shǒu	head; extn.—first; leader
chú	kitchen
cān	to eat; extn.—meal, fare
jù	utensil, implement, tool; to have, possess; furnish
cí	porcelain, china
qì	implement, utensil, ware; capacity, talent

jiào	to compare; extn.—comparatively, relatively; quite; rather
wǎn	bowl
chá	tea [brewed and ready to drink]
dié	small plate, small dish
bēi	cup; extn.—a glass
kuài	chopsticks
gēng	a thick soup; custard
chí	spoon
biàn	argue, dispute; debate
lùn	to talk about, discourse; extn.—opinion; determine
bài	to do obeisance; extn.—make a courtesy call
àn	to press, restrain, control; according to; to refer to
xí	practice, exercise; extn.—habit, custom; a surname
guàn	to be used to, be in the habit of
píng	bottle, vase, jar; extn.—flask

RATIONALE AND INTERPRETATION

Yàoshi (*want be*) is the equivalent of if, or in case. The second syllable is toneless.

Zhōumò means a weekend.

Jiā is used here in its basic sense of household or home.

Méi shì is the abbreviated form of **méiyǒu shìqing**, meaning *not having [any] business [to attend to]*, i.e., at a loose end.

Bāo jiǎozi (*wrap dumplings*) implies an invitation to a meal.

. . . géi nǐmen zhǎo máfan means to trouble you. Here is simply a polite response, and by no means a refusal to accept the invitation.

Méi nèi huíshì is an abbreviated version of **méiyǒu nà yíhuì shìqing**, which essentially indicates *no such matter exists*—in other words, "Nothing of the sort" or "Not at all." This is an alternative to **bù-máfan**.

Rènwéi means to consider, or to reckon and is an alternative for **xiǎng** (to think).

Wǒmen-de zuòfǎ bí nǐmen wàiguorén-de jiǎndān-de duō. This sentence may be analyzed through its three major components. The subject is **wǒmen-de zuòfǎ**, with **zuòfǎ** meaning method, a course of action, or ways of doing things. Next follows the amplifying phrase **bí nǐmen wàiguorén-de**, indicating *in contrast [to those] of you foreigners*.

This phrase provides the main thrust of the sentence and leads to the conclusion that the ways under reference are **jiǎndān-de duō** (*simpler by far*). **Jiǎndān** has the meaning of simple, uncomplicated or casual, when **dān** is coupled with the new component **jiǎn** (brief or simple).

Shǒuxiān is an expression used to mean firstly, or to begin with.

...**chúfáng yòng-de jiāhuo bìng bù duō** means in effect not many kitchen implements [are] in use, the reference being to the kitchen (**chúfáng**) implements (**jiāhuo**). The word **bìng**, from the compound **bìngqiě** (moreover), reinforces the meaning of **bù duō**, (not many) by adding emphasis and creating the nuance *by no means many*.

Qí tā (*besides it*), may be translated here as apart from which.

...**jiāli-de cānjù lián cíqì**. Two new terms to learn are the compounds **cānjù** (*food utensils*) meaning tableware, and **cíqì** (*ceramic ware*) meaning chinaware, or crockery. Typical articles are listed in the dialogue and Supplementary Vocabulary. **Jiāli-de**, which modifies the two main terms, meaning *in the home* or for domestic use, is self-explanatory. The word **lián**, occurring between the two main terms, is a conjunction signifying together with, and is often used as the equivalent of *and*.

Bǐjiào shǎo may be translated as somewhat fewer, since the compound **bǐjiào** means comparatively or relatively, and **shǎo** means few.

Búbìyào-de. Since **bìyào** (*must want*) is the term for essential or necessary, the prefix **bù** obviously creates the antonym unnecessary.

...**bù gēn nǐ biànlùn** means literally *not with you argue*. In the compound **biànlùn**, the main thrust of the meaning to argue or debate comes from the word **biàn**.

Wǒ lái bàifǎng nǐmen. **Fǎng** (to visit) is compounded with **bài**, which can have a similar meaning, to provide the polite term for calling on or visiting, thus serving as an alternative for **zhǎo**, which may also mean to visit.

Xíguàn. **Xí** and **guàn** have a similar import and, according to context, the meaning of this compound can vary slightly from custom or habit to habitual or usual practice.

Liǎng píngzi Shàoxīngjiǔ means just what it says: "two bottles [of] Shaoxing wine." **Píng** (bottle) serves as a MW; in general, a bottle is referred to as **píngzi**. A popular wine for the kind of occasion described is a yellow rice-wine, which is generally served warm (rather as sake is with

Japanese food). The best wine of this type comes from Shaoxing, which is near Hangzhou, about 100 miles down the coast from Shanghai. It is not unlike a medium sherry in flavour, and it is not nearly so potent as many other Chinese wines, which are also distilled from grain. Strangely enough, viniculture was not one of China's early accomplishments.

Xièxie nǐ-de hǎoxīn. Since **hǎoxīn** (*good heart*) means kind intentions, this clause is a means of expressing thanks in a context where "Thank you for your kindness," or "I'm much obliged" would be the English equivalent.

Kāifàn means in effect *to dish up the food*. **Kāifàn** may be also used as a figure of speech for time to eat.

SUPPLEMENTARY VOCABULARY

chāzi	fork
dāozi	knife
chízi	spoon
sháozi	ladle
pánzi	plate
chádié	saucer
yǐnliào	beverage
píjiǔ	beer
kāishuǐ	boiling water
liáng kāishuǐ	cold boiled water
kāfēi	coffee
cháyè	tea (i.e., loose tea)
qī chá	to make tea
dào chá	to pour tea
hē chá	to drink tea
yìwǎn chá	a cup of tea
cháhú	teapot
niúnǎi	milk
qìshuǐ	pop
yìwǎn fàn	a bowl of rice

tāng	soup, stock
tāngwǎn	soup bowl
wèidao	flavour
kǔ	bitter
yán	salt
xián	salty
báitáng	sugar (refined)
tián	sweet
cù	vinegar
suān	sour
là	spicy (hot)
jiàngyóu	soy sauce
nóng	strong
dàn	weak
píngguǒ	apples
xiāngjiāo	bananas
shuíguǒ	fruit
guǒzhī	fruit juice
pútao	grapes
táor	peaches
yālí	pears
shìzi	persimmons
júzi	tangerines/oranges
xīguā	watermelons
miànbāo	bread
shēngjiāng	ginger
bīngqílín	ice cream
wèijīng	monosodium glutamate (MSG)
miàntiáor	noodles

FOURTEEN

GOING
SHOPPING

"He who knows he is a fool is not a big fool."

Almost anywhere foreign tourists go there will be a **yǒuyì-shāngdiàn** (Friendship Store) available for shopping. This type of emporium has evolved over the past thirty years to cater solely to the needs of the visitor. The Chinese may not shop there. Hong Kong has one of the largest—and best—of these stores, but all the major cities have them. They house a concentration of most Chinese wares, especially handicrafts. This certainly saves time for the tourist, but then one misses out on seeing the way in which many things are made—and that is an experience in itself. Only Chinese products are sold at Friendship Stores, and only FEC is required for currency—although obviously foreign currency and travellers' cheques are negotiable as well. Prices are fixed and visible on all items, and usually the staff can converse in English—otherwise the guide may be co-opted to help out. This arrangement suits the local authorities, who naturally wish to avoid the embarrassment of strays, who cannot express themselves in Chinese, wandering about unattended. It also removes a lot of temptation for the black market by confining the movements of foreigners to certain small areas. However, this is not to say that one must only shop at the Friendship stores, or that one's needs cannot be satisfied elsewhere. Provided that the communication gap can be overcome, shopping throughout China is a great experience not to be missed.

Shopping can be approached in a number of ways. In addition to the convenience of the Friendship stores, the tourist has other options, depending on the itinerary. For instance, Suzhou is the obvious place to shop for silks, as it is the centre of sericulture and related activities. Shanghai abounds in manufacturers of a broad spectrum of goods, varying from furniture to tapestries and many handicrafts, including jade carving.

As is so often the case, most fabrication activities take place where the best resources are found. Wool from sheep and goats accounts for the preponderance of carpet looms in the North, while the humid climate of South China makes possible the dust-free atmosphere essential for lacquer handicrafts. In addition, the lac tree, grown mainly in those parts, supplies the quantities of varnish needed for fine lacquerware. While Fuzhou is the centre of lacquerware production in the South, Beijing in the North also has a thriving industry producing its own carved red lacquer. This has a matt finish, and the cinnabar bas-relief doubtless evolved because of the dry and dusty atmosphere predominating in North China, where the other lacquer form would be virtually impossible. Fujian province, with its abundance of granite, is the place to visit for people interested in stone carving, while exquisite carvings in many colours of agate and quartz are found mainly in the province of Heilongjiang. In fact, the list of merchandise is almost endless in such a large country so rich in materials worked by so many skilled artisans.

The dominant influence in much Chinese handicraft is obviously the traditional form of painting (**huìhuà**). It consists largely of landscapes, and symbols originating from religion, folklore, or history, contributing to the distinctive appearance of Chinese handicrafts. In addition, many of these artistic products blend well with western decor, thus giving pleasure wherever they are seen. If you have a specific location in which to hang a Chinese picture, if it is a scroll it is important to consider the length because dimensions vary considerably. If shortened the proportions could be upset. Also, many embroideries can best be displayed if they are properly framed once you get them home.

Traditional Chinese painting is essentially different from traditional Western paintings. Paintings in mural form date from 2,500 BC or earlier, and two millennia later silk and bamboo were used, since paper had yet to be invented. An early specimen of Chinese painting is to be found in the British Museum, in the form of a scroll painted about the fourth or fifth century AD. Chinese artists primarily relied on nature for inspiration. The earliest Chinese art forms had animal subjects only, with people and scenery being introduced later on. Portraiture as we know it scarcely existed. Since shadows on faces were not liked or understood, a full face view was usual, robbing the face of much of its expression. Portraits of emperors were produced for the admiration of future generations, chiefly emphasizing the colours and richness of the costumes. Landscape painting, too, was devoid of shadow. Landscapes were called **Shānshuǐ-huà**, being *mountain and water paintings*, since they always portrayed a river emerging from mountain ranges, the peaks of which were generally shrouded in mist. As the painting calls to mind a view, a Chinese painter's point often is: "First we look at the hills in the painting, then we look at the painting in the hills." Chinese artists did not use easels but painted flat on a table, thus continually looking down at their landscapes from a height. When contemplating nature, the Chinese observe the minutest details, which they love to portray. Examples of such details abound: bamboo leaves drooping under the weight of raindrops, the movement of the feathery fins and tails of goldfish as they swim, not to mention the gracefulness of birds on the wing. More often than not, the artist would commit such details to memory, then return to his studio to paint them. The brushes used for painting are the same as those employed for calligraphy, and the same technique of handling is used in both these art forms. To a large extent, the uniqueness of a Chinese painting resides not so much in what is depicted, but in what is omitted. In this sense, there is a strong link between painting and calligraphy, for it is claimed that in the twisting lines of the pine tree is to be seen the same principle of twisting used in Chinese characters, while in the wavy lines of rocks are to be seen the spaces found between the character strokes.

14.1   WINDOW SHOPPING

R: **Gùo liǎng tiān wǒ yào shàngjiē gěi péngyou dàihuiqù jǐge xiǎo lǐwù. Ní yǒu-méiyǒu gōngfu péizhe wǒ?**
In a couple of days I want to go shopping for a few presents to take back to my friends. Will you have time to go with me?

C: **Nà bù chéng wèntí. Zuìhǎo wǒmen zuò chūzū-qìchē dào Yǒuyì-shāngdiàn qù kànkan, hǎo-ma?**

That's no problem. We'd best take a taxi and have a look in the Friendship Store, shall we?

R: **Zhè dàgài jiùshi zuì fāngbiàn-de bànfǎ. Tāmen zhùcún-de huòwù yěshi zuì duōzhǒng duōyàng, duì-buduì?**

This is probably the convenient way of doing it. Their stock of merchandise is the most varied, too, right?

C: **Kěbushì-me! Búdàn tāmen-de chánpǐn zhìliàng hǎo, érqiě dōu hén kěkào. Nǐ yào mǎi shénme tèbié-de ma?**

Exactly! Not only is the quality of their products good, they're also very reliable. Anything special you want to buy?

R: **Wǒmen xiān qù kànkan yàngzi ba. Zhǐyào dōngxi bú tài dà, bú tài zhòng jiù xíng; yàoburán dà xíngli-de shíhou kǒngpà zhuāngbuxià.**

Let's look around first. As long as the things aren't too big or too heavy it'll be fine; otherwise I'm afraid I won't be able to fit them when I'm packing.

VOCABULARY

lǐ	ceremony, rite; extn.—etiquette, courtesy; gift, present
fū	man; husband
péi	to accompany; extn.—to take care of
zū	to rent, hire, charter, lease
qì	steam, vapour
yì	friendship
gài	approximate, general; categorically; department
zhù	to store, save up, lay aside
cún	to live, survive; extn.—to keep, store, accumulate; deposit
dàn	but, yet, nevertheless; extn.—only, merely
chǎn	to bear, produce; extn.—production, estate
ér	and, but, then (a literary part of speech)
kào	to lean on, lean against; extn.—get near; trust, depend on

zhì   nature, character; quality; matter, substance
liàng   capacity; extn.—amount, volume, quantity (alt. pron. **liáng**)

RATIONALE AND INTERPRETATION

Guò liǎng tiān is an idiomatic way of expressing *in a few days' time*. While meaning *[when] two days have passed*, it need not be taken to mean precisely two days, any more than *a couple of days* need mean exactly that number of days.

Wǒ yào shàngjiē—"I want to go shopping." The expression **shàngjiē** is literally *to go on [or up] the street*, as opposed to **jiēshang**, which actually means *on the street*.

. . . **gěi péngyou dàihuiqù** . . . Note the omission of the personal pronoun. Since the context makes it obvious whose friends are under consideration, **gěi péngyou** means *for my friends*. **Dàihuiqù** is a combination of the verb **dài** (to take or to carry) and the compound verb **huíqù** (*return go*). Either **qù** (to go), which implies taking, as in this case, or **lái** (to come), which implies bringing, may be compounded with **huí** to indicate the direction of the motion. In either case **huí**, in the sense of *to return* or *to restore*, reinforces the main thrust of **dài**.

. . . **jǐge xiáo lǐwù** means *a few small presents*. Since this sentence is a statement rather than a question, **jǐge** is obviously not being used as a QW [how many?], but conveys the idea of *a few*. **Xiǎo** (little) not only serves the purpose of defining the size of the gifts to be bought, but also modestly implies that nothing very grand or costly is contemplated. **Lǐwu** is a compound made up of **lǐ** meaning a gift or present, and **wù** (an article).

Gōngfu means [free] time, but only in the particular sense of *time to spare for leisure or other activities not already provided for in the regular routine of things*. This explanation is necessary since the term has a range of somewhat nebulous, abstract meanings, very much in line with the Chinese concept of time. **Gōngfu** is far less finite than any terms connected with the word **shí** (time).

Péizhe has the meaning of *accompanying*. **Péi** is not a new word, having been introduced in the compound **quánpéi**, signifying the national guide, or overall attendant, who *accompanies* [visitors over the] *whole* [country]. **Zhe** is the toneless suffix which, in effect, puts the *-ing* on the end of accompany. A less idiomatic translation of this passage would be: "Have you the time to spare for accompanying me?"

Nà bù chéng wèntí may be translated as: "That does not become a problem." You are familiar with **méi wèntí**, and this is a close substitute. The word **chéng** was introduced in Dialogue 10.1.

Zuò chūzū-qìchē. The function of **zuò** (to sit) in relation to travel is explained in Chapter 10.2. **Chūzū** means to hire or to lease, while **qìchē** is a motor vehicle, thus the combination refers to a taxi or cab. The whole phrase means to ride in a cab or to hire a taxi.

Yǒuyì-shāngdiàn means a Friendship Store. **Yǒuyì** (friendship) is coupled with the compound **shāngdiàn** meaning a shop or store, which refers to a large establishment rather than a small enterprise.

Qù kànkan means simply to go and take a look at.

Gài compounded with **dà** (big, as in **dàxiǎo** for size) is a term meaning probably, presumably, and thus by extension approximate, or broad outline.

Zuì fāngbiàn-de bànfǎ means the most convenient method, in as much as **bànfǎ** implies a means or way of doing something.

Zhùcún-de huòwù refers to the *storing of merchandise*. Incidentally, a word for stock or goods on hand is **cúnhuò**. The compound **zhùcún** means to keep in storage or to store.

Duōzhǒng-duōyàng means literally *many species, many kinds*, and is the equivalent of varied, diversified or abundant.

Kěbushì-me is a popular exclamation which means "That's right!" or—in a word—"Exactly!"

Búdàn . . . érqiě . . . This construction is equivalent in formation and use to the not only . . . but also . . . construction in English. **Búdàn** means literally *not only*, while **érqiě** means *but also, moreover* or *besides*.

Tāmen-de chánpǐn zhìliàng hǎo (*their products' quality good*) includes the two compounds **chánpǐn** (product, produce) and **zhìliàng** (quality).

Kěkào, meaning literally *able to be depended on*, is the appropriate equivalent of reliable, dependable or trustworthy, and is applicable to persons and objects alike.

Kànkan yàngzi is an expression which implies looking at things in general—from tendencies and likelihoods to appearances or samples. In the present context, the thrust is more specifically to see what is available or, simply, to look around.

Zhǐyào (*only want*) means so long as.

...**bú tài zhòng**. You are reminded that the character pronounced **zhòng**, meaning heavy, may be pronounced **chóng**, in which case it means to repeat.

...**jiù xíng**. You are also reminded that the character pronounced **xíng**, meaning satisfactory or O.K., may be pronounced **háng**, in which case it means a business, or trade. The use of **jiù** (then) in this context gives the meaning of it will be fine then.

Yàoburán means otherwise.

Dǎ xíngli-de shíhou. Some of the many uses of **dǎ** (to strike) have been dealt with. Here it is an idiomatic expression for packing or *to pack one's luggage*, since **xíngli** is the term for luggage. **-De shíhou** (*of time*) designates when.

Zhuāngbuxià. Here is a further example of a resultative verb—in this case, the likely outcome is negative. **Zhuāng** has the meaning of loading up or loading onto. **Zhuāngxià**, in this context of filling a case with various things, takes on the meaning to fit [something] in, since **zhuāng** indicates the action, while **xià** indicates the result. As we are considering the potential aspect, or the probability of accomplishment, **bù**—being negative—indicates the unlikelihood that the action will be completed under the wrong circumstances.

14.2   A VARIETY OF WARES

Calligraphy appeals less to the western visitor than it does to the Chinese, who can read it, and therefore better appreciate its connection with brush art. More likely to attract foreign interest are the fine forms of carving available in a wealth of materials, particularly ivory, wood, and jade. Jade, specifically nephrite and jadeite, varies so much in colour that it is a wonder so many people from other parts of the world will consider only green jade—the best of which is said to be the jadeite from Burma. Jade—regardless of its origin—is designated in numerous ways by the Chinese. For example, they use terms such as kingfisher, apple, spinach, or mutton fat, the latter term indicating a favoured form of white jade, used for what is called finger jade. These are carvings designed to be held in the hand and fondled as well as admired. One popular form is a replica of a distinctive type of gourd (fingered citron) known as "Buddha's fingers."

Cloisonné is known as **jǐngtàilán** in Chinese. This word is a combination of the name of a Ming emperor, Jingtai (1450 - 1457 AD), and **lán**, representing the blue colour for which the Ming Dynasty is renowned. This art form is believed to have originated during the sixth century in the Byzantine Empire, and was introduced into China during the Yuan Dynasty, the late thirteenth century. The experts contend that, notwithstanding the development during the preceding dynasty, it was in fact during the Qing Dynasty that the best cloisonné was produced, especially in Beijing during the reign of the emperor Kangxi (1662 - 1722 AD). The production process of making cloisonné is so labour-intensive and time consuming, it is remarkable that the end product is not more costly. When selecting items for purchase, the shopper should examine the polished surface carefully to ensure there is no pitting around the cloisons. Pitting not only detracts from the appearance of the work, it also indicates inferior quality.

Another artistic feature is the variety of Chinese screens for both indoor and outdoor use. On coming upon a main entrance to a courtyard, you will notice that very often there is a brick or stone screen just beyond that blocks the view. The intention is not necessarily so much to ensure privacy as it is to provide security—especially against evil spirits, which are said to be able to travel only in straight lines. Prospect Hill, just North of the Palace Museum, was said to have been situated deliberately in that spot (being an artificially created hill) to ward off the evil barbaric spirits from that direction. Perhaps the most famous of all outdoor screens in Beijing is the Nine Dragon Screen located in the Winter Palace, although its present site in the northwest corner has no obvious purpose of diversion. It is well worth seeing for its beautifully glazed façade. A similar screen is to be found in the Forbidden City, but the original of this one, erected in the Temple of Ten Thousand Buddhas, was destroyed long ago. The Chinese screens best known to the West are, of course, the folding screens with four to eight hinged leaves. Some stand as high as eight or nine feet. They are generally made of wood, and some are intricately carved, while many others are lacquered. They are seldom left plain; indeed, next to scrolls, they provide the most popular surfaces for the Chinese artists to work on. These screens serve a useful as well as an aesthetic purpose, however, being used as dividers in a large chamber to subdivide the space. While the size, weight, and cost of these works of art make them unlikely purchases for the average visitor, should you buy one, the Chinese will pack and ship it expertly, as well as taking care of the paper-work, which may well include a detailed description or history of the motif should you request it. The same applies to the purchasing of carpets, which can provide interesting conversation pieces for years to come, and may encourage further research into Chinese arts as a leisure pursuit.

In Chinese folklore, the dragon (**lóng**) is a benevolent creature; it is used also to represent the emperor, while the phoenix (**fèng**) denotes the empress. In the Chinese mind, dragons are somehow associated with dinosaurs, which are called **kǒnglóng** (*terrifying dragons*). There are three species of dragon, but the main one is **lóng**, whose element is the sky, and there are nine different fabled varieties. One could go on indefinitely about the different forms in which the dragon is portrayed, the significance of the numbers of its claws (maximum five) and the associated symbolism. According to legend dragons constantly pursue the Celestial Pearl, or the Sun. Whenever an eclipse took place, there used to be a superstitious fear that the sun was being devoured by the dragon. Consequently, the populace below set up a great cacophony with any and every noise available to frighten the dragon away. The effectiveness of this procedure was invariably proven when the sun finally reappeared. The dragon and phoenix are more frequently portrayed in embroidery or on porcelain than in paintings, along with the many Buddhist and Taoist symbols which contribute so richly to the motifs seen on much Chinese handicraft.

Finally, one brief word of caution is offered to visitors to be reasonably knowledgeable concerning their purchases. "All that glitters is not gold," (apologies to Thomas Gray) and often jade turns out to be soapstone, just as ivory is often camel-bone. This is not to suggest that there is a host of charlatans making counterfeit jewelry or fake antiques for the sake of duping the unwary shopper. In China, reproduction has been developed to a fine art in its own right. Probably on the premise that imitation is the sincerest form of flattery, there is an abundance of handiwork available for purchase which would be quite out of reach in value were it the genuine article. A **nèiháng** (*insider*) or a connoisseur should know the difference, but if you do not, then obtain a guarantee. Jade and soapstone are sometimes confused; however, there are two superficial tests that can be used to distinguish one from the other. Jade is a much harder substance, therefore soapstone will accept a scratch more easily. Also, jade, when held in one's hand, will not warm readily to the touch, but feel cool for a relatively long period. Of course price can also be an indicator, since good jade comes no more cheaply than would a good diamond. When buying any wooden products, whether carvings or furniture, make sure they are capable of withstanding climatic and atmospheric changes, as you will not want them to split or warp. The wood used is not necessarily kiln-dried, and even the hard wood of ebony can be affected by temperature and other changes.

R: **Wǒ yào mǎi jǐkuài jǐngtàilán, kěshi wǒ bú-zhídào dào nǎr qù zhǎo nèizhǒng dōngxi.**
I want to buy some pieces of cloisonné, but I don't know where to go to find that sort of thing.

C: **Nǐ yào-buyào wǒ dài nǐ qù kànkan yíge jǐngtàilán gōngchǎng? Zhèyàng ní jiù yóu xǔduō jīhuì xuǎn zuì hǎo-de wùpǐn. Érqiě tāmen-de jiàqian kěnéng bǐ língshòushāng-de piányi yìxiē.**
Do you want me to take you to see a cloisonné factory? This way you will have many opportunities for selecting the best wares. What's more, their prices are likely to be a bit cheaper than the retailers'.

R: **Shìma? Zhè shì zěnme huíshì? Wó lǎo shì zhǎo jīhuì shěng qián!**
Really, how's that? I'm always looking for a chance to save money!

C: **Yīnwei qǔxiāole jīngjìrén, jiàqian dāngrán jiù dī yìdiǎn.**
Because the middleman having been eliminated, the price is naturally a bit lower.

R: Hái yǒu-meiyǒu biéde gōngchǎng kéyi qù cānguān?
    Are there any other factories we could go and visit?

C: Wǒmen kéyi qù kànkan zhīzào dìtǎn. Yàoshi yǒu shíjiān yě
    kéyi kànkan jiājù zhìzàochǎng.
    We can go and see some carpet weaving. If there's time we could
    also look at a furniture manufacturer.

R: Zhèxie zhúyì wǒ dōu wánquán tóngyì. Duì dìtǎn huòzhě
    wéipíng shàng-de zhuāngshì-tú'àn wó zǎo jiù yóu xìngqù.
    I entirely agree with both these ideas. I've long been interested in
    the ornamental designs on carpets or screens.

VOCABULARY

tài	safe, peaceful
lán	blue; a surname
chǎng	factory, plant, mill, works; yard, depot
shòu	to sell; to carry out [an idea]
xiē	a little, few [indeterminate number]
shěng	to economize, save; omit; province
qǔ	to get, fetch, take; extn.—seek; choose, assume
xiāo	to disappear; extn.—eliminate, remove
dī	low; extn.—to lower, hang down
cān	to join, enter, take part in; consult
guān	to look at, watch, observe; sight, view, outlook, concept
zhī	to weave, knit
zào	to build, create; extn.—invent; train, educate
zhì	to make, manufacture; formulate; restrict, control
tǎn	blanket, rug, carpet
wéi	to enclose, surround; extn.—all around, around
píng	shield, screen
shì	decorations, ornament; extn.—to adorn, cover up
tú	picture, drawing; map, chart; extn.—plan, scheme
àn	table, desk; extn.—record, file; proposal, plan; case
xìng	mood; interest; excitement (alt. pron. xīng—promote)
qù	interest, delight

RATIONALE AND INTERPRETATION

Jǐngtàilán is the term for cloisonné.

Bù-zhīdào means don't know. However, there is one point concerning **zhīdào** which should be noted. Whereas in the affirmative the emphasis is placed on the *first* syllable of this term, in the negative the emphasis shifts to the *second* syllable.

. . . **dào nǎr qù**. Since **nǎr** is a QW meaning where, this phrase may be translated as "where to go."

Zhèizhǒng dōngxi. **Zhǒng** essentially stands for type or variety. The use of **yàng** (kind, sort), is also quite permissible; if **yàng** were used, "this sort of thing" would become **zhè yàng-de dōngxi**.

Gōngchǎng is a factory, works, or plant. **Gōng**, the term for work, is compounded with **chǎng**, the general term for factory.

Zhèyàng, means simply [in] this way, thus, or like this.

Nǐ jiù yǒu xǔduō jīhuì may be translated directly as *you then have many opportunities*. **Xǔ** serves to indicate perhaps, or, as in this case, somewhat, and since **duō** means many, the compound **xǔduō** means a lot of, or a great deal of. **Jīhuì** is the term for opportunity or chance, being the combination of **jī**, which primarily means a machine, but may also indicate opportunity as it does here, and **huì**, which has the same secondary meaning.

Wùpǐn. This compound is a general term for articles or goods. If reference to more specific types of goods is required, **pǐn** may be modified:

chánpǐn	produce, products
gōngyèpǐn	industrial products
shāngpǐn	merchandise, commodities
zhìchéngpǐn	manufactured goods or products

Érqiě is closely allied to **bìngqiě**, with possibly a wider application, since **érqiě** has the nuance of *taking a step farther* or *going a stage further*. It may be considered the equivalent of what is more.

Jiàqian kěnéng bǐ língshòushāng-de piányi yìxiē means "Prices are likely to be somewhat cheaper than the retailers'." **Jiàqián** means price, and **kěnéng** indicates either possibility or probability. **Bǐ** (to compare, contrast) indicates the comparative form of **piányi** (cheap), while **yìxiē** means a little or some; hence, these three words together signify somewhat cheaper (the English *than* is not necessary in the Chinese syntax). The comparison being made is with retailers' prices which brings us to the compound **língshòushāng**. The first element, **língshòu**, means virtually the same as **língmài** (retail), since **shòu** means to sell. The second element, **shāng** means trade, commerce, or business in general. Thus the new compound combines these two elements—**língshòu** and **shāng**—to give the word for a retailer. The particle **-de** provides the possessive apostrophe.

Shìma? Zhè shì zěnme huíshì? Here is a typical expression to indicate surprise, if not disbelief. **Nèi huíshì** was shown to mean such a thing or such an occurrence. **Nèi** is replaced here with the QW **zěnme**, giving the sense of "How could such a thing be?," or simply "How come?" Other ways of phrasing **zěnme huíshì** might be, "Is that so?" or "How is that?"

Wó lǎo shì zhǎo jīhuì means virtually "I am constantly seeking the opportunity. . . ." **Lǎo** signifies old, but also has the secondary meaning of long standing or constantly. Thus, in this context, it may be translated as always or all the time.

Shěng qián means precisely to save money. While the sense of **qián** is unequivocal, **shěng** has more than one meaning. Here it is used as the verb to save; if it were used to mean a province, it would be preceded by the name of the province. For example, the province of Shandong (previously spelled Shantung—the name given to a type of silk) would be referred to as **Shāndōng Shěng**.

Qǔxiāo jīngjìrén means to eliminate the middleman. The components of the term **qǔxiāo** consist of **qǔ** (to select), and **xiāo**, which means to remove. This new compound may therefore mean to cancel, to abolish, to eliminate, or to call off. **Jīngjìrén** means a broker or an agent or, in this case, middleman. This compound consists of known components; that is, **jīng**—to manage, **jì**—to record, and **rén**—person.

Dī yìdiǎn (*low a spot*) comprises **dī** meaning to lower, and **yìdiǎn** (or **yìdiǎr**, as often heard in Beijing), which means a little or a bit.

Cānguān means to look around, or to visit [for the purpose of looking around].

. . . **kànkan zhīzào dìtǎn. Kànkan** means to have a look or, simply, to see. The two new words, **zhī** (to weave) and **zào** (to make or create), form the compound **zhīzào**, the term for weaving. In this instance, the product of the weaving is **dìtǎn**. **Dì** means ground and, by extension, floor, while **tǎn** has the meaning of carpet. Hence we have the term for carpeting.

Jiājù zhìzàochǎng refers to a furniture manufacturer. **Jiā** (family or home), with **jù** (to furnish) forms the compound for furniture. In regard to the second compound, **zhìzàochǎng**, particular attention should be paid to the word **zhìzào**, so as not to confuse it with the word **zhīzào**. Here is a typical example of the importance of the correct tone, (refer to Vocabulary for the distinction between **zhī** and **zhì**). **Zào** is a useful word, serving a number of compounds dealing principally with building or creating. Nowhere is this aspect of the word more evident than in the compound **zhìzào**, which means to manufacture, to make, to create, to fabricate or to engineer. By adding **chǎng** we obtain the term for a manufacturing plant. **Zhìzàochǎng** is therefore similar in meaning to **gōngchǎng** (factory).

Zhèxie zhúyì wǒ dōu wánquán tóngyì. Zhèxie zhúyì—these ideas—is in fact the object, which has been placed at the head of the sentence to give it emphasis. **Wǒ** (I) is the subject, while **dōu** refers to the two suggestions just made and is thus translated as both, rather than all. **Wánquán** (entirely), **tóng** (same), and **yì** (intention) combine to form the expression **wánquán tóngyì**, signifying to agree or to approve entirely. By now you should have a sufficient vocabulary and insight into basic Chinese to understand how characters in a compound are identified. The Chinese generally revert to analogy in order to distinguish a specific character from others with identical pronunciation. Consider **tóngyì** as an example: **tóngyàng-de tóng** and **zhúyì-de yì** is how this compound would be defined, i.e. **tóng** as in **tóngyàng** (same kind), and **yì** as in **zhúyì** (idea). Any literate Chinese would be able to visualize at once which two characters were intended. To put it another way, imagine a Chinese who had not heard of a pathway. This you could define as path as in footpath, and way as in wayfare. In the remaining chapters this method will be used in connection with words you already know.

Dìtǎn huòzhě wéipíng shàng-de zhuāngshì-tú'àn means the ornamental designs on carpets and screens. **Tú'àn** is a new compound meaning a pattern or design. Addition of the modifier **zhuāngshì** gives the expression for ornamental designs or decorative patterns as seen on fabrics, carpets, or crockery, for instance. Although the primary meaning of **zhuāng** is to pack, it may also mean to dress up or to embellish. Thus here it complements **shì** (decoration), to give the term for ornamental or decorative. The ornamental designs in this case are those of the **dìtǎn**, or carpets, and the **wéipíng**, or beautiful folding screens, for which China is noted. Screens which have been painted, rather than carved, are often referred to as **huàpíng** (*picture screen*).

Wó zǎo jiù yǒu xìngqù. The term **xìngqù** meaning interest together with **yǒu** (to have) yields the equivalent of to be interested. **Zǎo** (early) indicates that the interest is of long standing.

SUPPLEMENTARY VOCABULARY

suànpán	abacus
shǒuzhuó	bracelet
tóngqì	brass or bronzeware
diāokèpǐn	carving or engraving
qípáo	Chinese style dress/cheongsam
gúdǒng, gǔwán	curios, antiques
ěrhuán	earrings
xiùhuā	embroidery
huángjīn	gold
xiàngyá	ivory
yùshí	jade
zhūbǎo-shíqì	jewelry
xiùkǒng-zhīpǐn	lace
qīqì	lacquerware
dēnglong	lantern
xiàngliàn	necklace/beads
nǔgōng, zhēnxiùhuā	needlework
túhuàr	painting
mián'ǎo	quilted coat
jièzhi	ring
duànzi	satin
huàjuǎn	scroll
túzhāng, chuōzi	seals (chops)
chóuzi	silk

bíyānhú, nèihuàhú	snuff bottle
dìzuò	stand (carved)
xiùxiàng	tapestry
dǐngzhen	thimble
wánjù, wányìer	toys
huāpíng	vase
jiàndìng	authentification
máobing	defect, flaw

FIFTEEN

LEISURE
AND PLEASURE

"Enjoy yourself, it's later than you think."

If **tǐyù-yùndòng** seems a long-winded word for sports, maybe it is because for the Chinese competitive sport is a new concept. When China became a republic, the western world's impact became increasingly apparent, particularly in sports. Up until then, Chinese were far more inclined towards recreation. However, all that has changed in the last twenty years or so, with Chinese athletes winning medals and acclaim especially in table-tennis! Through their special talent in acrobatics, which goes back many centuries, they have developed an aptitude for gymnastics, as well as the associated sport of diving. Also, ever since Mao Zedong's much publicized swim in the Yangzi River, swimming and other aquatic sports have increased immensely in popularity. Team sports such as basketball and volleyball have a much longer history. Contact sports have not yet been developed to any extent, with the notable exception of wrestling, which is an individualistic and traditional form of competition. Realizing the admiration the western world has for sporting excellence, and the respect their athletes can earn for China, the Chinese enjoy testing their abilities in international sports competitions. The Chinese have emerged in the world of sport, and their degree of competition has improved as a result of their endeavors. They also retain their traditional martial arts exercises which are enjoying increasing popularity in the West.

15.1   OUTDOOR AND INDOOR PURSUITS

R: **Xiánkòng-de shíhou, nǐ zuì xǐhuan gàn shénme?**
What do you like doing most with your leisure time?

C: **Nà děi kàn qíngkuàng. Yàoshi tiānqi hǎo-de huà, wǒ cháng dào gōngyuán qù sànbù, dàizhe xiǎo sūnzi chūqù yóuwán.**
That depends. If the weather is fine, I often go for a stroll in the park, and take my young grandson out to play.

R: **Guānyu tǐyù-yùndòng nǐ àihào shénme?**
What sports are you keen on?

C: **Yīnwei niánjì dà-le, chúle tàijíquán wǒ bù cānjiā shénme yùndòng. Kěshi bùguǎn shì zài jiāli kàn diànshì, huòzhě dào qiúchǎng qù wó kě zhēn xǐhuan kàn páiqiú bǐsài.**
Because of advancing years, I don't participate in any sport, apart from T'ai Chi shadow-boxing. But I really do like watching volleyball games, regardless of whether it's at home on TV, or at the sports ground.

R: **Wó běnrén duì dǎ bīngqiú gǎnjué tèbié xīngfèn. Jiā-li hái yǒu shénme yúlè?**
Myself I find ice hockey especially stimulating. What other pastimes have you at home?

C: **Yǒu-de shíhou wǒ tīng shōuyīnjī, yàoburán jiù kàn rìbào, huà-kān, zázhì, huòzhě kàn xiánshú.**
Sometimes I listen to the radio, otherwise I just look through the daily papers, pictorials or magazines, or do some light reading.

VOCABULARY

xián	unoccupied, idle, leisure; extn.—not in use, spare
sàn	to disperse, break up; extn.—distribute, dispel
bù	step, pace; extn.—stage, condition, state; walk, tread

sūn	grandson; generations below grandchildren; a surname
nǚ	female, woman
nán	male, man
yóu	to swim; extn.—travel, tour, wander, roving
wán	to play, have fun, amuse oneself; extn.—treat lightly
yùn	movement, motion; extn.—transport; fate
dòng	to move, touch, rouse; extn.—stir, start
ài	love, affection, be fond of
quán	fist; extn.—boxing, pugilism
shì	to look at, watch, regard; extn.—inspect
qiú	sphere, globe; extn.—ball
chǎng	place for public gathering; scene
sài	contest, competition; extn.—game, match; surpass
bīng	ice, to put on ice; extn.—feel cold
fèn	to act vigorously, exert oneself; extn.—raise, lift
yú	to amuse, give pleasure to; extn.—joy, amusement
lè	happy; extn.—laugh, enjoy (alt. pron. **yuè**—music)
yīn	sound; extn.—tone; tidings, news
huà	to paint, draw; painting, picture, drawing
kān	to publish, print; extn.—publication, periodical
zá	sundry, miscellaneous; extn.—to mix, mingle
zhì	aspiration, ideal; extn.—keep in mind; mark, sign, annals

RATIONALE AND INTERPRETATION

Xiánkòng-de shíhou. The word **xián** is used in combination with **kòng** to indicate leisure. You know that **-de shíhou** is generally translated as *when*. Since it serves to introduce a time clause, it invariably occurs at the beginning of a sentence.

Zuì xǐhuan means *most keen on* or *most fond of*.

Gàn shénme. Together **gàn** (to do) and **shénme**, the QW *what*, literally mean *to do what*. Thus **zuì xǐhuan gàn shénme**, meaning *what [you] like doing most*, gives the idiomatic rendering in the dialogue.

Nà děi kàn qíngkuàng means that *requires looking at circumstances* or—more appropriately—"That depends [on the state of affairs]."

Tiānqì hǎo means fine weather, being an allusion to good sky conditions.

. . .-de huà is an expression signifying *in terms of*. It is often used in conjunction with **yàoshi** (if), in which case it is virtually equivalent to the English word say in the following examples:

Yàoshi tā lái wǎn-de huà. . .   If, say, he arrives late . . .

Yàoshi wǒ bùnéng-de huà. . .   If, say, I'm unable to . . .

Yàoshi rén tài duō-de huà. . .   If, say, there are too many people . . .

. . . **cháng dào gōngyuán qù. Cháng** means often or usually, while **gōngyuán** means a park. **Dào** (to arrive) is modified by **qù** to indicate not only the action of going, but also that of reaching a given destination—in this instance, the park.

Sànbù (*scatter steps*) is a term meaning to take a walk, or to go for a stroll, thus explaining the purpose of the action. A similar term, meaning to ramble or just to wander around, is **liūda**.

Dàizhe xiǎo sūnzi means taking my young grandson. **Dài** (to take), is coupled with the suffix **-zhe**, to form **dàizhe**, which signifies tak*ing*. **Sūnzi** is the word for grandson, with **zǐ** emphasizing the male relationship. By a similar token, the term **sūnnǚ** would denote granddaughter, with **nǚ** emphasizing the female relationship. Offspring or children in general may be referred to as **érnǚ** or **zínǚ**, since both **ér** and **zǐ** mean the same in this context. The use of **xiǎo** (small) as a modifier simply indicates that the child is still quite young. Note that **-zi**, which occurs frequently as a diminutive suffix in numerous nouns (e.g., **dānzi, yàngzi, zhuōzi**), is the same as the **zǐ** under reference.

. . . **chūqù yóuwán** is to go out to play. The verb **chūqù** (*to go out*) is formed by combining **chū** (to emerge) and **qù** (to go or leave). (Compare this with **chūlái** meaning to come out.) **Yóu** (to swim) is often used to form compounds such as **yóuguàng** (to tour) or **yóulǎn** (to go sightseeing), which are allied to its secondary meaning. By extension of this concept, **yóu** implies amusement, play, or recreation. As **wán** is to be found in any number of terms to do with fun or amusement, it is easy to see how **yóu** and **wán** compound with each other to produce the meaning of playing or to play games. An alternative to **yóuwán** is the less formal **wárwar**, which is a popular term in Beijing. However, do not attempt to use either expression to cover the many ways that to play is used in English (e.g., to play tennis, or bridge, or the piano). In Chinese there are specific verbs for such activities.

Tǐyù-yùndòng is an expression used to denote either sports or physical exercise in general. **Tǐyù** (physical education) is linked with **yùndòng**, the meaning of which centers around movement, either in terms of motion (e.g., exercise), or activity (e.g., political).

Àihào is the compound formed by coupling the **ài** of **àirén** (spouse) with the **hǎo** of **nǐ hǎo** pronounced in the fourth tone. It means to be keen on or, by extension, liking or a hobby.

Niánjì dà-le means virtually age increase. **Niánjì** (*a year record or period*) is an alternative way of expressing **suìshù** (age), but they are not entirely interchangeable. **Dà** (big) in conjunction with **niánjì** indicates *great in years*.

Chúle tàijíquán... **Chúle** means apart from, besides or except for. **Tàijíquán** is the correct form for what English speakers generally refer to as T'ai Chi. It is composed of **Tài** as in **Tàitai** (Mrs.), **jí** as in **hǎo jíle**, and **quán**, which is the word for boxing. A direct translation from the Chinese would be *ultimate boxing*. This shadow-boxing is indeed considered to be the last word in self-defense.

Wǒ bù cānjiā shénme yùndòng. This statement is straightforward, except for the compound **cānjiā**, the components of which are **cān** as in **cānguān**, and **jiā** as in **Jiānádà**! **Jiā** means not only to add but, by extension, to augment or to take part in, as is the case here. **Cānjiā** is the term for to participate, to take part in or to attend.

Bùguǎn. Guǎn, in general terms, can mean to mind or to bother about; thus, the negative **bù** gives it the sense of never mind or simply *regardless*.

Zài jiāli kàn diànshì means "watching television at home." **Diànshì** is the term for television. **Shì** is a word often used in compounds connected with vision.

Huòzhě has a range of meanings; here it signifies or.

Qiúchǎng (*ball park*) is the term for a playing field, usually an open air area where any form of ball game may take place—not just baseball which, incidentally, is seldom played in China. To refer to a sports ground which might be open or enclosed, the Chinese use the term **yùndòngchǎng**. Such an area would usually provide for a wider range of activities, including individual and team sports. The word **chǎng** may be used in a number of compounds. The compound **chǎngzi**, for example, has the general meaning of a place for public gatherings, while other compounds, such as

bīngchǎng (rink or ice arena) or **wǎngqiúchǎng** (tennis court), are more specific.

Páiqiú bǐsài is a volleyball game. The term **páiqiú** (*push ball*) is made up of **pái** as in **ānpai**, and **qiú** as in **qiúchǎng**. **Bǐsài** consists of the components **bǐ**, meaning to compare, and **sài** (contest, competition), which provides the main sense of the term. When modified by the name of a sport, the compound **bǐsài** takes on the meaning of a match, game, or even tournament.

Wó běnrén . . . The word **běnrén** emphasizes the specific individual indicated by the pronoun, most commonly I. The appropriate English equivalent is I myself or personally.

Duì dǎ bīngqiú. **Duì**, as applied here, means concerning or with regard to, and is thus an alternative to **guānyu**. **Dǎ bīngqiú** means to play ice hockey. Since so many sports involve a striking action, it is understandable that **dǎ** should be used to represent the action. With **bīng** meaning ice, and **qiú** meaning a ball, the game of ice hockey is called literally *ice-ball*, which incidentally is also the term for a puck.

Gǎnjué tèbié xīngfèn. **Gǎnjué** means—among other things—to feel, or to perceive, while **tèbié** means special or especially. The first element of the compound **xīngfèn** is **xīng**, as in **xìngqu** (interests), although here **xīng** is uttered in the first tone, giving it the sense of promote; the second element is **fèn** (to rouse). These two elements combine to give the meaning of exciting, exhilarating or stimulating. Hence **xīngfèn** may be used to say particularly exciting, or even highly sensational.

Yúlè is used in the general sense to mean recreation, amusement, or entertainment. When speaking of a pastime or light diversion, the Chinese may simply use the term **wár** (to play).

Yǒu-de shíhou may be taken in its literal sense of *there are times*, or sometimes.

Tīng shōuyīnjī means to listen to the radio. **Shōuyīnjī**, meaning a radio set, is a new compound. The components are: **shōu** (to receive) as in **shōutiáo** (a receipt), **yīn** for sound, and **jī** for machine. This last word **jī** is a somewhat overworked term used generically to cover just about every appliance or contrivance, as well as machinery.

Kàn rìbào means to read the daily newspaper[s]. **Kàn** on its own has the general sense of to look at or to gaze upon. However, when used in conjunction with certain objects, **kàn** may assume a more specific meaning; hence, **kànbào** means to read the paper, just as **kànshū** means to read a book. Further amplification concerning the use of **kàn** (look at) may be useful. Consider this additional random selection of examples:

kànbìng	to see a doctor or, conversely
look at illness	to examine a patient
kànbuchūlái	cannot see clearly, or
look not emerge	not noticeable
kàn-miànzi	to do something as a favour,
watch face	or for the sake of appearances
kànzhe bàn	to act as one sees fit
seeing manage	

Huàkān, zázhì are two types of publications. **Huà** is possibly one of the most important words in Chinese from a cultural point of view. Oddly enough this one word has many English counterparts, but by now it will have been realized that this is characteristic of many Chinese terms. On its own, **huà** stands for a painting or drawing, and therefore generally any kind of picture. Thus **huà** will be found in numerous compounds. For example,

huàbào	illustrated newspapers or periodicals,
(*picture papers*)	pictorials
huàjuǎn, huàzhóu	a picture scroll
huàkān	pictorial magazine
huàtú	a picture
huàxiàng	a portrait, to portray

From this last example you may have deduced that **huà** is also a verb; indeed, the equivalent of to paint a picture or to draw a picture is **huà huàr**. Not surprisingly, the word for a painter or artist is **huàjiā**. Finally, the term **zázhì** is used to cover all types of magazines, not necessarily illustrated, but usually of a periodical nature.

Kàn xiánshū. The compound **xiánshū** is made up of **xián** as in **xiánkòng**, and **shū** (book); it is used to signify casual or light reading matter. Incidentally, the Chinese term for a novel or fiction is **xiǎoshuō[r]** (*little speak*), while **gùshi** means a story.

15.2   CHOICE OF AMUSEMENTS

Dramatic art in China currently occupies a position midway between classical Chinese literature and popular fiction. Both plays and novels are written in the vernacular rather than in the classical literary style; yet, since Chinese dramatic composition consists largely of poetry—albeit sometimes doggerel—it occupies a higher position in the literary hierarchy than does fiction. This literature of the imagination, as it is sometimes known, has exerted an influence over the Chinese masses as no classical literature ever succeeded in doing. Moreover, between the two World Wars, western influence was making itself felt in the literary sphere no less than in the sporting. In the 1930s, the works of Henrik Ibsen were translated and read, as were the plays of Arthur Miller in the late 1970s—to name but two writers who have a popular following in China. Despite the western stereotyping of Chinese as inscrutable, a bystander in a Chinese theatre would soon see that, in fact, the Chinese can be a profoundly emotional people, with a weakness for sentimental plots. Chinese drama consists mainly of a combination of spoken and sung dialogues. Comedies tend to be in spoken form while tragedies and dramas are more often sung. Thus, the spoken word is used as we would expect to find it in theatre, while the music and song can be likened to a Broadway musical, rather than to opera as it is usually understood. The conditions of the early Chinese open air theatres, where the actors had to compete with the din of the fair, are believed to have given rise to the use of drums and gongs, as well as the falsetto voice typical of Chinese opera. The percussion instruments primarily served to attract an audience, while only a high falsetto could penetrate the noise of the crowds and the animals. Often the plot is of the flimsiest nature, while the songs and the way they are presented are the real draw. The audience knows most of the stories by heart, and recognizes the characters as much by their conventional masks and costumes as by their dialogues. Unlike westerners, the Chinese have traditionally considered the opera to be as much for the masses as for the privileged upper classes. Opera plays an important part in the cultural life of the Chinese, particularly the illiterates who, until comparatively recently, formed a very large part of the population. Whether opera is experienced live, or through the medium of radio or TV, it gives them a sense of the drama of history, folklore and literature. Furthermore, it furnishes them with their moral notions of good and evil—a fact well recognized and used to advantage by propagandists seeking to influence the moral consciousness of the public.

R: **Gànwǎn-le huó, dàjiā dàgài gàn-má?**
What does everyone generally get up to after work is over?

C: **Dāngrán gèrén dōu bùtǒng, kěshi nǐ zìjǐ kàndechūlái zài xiūxi-de shíhou dàduōshù dōu xǐhuan chūqù huànhuan nǎojīn. Huàn jùhuà shuō, yàobushi jiēshang liūda-liūda, jiùshi qí zìxíngchē huòzhě zuò gōnggòng-qìchē dào gèchù qù wár. Xǔduō rén ài tīngxì, háiyou xǐhuan kàn diànyǐng-de, huòzhě guàngguang shìchǎng sōngsan yíxià.**
Naturally not everybody is the same, but as you can see for yourself the great majority, when at ease, like to go out for a change of scene. In other words, if not strolling through the streets, they'll be riding their bikes or taking the bus to go all over the place for their fun. Many people like to go to the theatre, others like the cinema or wandering around the bazaars for relaxation.

R: **Guàng shìchǎng yǒu shénme yìsi?**
What's the idea of going to the bazaars?

C: **Nǐ bú-zhīdào ma? Bǐfang shuō, zài Dōngān Shìchǎng yǒu jùyuàn, kéyi suíbiàn tīng jīngxì, huòzhě kàn záshuǎ. Kěshi wàiguorén, yīnwei hái bú dà dǒng Zhōngwén, dàbàn nìngkěn kàn mǎxi, shuāijiāo, biànxìfǎr, zhèizhǒng yúle.**
Don't you know? For instance, at the Dongan Bazaar there are theatres where one can listen to a Beijing opera or watch a variety show. But foreigners who don't yet understand much Chinese mostly prefer to watch a circus, wrestling, juggling, and this kind of amusement.

The hurly-burly of the fair has as much appeal for the Chinese as for anyone else in the world. While not quite the sort of thing seen in the West, with all kinds of equipment and rides, certain regular events create diversion enough for all tastes. Before and during the Chinese New Year there is a very popular event which takes place at Liulichang (Glazed Tile Factory) near the Qianmen Gate south of Tiananmen Square in Beijing. Another fair, in the north-eastern section of the city, is Longfusi, which features among its attractions Mongolian wrestling of the catch as catch can variety, or Greco-style wrestling.

For many decades there has been, in the heart of downtown Beijing, the Dongan Shichang (*Eastern Peace Bazaar*), so named in keeping with the nearby Chang'an Avenue. This bazaar resembles a mall, in the sense that it is a large, covered area which not only contains shops and kiosks selling practically everything under the sun, but also provides entertainment of many kinds, as well as a variety of eating places—including Donglaishun. A more modern term for a market is **shāngchǎng** (*commerce precinct*). This compound is a most appropriate equivalent for our shopping malls.

Excellence in Chinese culture and entertainment is not, however, vested in Beijing alone. A form of **záshuǎ** (variety show) which captivates a large number of visitors to Xi'an, who go there primarily to see the terracota army, is a spectacle you should not miss. This is a stage production in the People's Mansion, and consists of a representation of the music and dance of the Tang Dynasty (608-905 AD). This show has elegance, wit, and sophistication to charm the most discerning audience of any nationality. Ensure that your guide includes it in an evening's entertainment. Ballet enthusiasts may be aware that the Chinese, who love folk dancing, have developed a strong affinity to western ballet and modern dancing. As a result of this attraction, the Central Ballet of China, based in Beijing, has developed a delightful blend of traditional Chinese and modern western choreography.

VOCABULARY

huó	to live, alive, living; extn.—lively, vivid; movable; work
nǎo	the brain
jīn	muscle, sinew
liū	to slide, glide; extn.—to slip away; smooth
dá	to extend; reach; achieve

qí	to ride [in a saddle], sit on the back of
xì	a play, drama, show; extn.—Chinese opera
yǐng	shadow; image, reflection; extn.—film, trace
guàng	to stroll, ramble, roam
sī	to think, consider; deliberate; extn.—thought
sōng	pine [wood]; loose, slack; extn.—to relax; a surname
jù	drama, play
shuǎ	to perform [tricks], put on a show; extn.—to flourish
dǒng	to understand; extn.—to know
nìng	rather, would rather, better; a surname
mǎ	horse; a surname
shuāi	to fall, tumble, lose one's balance; extn.—throw, fling
biàn	to change, become different; extn.—transform, alter

RATIONALE AND INTERPRETATION

Gànwán-le huó. The two words **gàn** (to do) and **huó** (work) combine to form the compound **gànhuó**, meaning to be at work or to be on the job. This compound is often used in referring to manual labour, but in the comparatively egalitarian atmosphere of China today it has a wider application, and may refer to work in general. The other two components of the expression are **wán** (to complete), and the particle **-le**, which is used to indicate completion of the action. Thus by compounding the two verbs **gàn** and **wán**, and adding the particle **-le**, we obtain to have finished doing; then, by adding **huó**, we obtain the equivalent of when work is finished or after work is over.

Dàjiā dàgài gàn-má? This sentence means roughly "What does everybody usually do?" **Dà** as in **dàxiǎo** (size), and **jiā** as in **jiājù** (furniture) together form the term for everybody or all [people]. **Dàgài** means generally or usually. **Gàn** (to do), combined with the QW **má**, conveys the same meaning as the expression **gàn shénme**, but **gàn-má** is more colloquial. Incidentally, **gàn-má** also has an interrogative sense of not only why but, more emphatically, "whatever for!" For example:

Tā gàn-má zhènme wǎn?   Why [on earth] is she so late?

Gèrén bùtóng (*each person not alike*) is an example of how occasionally Chinese logic renders Chinese sentence construction different from English. Rather than stating "Not everyone is the same," the Chinese prefer to say "Everybody is not the same."

Nǐ zìjǐ kàndechūlái means "You can see for yourself." When the term **zìjǐ** is allied with a pronoun, it adds emphasis to it. Here the pronoun being **nǐ**, the combination **nǐ zìjǐ** means you yourself. The sentence also contains a resultative verb, **kàndechūlái**, which simply means to be able to see or discernible. To express the reverse idea, you would substitute **bù** for **dé**, and say **kànbuchūlái**, meaning to be unable to see or undetectable.

Xiūxi-de shíhou. Xiūxi has a fairly broad interpretation, covering everything from a [short] break or rest to an indeterminate interval for relaxation. By extension, we may interpret this to mean being at leisure or at ease or, quite simply, not busy.

Dàduōshù dōu xǐhuan chūqù means the majority like to go out. **Duō** as in **duōshǎo** (amount) and **shù** as in **shùzi** (figure) combine to mean the majority or most. By adding **dà** (big) to this compound we obtain the equivalent of the great majority or vast majority. **Dōu** (all) gives additional emphasis. **Xǐhuan** (to like) supports **chūqù** (to go out). Anyone who has visited China will have seen the crowds of people milling around the streets of an evening looking for a change of scene, and will understand this clause perfectly. The Chinese use the term **rénhǎi** to refer to a vast crowd, which is a metaphor identical to our "a sea of people"—but in China, the tide nearly always seems to be in!

. . . huànhuan nǎojīn. Huàn means to change or to exchange. It is duplicated to emphasize the fact that the activity goes on for an indefinite length of time. **Nǎojīn** (*brain muscle*) refers to the mind or brains and, by extension, it implies a way of thinking. However, this Chinese expression, far from meaning to change one's mind, signifies to give one's mind a rest through a change of scene, i.e., take a break.

Huàn jùhuà shuō is another Chinese expression using **huàn**, only a little more literally this time. This expression is used to convey the idea to say [something] differently or, more idiomatically, "in other words."

Yàobushi . . . jiùshi. This construction is used when expressing an alternative circumstance in the sense of "If not . . . [then] . . . ," the key words being **yào** (if) and **jiù** (then), both of which are used with **shì** (to be).

Jiēshang liūda-liūda. Liūda is a compound, meaning to stroll, to saunter, or to go for a ramble; that is, to walk essentially as a relaxation rather than to walk for a particular purpose. The duplication of **liūda** provides another example of emphasis on the duration of the action.

Qí zìxíngchē. Consider first the compound **zìxíngchē**. **Zì** as in **zìjǐ** (self), **xíng** as in **lǚxíng** (travel), and **chē** meaning a vehicle, all combine to give us the term for a bicycle (i.e. a vehicle propelled by oneself). **Qí**, meaning to ride, is applied only to riding astride, as in a saddle. To express the idea of riding on a seat, as in a bus, train, or aircraft, the word **zuò** (to sit) is used, and is, of course, more widely applicable than **qí**.

Zuò gōnggòng-qìchē means to ride on a bus. **Qìchē** applies to any fuel-driven vehicle such as a car. When it is modified by the compound **gōnggòng** (communal, public), made up of **gōng** as in **gōngyuán**, and **gòng** as in **yígòng**, the term for a bus or that type of public transport is obtained.

Dào gèchù qù wár. The **dào** (arrive) and **qù** (depart) relationship means to reach [a place] somewhere, while **gèchù** means various or different places, being made up of **gè** as in **gèwèi**, and **chù** as in **bànshìchù**. This may be interpreted, as in the dialogue, to indicate to go all over the place. **Wár** is used widely to mean not only to play, but also to have fun or, generally, to seek amusement.

Xǔduō rén. **Xǔ**, in the sense of somewhat, is joined with **duō**, meaning many, to form a compound which also means many, thus giving this expression the meaning many people.

. . . ài tīngxì. **Ài** covers several degrees of liking, from "to love" to "to be fond of." **Tīngxì** is an expression meaning to listen to the opera. **Tīng** means to listen, and is used in this context because many discriminating Chinese theatregoers attend more for the singing than for the acting; hence they talk of listening to rather than watching or seeing an opera. **Xì** is the traditional word for drama or opera in the grand style, and is used in a number of compounds with associated meanings. Here the expression is used in an idiomatic way to convey going to the theatre in general terms, as well as specifically going to the opera.

Xǐhuan kàn diànyǐng-de. By a similar token, **kàn diànyǐng** means going to the cinema, since **diànyǐng** (*electric shadows* or images) refers to the movies. **Xǐhuan** (to like) with the particle **-de** alludes to those who like going to the movies. Many Chinese still do, in spite of television.

Guàngguang shìchǎng sōngsan yíxià. The meaning of **guàng** (stroll, ramble) is similar to that of **liūda**, with the subtle difference that **liūda** does not necessarily imply a particular destination, while **guàng** does imply visiting a particular place for a stroll around and is consequently more akin to **sànbù**. This difference, however, does not merit too much concern. **Shìchǎng** signifies a bazaar or marketplace; its components are **shì** as in **shìzhèng** (municipal), and **chǎng** as in **shāngchǎng** (market). The purpose of going to the bazaar is described by the words **sōngsan yíxià**. **Sōng** (loose) is the opposite of **jǐn** (tight). By extension it means to loosen up or to relax, particularly when compounded with **sàn**. Another way of expressing to relax is **fāsōng** (*promote slack*), **fā** being as in **chūfā** (to set out).

...**yǒu shénme yìsi** means "what is the interest to be had in..." or "what's the point of...." The components of the compound **yìsi** are **yì** as in **zhúyì** (idea), and **sī** (thought). This term can mean an idea, opinion, wish, meaning, or interest—depending on context.

Jùyuàn means a theatre. (Another word for a theatre is **jùchǎng**.) **Jù** (drama) can also be compounded with **xì** to form **xìjù**, meaning a drama, play, or theatre in the generic sense.

...**kéyi suíbiàn tīng jīngxì**. **Jīngxì** refers to the Beijing opera specifically, since **jīng** (capital) is derived from the name Beijing. The use of **suìbiàn** is deliberate, as it is not unusual for people in the audience to come and go at will during the performance of an opera. The operas performed are epics of heroic proportions, and would be hard to endure from start to finish.

...**kàn záshuǎ**. The compound **záshuǎ** means a variety show, a show which could include all kinds of performances other than plays. Its components are **zá** (sundry) as in **zázhì**, and **shuǎ** (put on a show). The expression **kàn záshuǎ** is natural, since Chinese would do more than **tīng** (listen), they would also **kàn** (observe). **Záshuǎ**, alluding to any number of turns that a variety show might include—from acrobatics to rapid-fire and witty dialogues known as **xiàngsheng** (mimicry)—would require close attention to be fully appreciated. The Chinese audiences lap up such chat shows, which are spiced with puns and double entendre, in which they delight as much as the satire on which these are often based.

...**hái búdà dǒng Zhōngwén** means literally *still not greatly understand Chinese*. **Dà** (big) is used to tactfully modify the verb **dǒng** (to understand), while **Zhōngwén** refers to the Chinese language, tacitly implying Chinese culture as a whole. A Chinese would not expect a foreign visitor to be well-versed in Chinese culture, and would be careful not to give embarrassment by treating the visitor's ignorance as an appalling deficit.

Dàbàn means literally *the larger half* or *most*. This term is interchangeable with **dàduōshù**, given previously for majority.

Nìngkěn. This compound means to prefer. Its components are **nìng**, meaning would rather, and **kěn** (willing).

Mǎxì, shuāijiāo, biànxìfǎr. These are just three kinds of entertainment one might expect to find at a **záshuǎ**, or variety show. **Mǎ** (horse) and **xì** (show) form the compound **mǎxì**, meaning a circus. This type of exhibition, which is not necessarily of the three-ring variety, or confined exclusively to demonstrations of horsemanship, is rapidly gaining admiration around the world. **Shuāijiāo** is another new compound, meaning wrestling. Some of the best Chinese wrestlers come from Mongolia. **Biànxìfǎr** signifies jugglers, or conjurers, and China has some of the most fascinating performers of this type. The elements of this compound are **biàn** (to transform), **xì** as in **xìjù** (drama), **fǎ** (method) and, last but not least, the Beijing retroflex **r**.

Zhèizhǒng yúlè—*this kind of amusement* is placed at the end of the sentence to indicate the end of the list of examples.

SUPPLEMENTARY VOCABULARY

chéngguǒ	achievement
huàtīng	art gallery
bāléiwǔ	ballet
yīnyuètīng	concert hall
yīnyuè	music
yīnyuèduì	orchestra, band

zájì	acrobatics
gōngjiànshù, shèjì	archery
yùndòngyuàn	athlete
jìngjì	athletics
jiángpǐn	award
yǔmáoqiú	badminton, shuttlecock
lánqiú	basketball
guànjūn	champion (i.e., gold trophy medal)
jiàoliàn [yuán]	coach
píngdì huáxuě	cross-country skiing
liú bīnghú	curling
tiàowǔ	dancing
tiàoshuǐ	diving
jiàngxià huáxuě	downhill skiing
xiàngmù	event [sporting]
jījiànshù	fencing
huāyàng huábīng	figure skating
fànguī	foul
qiúmén	goal
tǐcāo	gymnastics
mànpǎo	jogging
páli	luge
mǎlāsōng sàipǎo	marathon race
jiǎngzhāng	medal
jìjūn	bronze medalist
yàjūn	silver medalist
dēngshān	mountaineering
biáoyǎn	perform
jìlù	record
défēn	score
huáxuě yùndòng	skiing
zúqiú	soccer, football
yóuyǒng	swimming
yóuyǒngchí	swimming pool
pīngpāngqiú	table tennis, ping-pong

duì	team
wǎngqiú	tennis
xuěqiāo huábīng	tobogganing
tiánjìng-sài	track and field
xùnliàn	training
cáipàn [yuán]	umpire, referee
jíhé dìdiǎn	venue

SIXTEEN

EMERGENCIES

> "Even those who won't burn incense in times of Prosperity clasp the feet of Buddha in the day of misfortune."

When visiting China take along an adequate supply of commercial brands of medicinal and hygiene products required to meet one's daily needs. Do not forget prescribed medication for any chronic condition, since it is essential to be self-sufficient. In addition, the wise visitor will take the precaution of having adequate insurance to cover any serious medical contingencies or hospitalization. All vaccinations should be up to date, and also be inoculated—especially against tetanus and hepatitis—for travel in the Far East.

It is essential to take certain other precautions as well, such as never drinking unboiled water. A number of the better hotels claim that their tap water is potable, but one is well-advised not to be lulled into a false sense of security. Fresh fruit should be washed with boiled water.

In fact, all uncooked foodstuffs are the safer for being washed before being eaten. You may notice that the Chinese often call for a bowl of boiling water at a restaurant in order to scald the tableware before use! It is axiomatic that a traveler going anywhere in the world (not only China) should be adequately prepared to stave off, or remedy, diarrhea or constipation, not to mention the common cold. These three maladies, among many others, can seriously detract from one's enjoyment of travel.

This chapter is deliberately confined to minor difficulties someone with only a basic knowledge of Chinese may be capable of handling.

16.1 FEELING INDISPOSED

[◯◯] R: **Wǒ bú dà shūfu. Wǒ tóu téng, sǎngzi yě nánshòu. Wàibiar guā dàfēng, suóyǐ wó xiǎng jīntiān zuì hǎo bù chūmén.**
I don't feel very well. I have a headache and a sore throat. It's blowing a gale outside, so I thought it would be best not to go out today.

C: **Kěxī nǐ méi zǎo yìdiǎr tōngzhī wǒ. Nǐ yào-buyào wǒ tì nǐ qù yàofáng mǎi yìdiǎr yào chī?**
Pity you didn't let me know a bit sooner. Do you want me to go to the pharmacy for you and buy you some medicine?

R: **Kěnéng wó gǎnmào-le, késhi búbì zháojí. Wǒ zhèr xiūxi yíxià jiù déle. Rúguǒ míngtiān shēntǐ hái bù shūfu, wǒ jiù xiǎng bànfǎ qù kànbìng.**
I may have caught a cold, but there's no need to worry. I'll be all right after a short rest. If I'm still not well tomorrow, I'll find some way to get seen to.

C: **Lǚguǎn-li dàgài huì yǒu shuō Yīngyǔ-de dàifu. Wǒ lìkè géi nǐ wènwen, hǎo-ma?**
There's probably a doctor in the hotel who can speak English. I can find out for you at once, if you like.

R: **Nǐ xiān bié nàme máng! Xiànzài wǒ méi fāshāo, wèikǒu hái bú cuò. Duō déng liǎng tiān zài shāngliang ba.**
You needn't be in such a hurry. At present I don't have a fever, and my appetite's not bad. Let's wait another couple of days and then talk about it.

VOCABULARY

shū	to unfold, stretch; extn.—leisurely; a surname
téng	pain, hurt, sore, ache; extn.—to dote on, love dearly
sǎng	throat, larynx; extn.—voice
nán	difficult, hard; extn.—bad (also pron. **nàn**—disaster)
shòu	to receive; accept; extn.—be subjected to; endure, suffer

guā	to scrape; extn.—shave; to blow (gust)
fēng	wind; scenery
xī	to pity; cherish, take care of
yào	medicine, drugs; extn.—generic for certain chemicals
mào	to emit, to give off; to risk
jí	anxious, impatient; extn.—urgent
rú	according to; as if; like; such as, for instance
guǒ	fruit; extn.—result, consequence; really
shēn	body; extn.—oneself, personally
yīng	English, Anglo-
bìng	ill, sick; extn.—disease; defect
shāo	to burn; extn.—cook, bake, roast; run a temperature
wèi	stomach
cuò	intricate, complicated; extn.—fault, wrong; rub

RATIONALE AND INTERPRETATION

...bú dà shūfu means, in essence, not very comfortable. You have seen that dà may be used to mean more than simply big or large; it can also be used to signify scale or quantity. Here it modifies shūfu, to create the sense of overly or greatly. Shūfu means comfortable and, by extension, is used in the idiomatic sense of to feel well. It is composed of shū (leisurely), and fú, as in yīfu. In the affirmative it means comfortable, in the sense of being at ease, whereas in the negative, the context should make it apparent whether it is being used to indicate ill at ease or—more figuratively—an indisposed feeling, i.e., unwell or just plain ill!

Wǒ tóu téng can be translated directly as "My head hurts" or, "I have a headache." Tóu is a word for head, an alternative word for which is nǎodai. Téng can be used to indicate a painful feeling anywhere you care to mention.

...sǎngzi nánshòu. Sǎngzi refers to the throat (internal). Nán is used here with its primary meaning of difficult or hard. Nàn (fourth tone) has an associated meaning of adversity or disaster, e.g., nànmín for refugees. Nánshòu (*hard to endure*) means to feel sore, being a combination of nán meaning difficult, or unpleasant, and shòu—to accept or endure. Thus, in this particular context, sǎngzi nánshòu is an appropriate way of expressing a sore throat; but if the throat is really painful, then substitute **téng** for **nánshòu**, since the latter would be an obvious understatement.

Wàibiar guā dàfēng. The word **guā** has two distinct meanings. In this instance **guā** applies to the wind (**fēng**), and therefore **guāfēng** means that the wind blows. **Dàfēng** simply means a great wind, and can be applied, therefore, to anything from a gale to a tropical cyclone. Indeed, it is the origin of typhoon in English. **Qǐ** is used to modify **guā** to indicate up, in the same way one would say a storm blew up i.e., **guāqǐ dàfēng**. Lastly, **wàibiar** indicates outdoors or outside.

Chūmén means literally *to go out the door*, therefore **bù chūmén** can be taken to mean either not to go out [of doors], or to stay in [doors]. (This expression is very close to the idiomatic expression **chū ménzi**, which signifies to marry. The latter is applied only to a woman since, as a rule, she is the one who leaves home to set up a new home elsewhere, possibly with her husband's family.)

Kěxī. **Kě** has been presented in a number of compounds in various chapters. The compound **kěxī** is a complete expression, not simply an adjective. The essence of the expression comes from **xī** (to pity). It is in effect an equational verb, the basic equivalent of which is pity or shame, or an exclamation of regret, such as "What a pity!" or "That's too bad!" In terms of sentence construction, its place is at the head of the sentence as it would be in English. It may also be used to mean unfortunately.

Nǐ méi tōngzhī wǒ—"You didn't notify me." **Tōngzhī** (to inform or notify) is modified by the phrase **zǎo yìdiǎr** (a little earlier). With the addition of the expression **kěxī**, the sentence means "It's a shame you didn't let me know a little sooner."

Wǒ tì nǐ qù means "I go on your behalf." **Tì nǐ** need not be followed by **géi nǐ** (for you), since the purpose of buying the medicine is implied at the end of the sentence by **chī** (i.e., for you to take).

. . . qù yàofáng mǎi yìdiǎr yào chī. The main word is **yào**, which is the generic term for medication. The Chinese actually speak of eating medicine, hence the use of **chī**. **Yàofáng** (*medicine house*) is the compound for pharmacy or drugstore, or even dispensary.

Kěnéng wó gǎnmào-le. "Possibly I caught a cold" is what this means. The common cold is as prevalent in China as anywhere else, and—as in English—may be referred to in different ways. **Gǎnmào**, which may be used either as a noun or a verb, is the term for a cold or flu. **Zháo**, an alternative pronunciation for **zhe**, meaning to touch or to feel, together with **liáng**, meaning cool or cold, provide the term **zháolíang** (*touch cold*), which is another way of saying to catch a chill.

Zháojí means to worry or to feel anxious. **Zháo** in this case is compounded with **jí** (anxious) to convey the nuance of becoming impatient, or even upset. The expression **búbì** (or **bié**) **zháojí** is therefore used to mean "Don't fret," or "No need to worry."

Xiūxi yíxià. The sentence **wǒ zhèr xiūxi yíxià** means "I'll rest here a while [in order to get better]." **Jiù déle** is similar to the expression **jiù xíng** (to be O.K.).

Rúguǒ means if, in case or in the event of, and may be used in the same way as in English.

...shēntǐ hái bù shūfu is to say, literally, *... body still not comfortable.* To designate the human body, the term **shēntǐ** is appropriate, consisting of **shēn** (body) and **tǐ** as in **tǐyù**. To refer to physical discomfort, as opposed to actual illness, you can say **wǒ shēntǐ bù shūfu** as an alternative to **wǒ bù shūfu**, since by extension **shēntǐ** refers to health as well. **Shēntǐ bù shūfu** may be translated as *feeling off colour*, whereas **yǒu bìng** means to be ill.

Wǒ jiù xiǎng bànfǎ qù kànbìng. **Kànbìng** may mean either to see a patient (from the doctor's point of view), or to consult a doctor (from a patient's viewpoint). **Xiǎng bànfǎ** means to think of a way. **Xiǎng** means to think, to consider or to intend, while **bànfǎ** (method, means, way) is the combination of **bàn** as in **bànshìchù**, and **fǎ** as in **zuòfǎ**. In the opposite vein, an expression often used is **Méi[yǒu] bànfǎ** meaning "It's hopeless!" Sometimes is heard **méi fázi** or—in Beijing—**méi fár bàn**, which is another way of saying "It can't be helped."

Lǚguǎn dàgài huì yǒu...dàifu means "The hotel probably has a doctor." **Dàgài** means presumably or most likely, and **dàifu** indicates a medical practitioner or doctor [of medicine]. The qualifying clause applied to the doctor (i.e., **shuō Yīngyǔ-de**) indicates that he should be *of* [the kind who] *speaks English.*

Wǒ lìkè géi nǐ wènwen. **Lìkè** means right away or immediately. **Wèn**

is the verb to ask. Duplication of the word **wèn** signifies to make enquiries or to ask around—hence to find out.

Nǐ xiān bié nàme máng. Máng means not only busy but also haste. **Bié máng** is an expression meaning "Don't rush it" or "No hurry." By inserting **nàme**, we get "No need for that [much] hurry." **Xiān** (first) is used here in the sense of yet. Consequently we have "You needn't be in that much of a hurry yet!"

Fāshāo, being the compound of **fā** as in **chūfā** and **shāo** (to burn), means to run a temperature or have a fever.

Wèikǒu hái bú cuò. Wèikǒu is a compound signifying appetite. As for **cuò**, while this word on its own has the sense of fault or wrong (i.e., something bad), **bú cuò** implies not bad or, conversely, pretty good! The use of **hái** in this instance shows that the patient's appetite is still as satisfactory as it should be.

Duō déng liǎng tiān. Déng liǎng tiān simply means *to wait two days*. Because the sentence begins with **duō** (many, or more), the sense is to wait two more days, or to wait another couple of days. This idea is reinforced by the suggestive particle **ba**, which gives "Let's wait two days longer."

Shāngliang means to talk over, to discuss, or to consult. The compound consists of **shāng** as in **shāngyè**, and **liàng** as in **zhìliàng**. It is often used as a substitute for the more commonplace **shuō** (to talk).

16.2   LOST PROPERTY

R: **Wǒ bú zhīdào zěnme huíshì, kěshi wǒ wàngjìle bǎ yǎnjìng fàng zài nǎr-le. Zhèr yǒu-meiyou shīwù-zhāolǐngchù?**
I don't know how it happened, but I've forgotten where I put my glasses. Is there a Lost and Found Office here?

C: **Yǒu, wǒ fùzé zhèijiàn shì. Nǐ yǎnjìngr diūle duójiǔ? Nǐ jìdezhù kěnéng diū nǎr-le ma?**
Yes, I'm responsible for that. How long ago did you lose your glasses? Can you recollect where you might have lost them?

R: **Dàgài zuótiān xịàwǔ ba. Píngcháng wó xiěxịn huòzhě kànshū-de shíhou cái dài yǎngjịng, suóyǐ zuótiān wǎnshang zài fàntīng-li yào kàn càidān wǒ cái fāxiàn yǎnjịng méiyǒu-le.**
It was probably yesterday afternoon. Normally I only wear glasses when I'm writing letters or reading, so it wasn't until last night in the dining room when I wanted to read the menu that I discovered my glasses were gone!

C: **Kǒngpạ̀ méiyǒu nǐ-de. Wǒ zhí yǒu zhè yífù tạ̀iyángjịng, búshi nị̌-de ba?**
I'm afraid I haven't got yours. I only have this one pair of sunglasses which aren't yours—are they?

R: **Búshi. Qịàhǎo jìngtou chụ̌fāng wǒ hái nạ́zhe-ne. Qíng nǐ géi wǒ jièshào yǎnjìngshạ̄ng, hǎo-ma?**
No. Fortunately, I still have the lens prescription. Would you please recommend an optician?

VOCABULARY

wàng	to forget; extn.—to overlook, neglect
yǎn	eye; extn.—to glance at; aperture
jìng	mirror, extn.—lens, glasses
shī	to lose, extn.—miss, let slip; mishap
lǐng	neck; extn.—collar; to lead, have jurisdiction over
fù	to carry on the back, bear; extn.—assume responsibility
zé	duty, responsibility; blame, reprimand
diū	to lose, mislay; extn.—to forget
zuó	yesterday
dài	to put on, wear; a surname
tīng	hall, court
qià	appropriate, proper; precisely
chǔ	to handle, deal with, manage (alt. pron. **chù**—place)

RATIONALE AND INTERPRETATION

Bù zhīdạ̀o zěnme huíshì is an expression indicating ignorance as to how something may have happened.

Wǒ wàngjìle bá yǎnjìng fàng zài nǎr-le. **Wàng**, meaning to forget, is often used on its own, but for emphasis it may also be compounded with **jì** (to remember) as in **dēngjì**. **Yǎnjìng** refers to glasses or spectacles. **Yǎn** (eye) is combined with **jìng**, meaning lens, and the resulting compound is sometimes heard with the suffix -**zi** (i.e., **yǎnjìngzi**), although in Beijing the pronunciation is more likely to be **yǎnjìngr**. All three versions refer literally to eye-glasses and should not be confused with **yǎnjing**, referring to the eye. The use of **bǎ** serves to emphasize the object by transposing it to a position in front of the verb. **Fàng zài nǎr**, modifying **yǎnjìng**, refers to where (**nǎr**) they were put (**fàng**). **Fàng** means to release which, by extension, leads to the meaning of put down or let go.

Shīwù-zhāolǐngchù refers to the Lost Property Office. The term consists of two parts, namely **shīwù**, meaning lost items, and **zhāolǐng**, alluding to an *announcement of the finding*. This is akin to our own expression of Lost and Found.

Fùze means to be in charge [of] or, by extension, to be responsible [for]. The elements of this compound are **fù**, which denotes the shouldering of responsibility, and **zé**, which provides the main sense of this term (**zérèn** is the word for responsibility). Because a person can be said to have taken a responsible attitude, **fùzé** can also be used in an appropriate context to mean conscientious.

Ní yǎnjìngr diū-le duójiǔ? Note the construction of this question: although it is the glasses which are lost, they are the subject, not the object, of the sentence. **Diū** (to lose) is combined with the interrogative aspect introduced by the QW **duó jiǔ** (*how long [a time]?*).

Jìdezhù. This resultative verb is the combination of two verbs with very similar meanings. **Jìde** means to remember or to recall, being **jì** as in **dēngjì**, and **dé** as in **déle**. **Jìzhù** means to bear in mind, using the same **jì** with **zhù** (stay). Hence **jìdezhù** means to recollect or remember, while the opposite idea would be expressed as **jìbuzhù**.

Kěnéng diū nǎr-le literally means *possibly lost where*. **Kěnéng** conveys the idea of probability or possibility, and in conjunction with **diū** (to lose) and the particle -**le** yields *could have been lost*. **Nǎr** is the QW and, since the context is obvious, it is not necessary to use **zài** (at), which might normally be associated with the QW.

Píngcháng means ordinarily, usually or normally. The components are **píng** as in **píngxìn**, and **cháng** as in **fēicháng**.

...**xiěxìn huòzhě kànshū-de shíhou.** "When I'm writing letters or reading." The term **xiěxìn** means to write letters, with **xiě** being to write and **xìn** being a letter.

Wǒ ... cái dài yǎnjìng means "I only wear glasses." **Cái** is used here in the sense of only, (i.e., only when reading or writing). **Dài** means to wear. However, it may not be used indiscriminately in this sense, for where some clothing is concerned a different word is used. **Dài** applies to spectacles, gloves, and hats, as well as wrist-watches, collars and neckties.

Suóyǐ zuótiān wǎnshang zài fàntīng-li... "Therefore last night in the dining room...." As a quick review: time clauses are generally placed at the beginning of a sentence, followed by the place (if applicable) or other qualifying clause.

...**yào kàn càidān** ... continuing with the same sentence, we have "wanting to read the menu," as **càidān** means a menu.

Wǒ cái fāxiàn yǎnjìng méiyǒu-le. "Only then did I discover I didn't have the glasses." The English presentation may differ slightly from the Chinese, for when the Chinese rendering is literally "It was only then...," an English-speaker might say "Not until then...." **Fāxiàn** means to discover, to find out or to notice; the components are **fā** as in **fāshāo**, and **xiàn** as in **xiànzài**. Note the **-le** at the end of the sentence, which indicates completion of the action; in this case, not to have [any more].

Wǒ zhí yǒu zhè yífù tàiyángjìng means "I only have this pair of sunglasses." Here the sun is referred to as **tàiyáng** (as compared with **rì**), a compound made up of **tài** as in **tàijíquán**, and **yáng** as in **yánglì**; hence **tàiyángjìng** for sunglasses. The MW **fù** is used in connection with gloves and glasses. **Zhǐ** (only) is the same as in **zhǐyào**.

Qiàhǎo means "as luck would have it" or fortunately. **Qià** (precisely), is joined with **hǎo** (good), and the resulting compound may be taken to imply by good luck rather than by good management!

Jìngtóu chǔfāng. The word for a lens is **jìngtóu**, **jìng** being as in **yǎnjìng**, and **tóu** as in **tóuténg**. **Chǔfāng** means to prescribe or a prescription, being the compound of **chǔ** (to handle), which is also pronounced **chù** (fourth tone), and **fāng** as in **dìfāng**. **Fāng** is used here in its sense of directions or instructions.

... **géi wǒ jièshào yǎnjìngshāng** conveys a request to "recommend an optician to me." While **jièshào** means to introduce, it also carries the sense of refer, and thus may be used to mean to recommend. **Yǎnjìngshāng** (*eye glass business*) is the term for an optician, using **shāng** as in **shāngyè**.

16.3   A PANIC CALL FROM HOSPITAL

Xiéhé Yīyuàn is the Chinese name for a hospital in the centre of Beijing which, until 1951, was referred to as the Peking Union Medical College (PUMC). It was established in 1914 by the China Medical Board and the Rockefeller Foundation, and supported by them for 37 years. It is credited with having had a profound influence on medical education and medical practice not only in China but throughout East Asia, and stands to this day a proud monument to Joint Harmony or Concord, from which it derives its Chinese name—**Xiéhé**. Its architecture alone is worth more than a casual glance, and it may be said to have been the forerunner of a blend of Western and Chinese design which can be seen in many of the more modern public buildings nowadays.

Modern hospitals are constantly being visited by western medical practitioners, who are interested in comparing techniques with the Chinese and are frequently impressed with the blend of traditional and modern treatments. While this blend may not appeal to some foreign patients, there can be no doubt that the Chinese medical staff will do their utmost wherever possible to assist a patient's recovery. If anything, they might be over-solicitous in their efforts to restore the patient to health, for they are quick to understand that the visitor is far from home and would naturally be anxious to return to the bosom of the family. There is unlikely to be a more caring person than a good Chinese friend.

OO   R: **Wó yǒu jíshì qíng nǐ bāngmáng!**
             Please help me with an urgent matter!

C: **Kuài shuō-ba! Nǐ zài nǎr ne?**

Hurry up and tell me where you are.

R: **Wó liǎngtiān-zhīqián fāzuò-le xīnzàngbìng, jiù jìnrù-le Xiéhé Yīyuàn. Kǒngpà wó děi duō dānwù jǐtiān, fǒuzé búyào zhèyàng máfan rénjia.**

I had a heart attack two days ago and was admitted to the Xiehe Hospital. I'm afraid I'll be delayed a few more days, otherwise I wouldn't bother people like this.

C: **Nǎr-de huà! Nǐ yào wǒ tōngzhī dàshíguǎn ma?**

What a thing to say! Do you want me to notify the embassy?

R: **Duì. Qǐng tāmen géi wǒ mèimei dǎge diànbào. Zuìjìn-de qīnrén zhí yǒu tā yíge rén. Wǒ xīwàng tā hé dàshǐ yíkuàr kéyi gǎnbàn wǒ huíguó-de zhǔnbèi.**

Right. Ask them to send a cable to my younger sister. She is my only next-of-kin. I'm hoping that she, together with the ambassador, can expedite arrangements for me to return home.

C: **Nǐ fàngxīn ba. Dǎwán-le diànhuà yǐhòu wǒ gánjǐn guòqù zháo nǐ.**

Leave it to me. After I've made the phone calls I'll get over to see you at once.

VOCABULARY

jìn	to advance; extn.—enter, go into
rù	to enter; extn.—to join, be admitted into; income
xié	joint, common; extn.—assist
hé	gentle, kind; extn.—harmonious, peace; and; a surname
dān	to delay; extn.—to indulge in, abandon oneself to
wù	mistake, error; by accident; harm; extn.—to miss
fǒu	not; negate, deny
shǐ	to use, employ, cause, enable; send; extn.—envoy, courier
mèi	younger sister, sister
qīn	parent; blood relation; next of kin; oneself

RATIONALE AND INTERPRETATION

Wó yǒu jíshì qíng nǐ bāngmáng means in effect "I have an urgent matter requiring your assistance." With **jí** from **zháojí**, and **shì** from **shìqing**, we get an urgent matter or an emergency for which assistance (i.e. **bāngmáng**) is requested.

Kuài shuō-ba states virtually "Get on with what you're saying!"

Nǐ zài nǎr ne—"Where are you?" **Ne** is not essential, but serves roughly the same purpose as just now, or at present; in other words it emphasizes current whereabouts.

Liǎngtiān zhīqián refers to two days previously or two days ago, since **qián** has the meaning of before or preceding, as in **yǐqián**.

Fāzuò xīnzàngbìng means to have a heart attack. **Fāzuò**, comprising **fā** as in **chūfā** and **zuò** as in **zuòfǎ**, has the sense of breaking out or showing the effect, thus serving as the equivalent of to have (as hysterics or a fit of anger or, in this case, a heart attack). **Xīnzàng** refers specifically to the heart as an internal organ, and is composed of **xīn** as in **dānxīn**, and **zàng** meaning an organ, (the alternative form for **zāng**). By adding **bìng** (illness) the term for a heart attack is obtained.

. . . **jìnrù Xiéhé Yīyuàn**. **Jìnrù** means to enter or to go into and, by extension, to be admitted to a hospital (**yīyuàn**). Incidentally, **zhùyuàn** is the term for hospitalized, composed of **zhù** (to stay), and **yuàn** as in **yīyuàn**, while the expression for hospital treatment is **zhùyuàn-zhìliáo**.

Wó děi duō dānwù jǐtiān. The key word is **dānwù**. While its actual meaning is to be delayed or to be held up, when one analyses the components there is a suggestion that dilly-dallying is the cause of the delay! The word **duō** preceding **dānwù** indicates delay of a few more days (**jǐtiān**). **Děi** (also pronounced **dé**), when pronounced as it is in this case, takes on the sense of must or have to. All in all, this sentence therefore means "I'll have to stay on a few more days."

Fǒuzé búyào zhèyàng máfan rénjia serves as an apology for being a nuisance. **Fǒuzé** means or else, if not or otherwise. The rest of the sentence consists mainly of **máfan** (to bother), and **rénjia** meaning people [in general], with **rén** as in **rénmín** and **jiā** as in **jiājù**.

Nǎr-de huà is an exclamation to the effect of "What makes you say that," or "What a thing to say!"

Tōngzhī dàshǐguǎn means simply "to notify the embassy," comprising **tōngzhī** (to inform) and **dàshíguǎn** (embassy). **Shǐ**, the second syllable of **dàshíguǎn**, takes on its extended meaning of envoy. The term **dàshǐ** (*great envoy*) refers to an ambassador, and is compounded with **guǎn** (office), as in **fànguǎn**, to give the meaning of embassy.

Géi wó mèimei dǎge diànbào means "Send a telegram to my younger sister." **Mèimei** is the term for a sister younger than oneself.

Zuìjìn-de qīnrén refers to next of kin, being literally *nearest relative*.

. . . **zhí yǒu tā yíge rén** means "She is the only person."

Wǒ xīwàng tā hé dàshǐ yíkuàr . . . This is a straightforward presentation of "I hope she and the ambassador together. . . ." One meaning of **hé** (and) in this case, is reinforced by **yíkuàr** (together). **Xīwàng** means to wish, hope for or expect.

. . . **kéyi gǎnbàn wǒ huíguó-de zhǔnbèi**. **Gǎnbàn** means to expedite, and is composed of **gǎn** as in **gǎnkuài**, and **bàn** as in **bànfǎ**. **Wǒ huíguó-de**, the clause modifying **zhǔnbèi** (arrangements), alludes to the purpose of the arrangements (i.e., for my returning home), since **huíguó** refers to a *return to [one's own] country*.

Nǐ fàngxīn ba. **Fàng** as in **fàngjià**, and **xīn** as in **dānxīn** combine to make up the expression to be at ease or to rest assured, which in effect is the opposite of **dānxīn** (*to be anxious*). Here then, is the equivalent of "Set your mind at rest" or, in other words, "Leave it to me."

Dǎwán-le diànhuà yǐhòu—"After the phone calls have been made." Just as **yǐqián** means before or previously, so **yǐhòu** means after or later.

Wǒ gánjǐn guòqù zháo nǐ. While the term **gǎnkuài** means quickly, **gánjǐn** implies a somewhat greater degree of urgency (i.e., immediately or at once) and is appropriate to this situation. **Guòqù** (*pass leave*) implies getting across [town to the hospital].

SUPPLEMENTARY VOCABULARY

fùbù	abdomen
gēbei	arm
ěrduo	ear
tuǐ	leg
pífu	skin
dùzi	stomach

zhēncì [liáofǎ]	acupuncture
kàngshēngsù	antibiotics
guǎizhàng	crutches
yá-yīshēng	dentist
yǐnshí	diet
jíjiù	first aid
yàojì	medication
dānjià	stretcher
tǐwēnjì	thermometer (clinical)
zhìliáo	treatment
bìngfáng	ward, sickroom
lúnyǐ	wheelchair
guòmǐn	allergy
biànbì	constipation
xièdù	diarrhea
tóuyùn	faint, dizzy
ěxīn	nausea
hūxī jícù	short of breath
niǔshāng	sprain
zhǒngzhàng	swelling
yáténg	toothache
kuìyáng	ulcer
shuāiruò	weak, feeble
shāngkǒu	wound, cut

SEVENTEEN

POTPOURRI

"Better one bite of the peach
of immortality than a whole
basketful of apricots."

The Chinese, like other peoples, have from distant ages worshipped the supernatural. Fifteen hundred years before Christ, ancestor-worship existed; and by a thousand years later rulers had adopted the title of Son of Heaven. Confucianism should never be confused with religion, for it is essentially a philosophy based on a code of ethics, and involves no idolatry. Sacrifices in Confucian temples were offered to the memory of the Master, but he advocated no more than a cult based on ancestor worship, and lofty principles of chivalry and moral obligations according to one's place in society. Confucius lived from 551 to 479 BC, and his Anglicized name derives from **Kǒng Fūzǐ**, meaning Master Kong. He is revered for his own writings, and his discourses—known as Analects—were recorded by his disciples, the most renowned of whom was Mencius (372-289 BC).

A philosophy known as **Dào** (Taoism)—the Way—the earliest form of religion recorded in China, dates back to the sixth or seventh century BC, the time of its traditionally acknowledged founder **Láozǐ** (previously spelled Lao Tzu). This religion was paramount in the China of the Qin and Han dynasties, and to this day many Chinese scholars maintain that it has exerted greater influence over the Chinese than Buddhism. The Buddhist religion was introduced into China from India through Central Asia during the first century AD. Both religions coexisted for a number of centuries thereafter. Nowadays, to the outsider, their symbolism and practices appear intertwined as relics of past religions, and of little more

227

than academic interest. While Taoism and Buddhism may appear identical, some superficial differences are discernible, if only in the names of their temples. For example, in the Chinese language the word **guàn**, which stands for temple, is used only in connection with Taoist places of worship. The word **miào** denotes temples where the Buddhists, or Lamas (followers of a Tibetan form of Buddhism) worship, as well as temples dedicated to the memory of Confucius.

Both Buddhist temples and Muslim mosques may also be known as **sì**; for instance, the Temple of the Sleeping Buddha is called Wofosi, while the main Islamic mosque in Beijing is called Qingzhensi. Two powerful religious influences from outside of China which must be recognized are the Islamic and Christian faiths. Muslim and Nestorian followers, plying the caravan routes between Asia Minor and China during the seventh century, started the new theological trend. Currently the faith of Islam is maintained by many of the minority tribes of the hinterland, and also numerous Northern Chinese, though not with the same radical fervor as manifested by the people of the Middle East. Christianity did not become established until comparatively recently. Although it is claimed that Richard the Lion-Hearted, on his way through France to the Crusades, received the Holy Sacrament from the hands of a Chinese Nestorian priest, Catholicism did not take hold in China until some four centuries later. In 1582, the Italian Jesuit priest, Matteo Ricci, was received into the Ming Imperial court of Emperor Wanli. It is likely that there are more Chinese of the Catholic faith than of all the Protestant denominations put together. Historically speaking, however, it may be argued that Christian missionaries, for all their dedication, do not enjoy an enviable reputation in China, with the possible exception of the Society of Friends (Quakers) and the Salvation Army, who gave much more to the Chinese than they gained from them.

The modern Chinese may arguably be considered to be largely agnostic, but a number of Chinese do observe certain religious practices. Whether to placate fate or gain favor with their gods, they attempt to allay various superstitions at different religious festivals. As a Communist nation, China is—by definition—atheistic, but providing religious practices do not conflict with the authority of the State, religious groups are recognized. That there is a policy of freedom to pursue religious beliefs may be true, but to what extent such freedom actually exists is not really definable. Since October, 1979, public worship has been tolerated, and about half a dozen religious associations are now officially recognized. Despite this, many of the temples open to tourists are simply interesting sights for people of all kinds, including many Chinese, to admire and photograph. Some become active on special festive dates, and there are a few still in constant use as places for spiritual inspiration or worship. Consequently, when visitors come across Chinese at worship, this is a time for sensitivity and respect rather than curiosity. A prayer to Guanyin, a Bodhisattva often referred to as the Goddess of Mercy, is no less devout than a prayer to the Virgin Mary.

A modern young Chinese does not necessarily have any particular spiritual leanings. Nowadays, where worship exists, it is probably maintained only by some of the older generation who survived the Cultural Revolution (1966-1976). In the face of modern upbringing in schools and also peer pressure, relatively few youngsters have been influenced by their parents' religious practices. It is unlikely that such offspring would openly follow any faith, traditional or Christian.

17.1   REGARDING WORSHIP

R: **Jìshì míngtiān xīngqīrì búshi xiūxi yìtiān ma? Wó xiǎng qù zuò lǐbài. Fùjìn yǒu-meiyǒu jiàotáng?**
As tomorrow is Sunday, won't we be having a day's rest? I'd like to go to church. Are there any churches nearby?

C: **Kěnéng yǒu ba. Wǒmen qù lǚguǎn fúwùtái wènwen ba. Yàoshi tāmen bú-zhīdào, kéyi gěi dàshǐguǎn dǎ diànhuà gēn tāmen dǎting yíxià.**
There probably are. Let's go and ask at the hotel Reception. If they don't know, we could give the embassy a phone call and inquire.

VOCABULARY

jì	already; since, as, now that
táng	the main room of a house; extn.—hall, auditorium

RATIONALE AND INTERPRETATION

Jìshì míngtiān xīngqīrì means *as tomorrow is Sunday*. **Jìshì** is made up of **jì** (since) and **shì** (to be), and conveys the sense of since, as, now that, or even, it being the case.

...**búshi xiūxi yìtiān ma?** is in effect a rhetorical question, with **xiūxi yìtiān** as meaning *rest for a day*. **Búshi...ma** means "isn't that so?"

Zuò lǐbài (*make worship*). **Lǐ** as in **lǐwù** (gift), used here with its primary meaning of a ceremony, is conjoined with **bài** as in **bàifǎng**, in its primary sense of worship. The compound **lǐbài** therefore means religious worship, and is reinforced by **zuò** (to make). By extension, it may be translated as to go to church or church service since it was frequently used in a Christian context. In the modern political climate, the term is not often heard, and if the concept of worship is referred to, the term may vary according to the religion involved. For example, **shāoxiang** (*burn incense*) relates to worship before an idol.

Fùjìn means nearby or in the vicinity.

Jiàotáng is the term used for both church in a general sense, and specifically a cathedral. It is made up of **jiào** as in **jiàoshòu** (professor)—albeit in its secondary meaning of religion, in the extended sense of teaching—and **táng** (hall). It is not surprising that **jiàotáng** refers exclusively to Christian places of worship when we consider the word **jiàohuì**, which refers to Christianity. The latter compound, with **huì** meaning assembly or a meeting, is possibly an allusion to the fact that Christian services take place at regular times (not usually the case in temples, where worshippers may come and go at will).

Lǚguǎn fúwùtái refers to the reception desk or counter in a hotel (**lǚguǎn**). **Fúwù**, meaning to give service, consists of **fú** as in **yīfu**, but with its alternate meaning to serve, and **wù** as in **cáiwù**, while **tái** (counter) completes the compound.

Wènwen. The duplication of **wèn** (to ask) merely indicates that the action is of brief duration; in other words, a casual, as opposed to an in-depth, inquiry.

...**gēn tāmen dǎtīng yíxià**. In contrast to asking a simple question at a hotel reception desk, a phone call to the embassy implies pursuing an inquiry more seriously, and thus calls for a weightier term like **dǎtīng**. Much has already been said about **dǎ** (to beat), which is compounded here with **tīng** (to listen). The use of **yíxià**, like duplication of a verb, may signify an action of brief duration. Thus, an acceptable substitute for **yíxià** would be **dǎtīng dǎtīng**.

17.2 HOW ABOUT A PARTY?

R: **Yuèdǐ èrshíqí-hào yuē-hǎole qiāndìng hétong, duì-buduì?**
The 27th of this month has been agreed to for signing the contract, right?

C: **Duìle. Nǐ yào tíchū shénme yìjiàn ma?**
Yes. Do you want to make some suggestions?

R: **Wǒ-de huǒbàn yǐwéi nèitiān wǎnshang zhèng hǎo jiè jīhuì yuēqǐng hézuò-de Zhōngguo péngyou gēn wǒmen yìqǐ qìngzhù yíxià zhèihuí shì. Nǐ kàn zěnme yàng?**
My partner feels it would be most appropriate on that evening to invite participating Chinese friends to join with us in celebrating this occasion. What do you think?

C: **Nà hǎo-jíle! Nǐ yuànyì wǒ géi nǐ ānpai yànhuì ma?**
That'd be great! Would you like me to arrange a banquet for you?

R: **Wǒ bù yīnggāi bǎ zhèxiē shìqing dōu tuī dào nǐ shēnshàng, kěshi wǒ zìjǐ zhēn búhuì bàn. Zhèyàng bù hǎo-yìsi, dànshi lián qǐngtie wǒ dōu búhuì xiě.**
I shouldn't burden you with all this, but I really don't know what to do. This embarrasses me, but I can't even write the invitations.

C: **Méi guānxi. Hùxiāng bāngmáng shì yīngdāng-de.**
Never mind. It's only right for us to help each other out.

R: **Nà wǒ fēicháng gǎnxiè-le. Zhè jiù shèngxia yíjiàn shì wǒ hái bàndedào.**
I'm most grateful. That leaves me just one matter I can still deal with.

C: **Nǐ shuō shénme?**
What are you saying?

R: **Wǒ xīwàng dàodǐ hái huì tāo yāobāo!**
I hope in the end I can still foot the bill!

VOCABULARY

dǐ	bottom, base, end; extn.—below, under
yuē	to make an appointment, arrange; pact; approximate
hé	to close, shut; extn.—join, combine; agree; suit
bàn	companion, partner; extn.—to accompany
yuàn	to hope, wish, desire; extn.—be willing
yàn	to entertain [to a dinner]; extn.—banquet, feast
tiě	invitation; note, card
hù	mutual, each other
shèng	surplus, remnant
xī	hope; rare, scarce
wàng	to look over; to expect, hope; reputation
tāo	draw out, pull out; extn.—scoop out
yāo	waist; small of the back; pocket

RATIONALE AND INTERPRETATION

Yuèdǐ èrshiqí-hào indicates the 27th of the month, with the current month being implied. **Dǐ**, with its meaning of end or bottom, refers to the month's end. While not essential, **yuèdǐ** serves a similar purpose to **jīntiān** (today) when the latter is used in an expression like **jīntiān wǎnshang** (*today evening*), since it is not possible to say *this* evening, as such.

...**yuē-hǎole qiāndìng hétong. Yuē** means to make an appointment. The use of **hǎole** shows that the action has been completed satisfactorily; in other words, agreement has been reached. What has been agreed to is **qiāndìng hétong**, i.e., *[the] signing [of the] contract*. **Qiāndìng** consists of **qiān** as in **qiānmíng**, and **dìng** as in **yídìng** (definite), and means to sign or to conclude (e.g., a treaty). **Hétong** means a contract, it consists of **hé**, which has the sense of to agree or to suit, and **tóng** as in **tóngyì**, also meaning to agree.

. . . **tíchū shénme yìjiàn** means literally *to put forward what opinions*. **Tíchū** is made up of **tí** as in **tíxiāng**, and **chū** as in **chūlái**. **Shénme** is a QW modifying the term **yìjiàn**, which consists of **yì** as in **tóngyì**, and **jiàn** as in **zàijiàn**, and means an idea, view, opinion or, as in this case, a suggestion.

Wǒ-de huǒbàn signifies *my partner*, and is also used sometimes to mean companion. **Huǒbàn** consists of **huǒ**, as in **huǒshi**, and **bàn** meaning partner.

Yǐwéi means to regard as, to consider, or to feel. The compound consists of **yǐ** as in **yǐhòu**, and **wéi** as in **rènwéi**. While **yǐwéi** and **rènwéi** are similar to some extent, **yǐwéi** has the nuance of supposition, whereas **rènwéi** is more emphatic—being based on conclusion.

Zhèng hǎo jiè jīhui. **Zhèng** means just right or precisely, and **hǎo** means good. Together these words furnish the meaning just right or appropriate. The expression **jiè jīhui** (*borrow opportunity*) provides the equivalent of a favourable, or opportune [moment].

Yuēqǐng means to invite, and combines the word **yuē** with **qǐng** which needs no explanation. The compound implies a formal invitation stipulating a date, time, and place, and the term is therefore naturally related to **qǐngtie**.

Hézuò is the compound formed from **hé** (to agree) and **zuò**, meaning to do, to engage in or to make. Its meaning is literally *to work together*, hence to collaborate or to cooperate, and it is a useful term often employed in joint or cooperative ventures.

. . . **yìqǐ qìngzhù yíxià zhèihuí shì**. The main expression here is **qìngzhù**, which means to celebrate. The object of the celebration is **zhèihuí shì**, where **shì**—as in **shìqing**—means a matter or affair, and **huí** stands as a MW signifying occasion, thus **zhèihuí shì** implies *the occasion of this affair [of the contract signing]*. **Yìqǐ** is synonymous with **yíkuàr** (together), and designates primarily *the same place*. Thus, by extension, it can also mean in all, all together, or simply together. The term consists of **yī**—which is **yī** (one) pronounced in the fourth tone—and **qǐ** as in **duìbuqǐ**.

Nà hǎo-jíle is a response indicating enthusiastic approval.

Yuànyì is a compound of **yuàn** (to desire) and **yì** as in **yìsi**. While its primary meaning is to be willing to, by extension it also has the associated sense of *to like to*, as in this case.

Ānpai yànhuì means *to arrange a banquet*. **Yànhuì** is a compound consisting of **yàn**, meaning a feast or dinner, and **huì**, which means to meet or to assemble.

Yīnggāi, meaning should, must or ought to, is interchangeable with **yīngdāng**.

... **bǎ zhèxiē shìqing dōu tuī dào nǐ shēnshang** means to push all these matters onto your shoulders (*body*). Note the use of **bǎ**, which enables the object **zhèxiē shìqing** to be placed before the verb. The expression **tuī dào nǐ shēnshang** should not be hard to understand once it is known that **tuī**, as in **tuījiàn** (recommend), has the primary meaning of to push. The Chinese tend to speak in general terms of taking on [responsibility] or bearing [a burden], rather than in more physically specific terms such as in the English expression "to shoulder [a load]." If a physical reference is used, it is usually a general one (e.g., to load onto a body rather than onto the back or shoulder); hence the concise equivalent to burden given in the dialogue.

Wǒ zìjǐ zhēn búhuì bàn means literally *I myself truly am unable to do [it]*. **Zìjǐ** means oneself, and in Beijing a local variant **zìgěr** is often heard. Note the word **huì**, used in its secondary sense of *to be able* in terms of having acquired the necessary skill. Here it is used in the negative, implying that the inability [to cope with the situation] is brought about by lack of experience.

Bù hǎo-yìsi. The Chinese expression **bù hǎo-yìsi** means *to be ill at ease* or *embarrassed* and thus, by extension, to hesitate or to find it difficult. Chinese etiquette dictates that a person must avoid causing or showing embarrassment if at all possible. Nonetheless, as a psychological ploy in appealing to a friend's sensitivity or understanding, an admission of guilt for possibly giving offence is one form of gentle persuasion to enlist that friend's assistance. This is the intention demonstrated here, for not only is the speaker admitting to inadequacy to meet a particular situation, but the burden brought about by this shortcoming is also being placed un-blushingly on a friend.

Dànshì means but, still, or nevertheless, and is often used as a substi-tute for **kěshi** (however). It is made up of **dàn** as in **búdàn**, and **shì** (to be), which is common to both terms.

Lián qǐngtie wǒ dōu búhuì xiě means "I can't even write the invita-tions." **Qǐngtie** comprises **qǐng** (to invite) and **tiě**, which has the basic meaning of an invitation. **Xiě** (to write) serves the same purpose as in **xiěxìn**; but here, instead of **xìn** (letters), the object of the writing is **qǐngtie** (invitations). **Lián . . . dōu búhuì** is an emphatic denial of the ability [to do something], i.e., to write the invitations. **Lián** (to include) by extension means even, and is used in conjunction with **dōu** (all) to pro-duce the equivalent of to not even be able to write at all. The tacit admis-sion is that not only is the speaker ignorant of the proper form for issuing an invitation but is also unable to write characters.

Hùxiāng bāngmáng shì yīngdāng-de. The compound **hùxiāng** is a useful one, consisting of **hù** (mutual) and **xiāng** (first tone), which gives full significance to the meaning each other or mutual[ly]. **Xiāng** may also be pronounced **xiàng** (fourth tone) as in **xiàngjī**. The combination of **hùxiāng** and **bāngmáng** (to assist), conveys the idea of mutual assistance or helping each other.

Fēicháng gǎnxiè means *extremely grateful*. **Fēicháng** means particu-larly, most, or especially, a useful term to know when superlatives are needed. **Gǎnxiè** is a somewhat formal expression of gratitude. The com-pound consists of **gǎn** meaning to feel, and **xiè** (to thank) as in **xièxie**, and therefore means to be grateful, gratitude or thanks.

Jiù shèngxià yíjiàn shì. Shèng means primarily surplus and thus, by extension, **shèngxià** means to be left [over], or to remain. The sense here is therefore "Just one matter remains."

Wǒ hái bàndedào is a further example of potential resultative verbs, so often used in Chinese. **Bàn** (to do, to attend to) as in **bànfǎ** (method), and **dào**, meaning to reach or to arrive, together mean to accomplish or to get something done. The addition of **dé** indicates the positive potential thus providing the sense of "[something] I can still do."

Wǒ xīwàng dàodǐ hái huì tāo yāobāo. This is intended as a humorous response. **Xīwàng** means to hope, to wish, or to expect. Both components of the compound include the essence of hope. **Dàodǐ** consists of **dào** (to reach) and **dǐ** as in **yuèdǐ**, which combination provides the meanings of *in the end* or *finally*, and, by extension, in the final event. **Hái huì** simply means still able. **Tāo yāobāo** is the equivalent of the idiomatic phrase *to foot the bill*. Literally the expression means to draw out the wallet, or a freer rendering would be to fork out from one's own pocket! **Tāo** means to draw out or to dig [or fish] out. **Yāobāo** (*waist purse*) alludes to the money belt worn in olden times when money was kept in a compartment in the waist belt or girdle, but now it stands for a wallet or purse, recently revised in the form of the hip-bag.

17.3   VISITING A SCHOOL

Chinese children, like all others, seem to fall into two main categories—either extremely shy, or quite uninhibited and precocious. Generally speaking they are quite outgoing, for Chinese adore children and appear not to inspire fear of strangers. Foreigners, though, may be a different matter! However enchanting a child, do not be tempted to give more than an encouraging pat on the head. Even at an adult party do not permit yourself to show enthusiasm by back-slapping, hugs, or other familiarities, for such gestures can be misinterpreted in more ways than one. The Chinese still entertain a number of misconceptions about foreigners, and therefore each side needs to be sensitive to the possibility of an adverse reaction by the other. Being alert to the body language of the Chinese should help you to avoid embarrassment. Although the Chinese are reputed to be inscrutable because of masked facial expressions, hand movements—like those of people of all ages from any part of the world—can be quite revealing!

C: **Guò jǐtiān, jiǎrú tiānqì hǎo-yìdiǎr wó xiǎng dài nǐ qù fǎngwèn yíge yòu'éryuán. Kànkan xiǎo háizi zhēn yǒu yìsi.**
In a few days, if the weather improves, I thought I'd take you to visit a kindergarten. Watching youngsters is great fun.

R: **Wó lǎo pànwàng zhuāzhù zhèige jīhui. Wǒ dài xiàngjī pāi jǐzhāng zhàopiàn, kéyi ma?**

I've looked forward to getting this chance for a long time. Could I take a camera to get a few snapshots?

C: **Wǒ rènwéi zhè búhuì chéng wèntí.**

I reckon this shouldn't pose a problem.

R: **Nàme wó kěndìng duō ná jiāojuǎr. Yàoshi dài xiǎo lùyīnjī, zěnme yàng?**

Then I'll be sure to take more rolls of film. How would it be if I took along a small tape recorder?

C: **Nà yàng-de huà, wǒ gùyì-de yāoqiú jiàoshī ràng xiǎohár géi wǒmen chànggér.**

In that case, I'll make a point of asking the teacher to get the kids to sing us some songs.

R: **Bùguǎn zěnmeyàng, zài jiàoshì-lǐ huòzhě zài cāochǎng-shàng zhàozhe xiǎohár wánshuǎ, yíqiè yídìng dōu hén hǎowár. Yàoshi zhàopiàn zhào-de hǎo, wǒ kéyǐ duō jiāyìn jǐzhāng sònggěi jiàoshī.**

Whether the kids are in the classroom or playing in the playground, they are bound to be fun to photograph. If the snaps are good, I can get some extra prints to give to the teachers.

C: **Ní xǐhuan nàyang bàn, tāmen yídìng fēicháng gāoxìng.**

If you'd like to do that, they're sure to be highly delighted.

VOCABULARY

yòu	young, under age; extn.—children
ér	son; extn.—child, youngster; diminutive suffix
hái	child
pàn	to hope for, long for, expect
zhuā	to grab, seize; scratch

pāi	to clap, pat, beat; shoot a film
jiāo	glue, gum, rubber; extn.—film
juǎn	to roll up; a roll, spool, reel; [MW]
lù	to record, copy; employ; register
yīn	sound; extn.—tone; tidings, news
gù	incident, happening; extn.—cause, reason; on purpose
qiú	to beg, entreat; request; extn.—demand; strive for
ràng	to give way, yield; to offer; allow, let
chàng	to sing; extn.—call, cry out
gé	song; extn.—to sing
cāo	to grasp, hold; to do; extn.—operate; drill, exercise
yìn	seal, chop, stamp; extn.—to print, engrave
gāo	tall, high; a surname
mǎn	full; extn.—reach the limit; completely; satisfied

RATIONALE AND INTERPRETATION

Guò jǐtiān is an allusion to the near future, meaning *[when] a few days have passed*, or, in other words, "in a few days' time."

Jiǎrú tiānqì hǎo-yìdiǎr. This is another way of saying yàoshi tiānqì hǎo-de huà. Both jiǎrú and yàoshi can mean if, supposing or in case. Jiǎ may be pronounced in the fourth tone, in which case it means a holiday, but in the third tone it means fake or artificial. By extension this meaning leads towards supposing or if, particularly when jiǎ is coupled with rú as in rúguǒ. Tiānqì refers to the weather, while hǎo yìdiǎr means a little better, implying that an improvement in current weather conditions is either imminent, or at least desired. The Chinese terms for meteorology and weather may be used more or less interchangeably, as these two terms are in English. However, there is a need to differentiate between weather (tiānqì), and climate (qìhou). Qì is as in kèqì, and hòu is as in shíhou. Interestingly, too, qìhòu is used in the broadest sense of climate, to include economic or political climates. The Chinese equivalent of climatology is qìhòuxué, while meteorology is known as qìxiàngxué, with xiàng meaning image.

. . . dài nǐ qù fǎngwèn yíge yòu'éryuán. One of the many homonyms of dài in use here is as in xiédài and means to take [along]. Fǎngwèn means to visit, but implies to call on or to interview a person or organization, rather than to enjoy a friendly or casual visit of a more personal nature. The compound is made up of **fǎng** as in **fǎnghuá**, and **wèn** as in **wèntí**. The object of the visit is **yòu'éryuán** (a kindergarten or nursery school). **Yòu** and **ér** when used together mean child or infant. The addition of **yuán** (*recreation ground*), as in **gōngyuán**, indicates the nature of the place.

Háizi on its own simply means a child. **Xiǎo haizi** obviously means a small child or youngster. As with **rén** (person), it is necessary to prefix **háizi** with **nán** (male) for a boy, or **nǚ** (female) for a girl; thus for two little girls you would say **liǎngge xiáo nǚ-háizi**.

Zhēn yǒu yìsi means literally *truly of interest*. However the expression may be interpreted more liberally as significant, meaningful, or interesting, or even great fun—as in this instance. The meaning of **yìsi** when applied in a positive sense in this context differs significantly from that of the negative use shown in **bù hǎo-yìsi** in the previous dialogue.

Wó lǎo pànwàng zhuāzhù zhèige jīhui. **Lǎo** is used to mean old in the sense of long standing, rather than elderly. **Lǎo péngyou**, for example, signifies an old friend. **Lǎo** modifies the compound **pànwàng** (to look forward to or to long for), which is not to be confused with **xīwàng** (to hope, or to wish). Despite their common root in the second syllable, these two terms should not be considered interchangeable. Since **pàn** means to long for, and **wàng** is as in **xīwàng** (to hope), there is a nuance of greater intensity in **pànwàng** than in **xīwàng**, which conveys little more than anticipation of the action to come. Although **zhuāzhù** is not in very common use, it is nonetheless a useful word to know. It can mean anything from grasp or seize to grip or capture, and consists of **zhuā** as described, and **zhū** as in **zhūyuàn**. **Zhù**, with its basic meaning of staying, by extension has the nuance of holding firm or steady, which is its purpose in this case. Thus we get a translation: "For ages I've longed to grab a chance like this."

... **dài xiàngjī** simply means to take a camera.

Pāi jǐzhāng zhàopiàn. The key word is **zhàopiàn**, where **zhào** is as in **hùzhào** (passport), and **piàn** is as in **míngpiàn** (card), and it means a photograph or snapshot. **Zhāng** is a MW for **zhàopiàn**, while **jǐ** means several or a few and modifies **zhàopiàn**. **Pāi** applies in the sense of *to snap* as it is used in photography, and means to take a picture. Thus, the full expression is the equivalent of *to take a few snaps*.

...**kěndìng duō ná jiāojuǎr** means in essence...definitely take more rolls of film. **Kěndìng** expresses a firm intention. The term **jiāojuǎn[r]** (*gum roll*) refers to rolls of film. **Jiāo** means film while **juǎn** means a roll, and may be used as a MW for film. **Duō** (more) in conjunction with **ná** (used here as a substitute for **dài**, since they both mean to take) signifies taking extra [rolls of film].

Lùyīnjī (*record sound machine*) is a tape recorder.

Nà yàng-de huà (*that kind of speech*) may mean "in those terms" or "in that case," and serves as an alternative for **nàme**.

Gùyì-de yāoqiú. **Gùyì** means intentionally or for a special purpose and therefore, by extension, "to make a point of." **Yāoqiú** means to demand, to require or simply "to ask [as a favor]." By extension it can also imply to call for [a course of action]. It consists of **yāo**, seen here in the first tone, but better known as **yào** (to want) in the fourth tone, as in **yàoshi**; and **qiú**, whose meaning extends from a request to an entreaty. Should you use this particular word **yāoqiú**, a Chinese would be hard put to decline the request if he is at all able to oblige.

Jiàoshī ràng xiǎohár....**Jiàoshī** is the word for a teacher and is similar to **lǎoshī**, a term used when addressing a teacher. **Xiǎohár** is the Beijing equivalent of **xiǎo háizi**, meaning small children, or kids. **Ràng** has a variety of meanings. These range from allowing to letting or causing in the same way that **jiào** (to call) can be used.

Chànggē[r] means to *sing songs*. Children in China, like those the world over, learn to warble little ditties and songs, which they love to show off at the slightest excuse. To sing a national anthem is referred by **chàng guógē**, while the anthem itself can be identified by preceding the term **guógē** with the nationality involved; for example, **Fǎguó guógē** refers to the Marseillaise.

Bùguǎn zěnmeyàng means no matter what, or regardless of what happens.

...**zài jiàoshì-lǐ huòzhě zài cāochǎng-shàng** means "in the classroom or in the playground." **Jiàoshì** is not to be confused with **jiàoshī** (teacher), for although **jiào** (to teach, or to instruct) is common to both,

shì in this case means a room, as it does in **bàngōngshì** (office). **Cāochǎng** consists of **cāo**, which means to exercise or to drill, and **chǎng** as in **qiúchǎng**, meaning a playing field. Note that in the case of the classroom, **lǐ** is used to denote in, while for the playground **shàng** is used, indicating on. This is best explained by pointing out that **lǐ** refers to being inside an enclosure, while **shàng** infers to being on an open space. In a similar manner, Chinese refer to a [marker] in a book, i.e., **shū-lǐ**, but they would otherwise refer to the words on [the pages of] a book, i.e., **shū-shàng**.

...**zhàozhe xiǎohár wánshuǎ** refers to photographing the children at play. **Zhào** is as in **zhàopiàn** or **zhàoxiàng** (to take photographs), while **zhe** as a suffix indicates extended action, i.e., photograph*ing*. **Wánshuǎ**, meaning to play or to have fun, consists of **wán** as in **yóuwán** and **shuǎ** as in **záshuǎ**.

Yíqiè yídìng dōu hén hǎowár. In this clause, taken item by item, **yíqiè** means everything, **yídìng** means certainly, **dōu** means all, while **hén hǎowár** means very amusing or fun.

Yàoshi zhàopiàn zhào-de hǎo is literally *if the films are well photographed*. This may seem a labored way of expressing what is given in the English version of the dialogue, but explicitness is sometimes necessary in the Chinese construction. Note the difference between **jiāojuǎr**, which refers to the rolls or spools [of film], and **zhàopiàn**, which alludes to the printed photographs.

Duō jiāyìn jǐzhāng... The meaning of the term **jiāyìn** (*additionally print*) when applied to the photographs is easily enough understood.

...**sōnggěi jiàoshī** means to send or to give to the teachers.

Gāoxìng (*highly excited*) means more "to be pleased" than, say, elated, as the expression might suggest. The term is made up of **gāo**, meaning high or lofty, and **xìng** as in **xìngqù** (interest); in essence it also means delighted, happy or simply glad. In terms of satisfaction, a similar expression to **gāoxìng** is **mǎnyì**, which implies pleased or satisfied. The word **mǎn** means full, to reach the limit or completely, and **yì** is as in **yìjiàn** (opinion).

☐ ◯◯   SUPPLEMENTARY VOCABULARY

Fójiào/Fójiàotú*	Buddhism/Buddhist
Jīdūjiào/Jīdūjiàotú	Christianity/Christian
Tiānzhǔjiào/Tiānjǔjiàotú	Catholicism/Catholic
Yēsūjiào/Yēsūjiàotú	Protestantism/Protestant
Huíjiào/Huíjiàotú	Islamism/Muslim
Dàojiào/Dàojiàotú	Taoism/Taoist
xìnyǎng, xìnniàn	belief, faith
xìntiáo	creed, precept
dàoli	principle; reasoning, contention
zōngjiào	religion
mùshi	clergyman [Protestant]
héshang	priest, monk [Buddhist]
shénfu	priest [Roman Catholic]
lǐbàitáng	church
tǎ	pagoda
miào	temple [Buddhist or Confucian]
sì	temple [Buddhist or Muslim]
guàn	temple [Taoist]
xiéyì	agreement
fēngsú	custom
chōngxǐ jiāojuǎr	film developing
fàng fēngzheng	kite flying
dǒu kōngzhú	play a diabolo
cángmāor	play hide and seek

---

*Tú means follower, also disciple or pupil.

EIGHTEEN

ON DEPARTURE

"Friends can be found all over the world, and all under heaven are as neighbours."

The Chinese do not normally stay long after a formal meal or banquet. It will be quite apparent that once the party is over, it is perfectly in order to thank the host and leave. Four dialogues representing different ways of taking leave of one's host are presented in this chapter. The first example is quite informal, while the next three, which can be adapted to suit the occasion, demonstrate an increasing degree of formality.

18.1 TAKING ONE'S LEAVE

R: **Tiān bùzǎo-le. Wǒ gāi huíjiā-le.**
It's getting late. I ought to be getting home.

C: **Mànzǒu, a! Nǐ bú duō zuò yìhuěr ma?**
There's no hurry. Won't you stay a bit longer?

R: **Kàn wàibiar-de yàngzi kěnéng yào xiàxuě. Háishi gǎnkuài zǒu ba, shěngzhe chūshì.**
From the way it looks outside, it might snow. It would be as well to go at once to avoid mishaps.

C: **Duìle, kàn gāisì-de tiānqì bù zěnme hǎo. Nà jiù bù duō lịú
      nǐ-le. Duōduọ bǎozhòng.**
      You're right, the wretched weather doesn't look too good. In that
      case I won't hold you up. Take good care of yourself.

VOCABULARY

gāi	ought to, should; extn.—deserve; owe
sǐ	to die; extn.—death; extremity; inflexible, fixed, rigid
màn	slow; extn.—to postpone, defer
xuě	snow

RATIONALE AND INTERPRETATION

Tián bùzǎo-le, while meaning literally *the day is not early [any more],* is better translated as "Time is getting on," or "It's getting late."

Wǒ gāi huíjiā-le. The word **gāi** is often compounded with **yīng,** as in **yīngdāng,** to which it bears a close resemblance, since both words mean ought or should. **Gāi,** however, with the nuance of must, is slightly more insistent. Since **huíjiā** means to return home, the sentence as a whole can be translated as "I ought to get back home." The degree of urgency being self-evident, the expression may be used as the equivalent of "I must be getting back."

Mànzǒu a! This is an expression which can be used in two ways. While literally it means *to go slowly,* it may be considered equivalent to "Don't go yet" or "Do stay a little longer," which is the sense in this particular case. However, if the visitor is actually on the point of departure, and the host says **mànzǒu, mànzǒu,** he is bidding goodbye, since the expression then assumes the near-literal meaning "Take it easy," "Mind how you go," or simply "Take care"—as, for instance, in slippery winter conditions.

Nǐ bù duō zuò yìhuěr ma? Here is a straightforward amplification of the above invitation to stay longer. **Zuò yìhuěr** means *to sit a while,* and **duō zuò yìhuěr** then obviously signifies to sit a little longer. The negative **bù** is used simply to emphasize the invitation, giving it the sense of "Won't you stay a little longer?"

Kàn wàibiar-de yàngzi means literally *look at the appearance [of the] outside.*

Kěnéng yào xiàxuě means literally *the possibility [of] wanting to snow.* **Xià** is often used in the sense of to descend, but where precipitation is concerned, it is the equivalent of fall, as in rainfall, or snowfall. Hence the following compounds:

xiàbáozi	to hail
xiàxuě	to snow
xiàyǔ	to rain

Háishi gǎnkuài zǒu ba. The suggestive particle **ba** emphasizes the point of the remark that "It would still (**háishi**) be as well to go (**zǒu**) quickly (**gǎnkuài**)."

Shěngzhe chūshì. You may recall that **shěng** is a character serving a dual purpose. Its primary meaning to economize or to save may, by extension, be taken to mean also to avoid, as in this case. The suffix **zhe** indicates continuation of action. **Chūshì**, consisting of **chū** as in **chūqù**, and **shì** as in **shìqing**, means to have an accident or to meet with a mishap.

. . . gāisǐ-de tiānqì bù zěnme hǎo. Here is another expression using **gāi**. **Sǐ** means to die, and thus the compound **gāisǐ** (*ought to die*) becomes an exclamation or mild expletive, such as darned, damned, or merely wretched. As is often the case the world over, the expletive is directed at the weather, i.e., **tiānqì**, which in this case is not very promising—**bù zěnme hǎo** (*not much good*).

Nà jiù bù duō liú nǐ. **Nà jiù bù** is an abbreviated form of **nàme wǒ jiù bù**, which means "In that [case] I won't . . ." **Duō liú** (*more keep*) indicates "to detain [any] longer."

Duōduō bǎozhòng. This is an idiomatic expression which means "Look after yourself." **Duō** (more) duplicated implies more and more. **Bǎo**, from **bǎohu** (safeguard) is combined with **zhòng**, meaning weighty in the sense of considerable value; hence "Take good care of yourself."

18.2   MORE LEAVE-TAKING

R: **Shízài bàoqiàn, wǒmen shīpéi-le, hái děi dào biéchù qù.**
I apologize for us leaving now, but we have to go on somewhere else.

C: **Méi guānxi, wǒ sòng nǐ dào ménkǒu.**
    Never mind, I'll see you to the door.

R: **Nǐ hái yǒu xǔduō kèren děi zhāodài. Bú sòng, bú sòng.**
    You still have lots of guests to entertain. Don't bother to see us out.

C: **Mànzǒu, mànzǒu. Qǐng tì wǒ wènhòu nǐ àirén.**
    Take care! Goodbye. Please remember me to your spouse.

VOCABULARY

bào	to hold [in the arms]; extn.—to harbour, cherish
qiàn	apology

RATIONALE AND INTERPRETATION

Shízài bàoqiàn (*really apologize*). This is an expression of regret consisting of two compounds. **Shízài** is ordinarily used to mean true, real, really or honestly; by extension it may also mean in fact, or as a matter of fact. It consists of **shí**, as in **shíyè**, and **zài**, as in **zài zhèr**. **Bàoqiàn**, meaning to regret or to be sorry, consists of **bào** meaning to harbour, and **qiàn** an apology. The formal term used for an apology is **dàoqiàn**, with the verb **gěi** (to give); for example, **gěi nín dàoqiàn** means "to offer you an apology."

Shīpéi means in effect "to take one's leave." The two elements of the compound are **shī** as in **shīwù**, and **péi** (to accompany). Literally the compound means *to miss keeping company* and is an appropriate expression to use when leaving a gathering or a party.

Biéchù means another place or elsewhere. The compound consists of **bié**, as in **tèbié**, and **chù**, as in **bànshìchù**.

Méi guānxi is a polite rejoinder meaning "It doesn't matter," or "Never mind," in the sense of [the matter] being of little consequence (**xiǎo yìsi**), or "Think nothing of it!"

Wǒ sòng nǐ dào ménkǒu. The two key words are **sòng** and **ménkǒu**. In reverse order, **ménkǒu** (*door opening*) is the term for doorway or entrance—being **mén** for door or gate, and **kǒu** for mouth or opening—while **sòng** means to deliver. Thus, by extension, to deliver someone to the door is the way to express "to see someone out."

...**xǔduō kèren děi zhāodài**. **Xǔduō** means many, **kèren** means guests or visitors, and **zhāodài** means to entertain.

Bú sòng, bú sòng is a polite expression meaning "Don't bother to see me out" or "We know our own way out."

Qǐng tì wǒ wènhòu nǐ àirén. Here only the term **wènhòu**, consisting of **wèn**, as in **wèntí**, and **hòu** as in **shíhòu**, needs amplification. It is a polite expression meaning "to give one's regards" or "to ask after [somebody]." **Àirén** refers to the spouse of either sex. It is the object of **wènhòu**, which may be replaced by any suitable alternative. **Wènhòu**, as a method of sending regards, has a variant **wènhǎo**. **Wèn** as in **wèntí** is common to both, while **hǎo** is as in **hǎoxīn**. **Wènhòu** and **wènhǎo** are interchangeable as shown in these examples:

Tā xiàng nǐ wènhòu.	She sends you her regards.
Qǐng tì wǒ wèn tāmen dōu hǎo.	Please extend my greetings to them all.

You will note from the last example that it is possible to split the compound **wènhǎo** to accommodate the object **tāmen**. **Wèn...hǎo** is less formal and so may be interpreted more as "Please wish them all the best for me," or "Say hello to them for me."

18.3   A POLITE EXIT

R: **Qǐng yuánliàng, kěshi wó děi gàocí.**
        Please forgive me, but I must take my leave.

C: **Yǒu jīhuì qǐng zài lái duō tántan. Wǒ sòngsong nín.**
        When you get a chance, do come again for another talk. I'll see you out.

R: **Búbì máfan-le, qǐng nín liúbù.**
        There's no need to bother, please don't come any further.

C: **Nàme, jiù zàijiàn-le.**
        In that case, till we meet again.

VOCABULARY

yuán	primary, original; to excuse, pardon; a surname
liàng	to forgive; understand
cí	to take [one's] leave
tán	to talk, to discuss; a surname

RATIONALE AND INTERPRETATION

Yuánliàng has virtually the same impact as **duìbuqǐ**. The two expressions are not interchangeable however, as **yuánliàng** is principally used to mean to forgive, or to pardon, whereas **duìbuqǐ** simply means "Excuse me."

Gàocí (*report departure*) is a more formal expression than **shīpéi**. This compound, which also means to take leave [of one's host], consists of **gào** as in **gàosu** and **cí**, meaning to take [one's] leave.

Yǒu jīhuì qǐng zài lái duō tántan means "[When] there is an opportunity please come again for more discussions." **Jīhuì** is the term for chance or opportunity. Its elements are **jī** as in **fēijī** (but under its secondary meaning of chance rather than machine), and **huì**, which also has a secondary meaning of opportunity or occasion. **Tán**, when duplicated, implies informal conversation or a talk, since the duplication—as usual—renders the term less formal.

Sòngsong nín serves the same purpose as the expression **sòng dào ménkǒu**; that is, to accompany the departing guest. It is the appropriate response to **gàocí**.

Búbì máfan . . . qǐng liúbù. Búbì máfan, the first part of this expression, meaning "No need to trouble [yourself]," should now be familiar. **Liúbù,** composed of **liú** as in **liú huà**, and **bù** as in **sànbù**, is a courteous expression, meaning literally *to save steps*, thus providing a turn of phrase put more idiomatically as "Don't bother to come any further."

Zàijiàn is the expression probably used most to say goodbye in Chinese. It is closely akin to the French "au revoir," having the meaning *[till we] meet again.*

18.4   A FINAL FAREWELL

C: **Nín dǎsuàn něi tiān huíguó?**
When do you plan to return home?

R: **Xià xīngqīsān wǒmen jiù dòngshēn.**
We'll be leaving next Wednesday.

C: **Āiyā! Zhēn kěxī nèitiān wó yǒu biéde shìqing, suōyǐ bùnéng dào fēijīchǎng qù gěi nín sòngxíng.**
Oh dear! What a shame I have something on that day, so I shan't be able to see you off at the airport.

R: **Búbì nánguò. Jiānglái wǒmen zóngděi tōngxìn. Míngpiàn-shang yǒu wó zǒng gōngsī-de dìzhǐ.**
Don't feel badly. We are bound to be exchanging correspondence in the future. My head office address is on my card.

C: **Nàme wó děng nín-de láixìn. Tóngshí zhù nín Yílù Shùnfēng.**
In that case, I look forward to getting your letters. Meanwhile, I wish you Bon Voyage.

R: **Qǐng dài wǒ xiàng fūrén zhìyì.**
Please give my regards to your good lady.

C: **Zàihuì, zàihuì.**
Goodbye.

VOCABULARY

něi	which, what, [QW]; (alt. pron. **nǎ**)
jiāng	to support, take; be about to, going to, will, shall
sī	to take charge of, manage; a surname
lù	road, way; extn.—journey, route; surname
xiàng	towards; extn.—turn toward, face; a surname
zhì	to send; extend; extn.—to cause, incur

RATIONALE AND INTERPRETATION

Nín dǎsuàn něitiān huíguó? Dǎsuàn means to intend or to reckon on, and consists of **dǎ** as in **dǎtīng**, and **suàn** to calculate or reckon. **Huíguó** (*return country*) signifies "to go back [to one's] home[land]." The compound **něitiān** asks which day or, more generally when.

Dòngshēn (*move body*) is an expression used to mean to set out or depart—generally used in connection with a relatively long journey rather than a short trip. **Dòng** (to move) is compounded with **shēn** as in **shēntǐ**. **Shēn** means body in the widest sense, and applies to a structural body as much as to the human body. For example:

jīshēn	aircraft fuselage
chēshēn	car or truck body
chuánshēn	ship's hull

Āiyā! Zhēn kěxī nèitiān wó yǒu biéde shìqing. The first three words—**āiyā** (Oh dear!), **zhēn** (true) as in **zhēnzhèng**, and **kěxī** (a pity)—form the equivalent of the exclamation "Oh dear, what a pity!" The remaining terms provide the meaning "I have other business that day." Remember that the compound **shìqing** means matter or affair.

Fēijīchǎng is the compound used to denote an airport or airfield.

Sòngxíng is a term used in the sense of giving someone a send-off on a journey, rather than seeing someone to the door. **Xíng** has the meaning to go, as on a trip.

Nánguò consists of **nán** as in **nánshòu**, and **guò** as in **guòzhòng**. It means to feel sorry, feel badly, or be grieved.

Jiānglái wǒmen zóngděi tōngxìn. Jiāng is used to indicate action to come, and the compound it forms with **lái** (to come) means the future or in future. **Tōngxìn**, formed of **tōng** as in **tōngzhī** and **xìn** for a letter, means to write letters or to correspond. **Zóngděi** means inevitably and, by extension, to be bound to. The term is made up of **zǒng**, in its sense of always or invariably, and **děi** meaning must.

. . . **zǒng gōngsī-de dìzhǐ.** Here is another use of **zǒng**, where its meaning is similar to **zǒngjī** (main switchboard). **Gōngsī** means a firm or a company, consisting of **gōng** as in **gōngyuán**, and **sī** (department). Using **zǒng** in conjunction with **gōngsī** gives the equivalent of head office or home office. **Dìzhǐ** means address, so all in all we have head office address.

. . . **děng nín-de láixìn** means "to await your letters." **Děng** (to wait) in this context implies to look forward to. . . . **Láixìn** (*come letter*) refers to incoming mail.

Tóngshí (*[at the] same time*) means meanwhile, and is formed from **tóng** as in **tóngyì**, and **shí** as in **shíjiān**.

Zhù nín Yílù Shùnfēng is a way of wishing someone a good trip, i.e., bon voyage or "a speedy return home." **Zhù** stems from the compound **zhùhè** to congratulate. **Zhù** is used here in the sense of to wish as, for instance, in the toast **Zhù nǐ jiànkāng**—"[We] wish you good health!" **Yílù** may mean a road or, by extension, a journey. The term **shùnfēng** is made up of the words **shùn** as in **shùnlì**, and **fēng** as in **fēngshuǐ**. **Shùnfēng** refers to a favorable wind. This is doubtless an allusion to ancient times, when flat-bottomed junks made better time with a following wind, but it is still used in these days of air travel for much the same reason. A variation of this expression is **Yílù Píng'ān**, meaning "Have a safe journey" or "Have a pleasant trip." **Píng'ān** essentially means safe and sound, being composed of **píng** is as in **píngcháng**, and **ān** as in **ānquán**. A suitable toast at a farewell banquet for the departing guests is: **Zhù nǐmen lǚtú yúkuài**, meaning "Wishing you a pleasant journey." **Lǚ** is as in **lǚxíng**, and **tú** is as in **chángtú**; these two words when compounded take on the meaning of a journey. **Yúkuài** consists of a homophone to **yú** (to amuse) which means cheerful or happy, and **kuài** as in **gǎnkuài**. **Kuài** also has the meaning of happy or pleased, and is often compounded with **lè** as in **yúlè**, thus providing **kuàilè**, which is another word for happy or joyful.

Qǐng dài wǒ xiàng fūrén zhìyì. This is a rather formal way of giving one's regards. **Dài**, as in **dàibiǎo** means to substitute, and is sometimes compounded with **tì**. **Xiàng** is used here to mean simply to, rather than towards, its primary meaning. **Fūrén** is a formal title used for married ladies, and in usage conforms with Madame, Lady or Mrs. (when referring to an official or public figure). The term consists of **fū** as in **dàifu**, and **rén** as in **zhǔrén**. **Zhìyì** is a formal expression meaning to extend best wishes or greetings or, in the most formal interpretation, "to present one's compliments." The compound consists of **zhì** (to send), and **yì** as in **tóngyì**.

Zàihuì is a formal style of leave-taking, but means exactly the same as **zàijiàn**, which is the usual way of saying goodbye. **Huì**, as in **jīhuì**, has as its primary meaning to meet or to assemble.

▣ SUPPLEMENTARY VOCABULARY

dàodá	arrival
qǐchéng	departure
chēzhàn	depot, bus station
háigǎng	harbour, port
huǒchēzhàn	railway station
línju	neighbour
fùjìn	neighbourhood
láiwǎng-de xìnjiàn	correspondence
jiélüè	memo

NINETEEN

IN CONCLUSION: JIĀ YÓU

"One step, one footprint."

Jiā Yóu, which means literally *to add oil*, may be applied in several ways. **Yóu** is used here as an abbreviation of **qìyóu** (gasoline). Thus **jiā yóu** may be used to mean anything from "Step on it" (though not necessarily pedal to the metal), to "Press on" or "Go for it"—as intended here!

The Chinese sense of fun is certainly apparent at a party, and everyone is encouraged to contribute to the general merriment which frequently follows any but the most formal banquet. While excellence is naturally appreciated, any shortfall in performance is handsomely overlooked and everybody enjoys applauding everyone else. So now is the time to polish up on a snappy party piece, regardless of whether it is a little pantomime such as: "I'm a little teapot, short and stout..." or a ditty of some kind. Chinese visitors to the West often warble in unison their interpretation of Red River Valley. You have already been introduced to a Chinese version of Ten Green Bottles at the end of the Counting section; and perhaps this simple version of Happy Birthday in Chinese will prove useful some day!

> **Zhù nǐ shēngrì kuàilè**
> **Zhù nǐ shēngrì kuàilè**
> **Zhù nǐ yúkuài-de shēngrì**
> **Zhù nǐ shēngrì kuàilè.**

...yuè lái yuè duō!
(i.e., ... and many more!)

For an encore, here is a free translation of the refrain to "You are My Sunshine" for you to learn:

Nǐ shì wǒ yángguāng,
Suóyǒu-de yángguāng,
Rúguǒ yǒu yīntiān,
Dōu méi guānxì.
Nǐ bìng bù-zhīdào
Wǒ duóme ài nǐ,
Qǐng bié bǎ
Wǒ yángguāng qǔxiāo!

On a more serious note, there is a likelihood that, once you have spent some time with the Chinese in their own surroundings, you will have had some experiences which are at variance with what has been written here. This need not come as any surprise when you consider the size and complexity of China, the most populous country in the world. It would be virtually impossible to provide an insight into all aspects of Chinese life. In fact, however, it is the more superficial facets of Chinese customs which tend to differ, rather than the main features of the Chinese character. These are a proud people; some Chinese might even appear to be arrogant. Such variations exist in all societies. However different life in China may appear to be, the people are essentially friendly, hospitable and good humoured.

The average visitor is, of course, largely confined to witnessing life in the urban areas, which are currently more advanced and prosperous than the vast rural expanses. While the countryfolk may be more conservative and, as in so many countries, less sophisticated than their urban counterparts it is in the countryside that the backbone of the nation is to be found. The nóngmín (farming people), or peasants, tend to get overlooked. Nonetheless, it it is among these people that the real fortitude and resilience of China may be perceived. Their way of life may be cruder, and undoubtedly less privileged, but it may justly be claimed that it is these harsher conditions which have tempered their character throughout the centuries. Whatever the setbacks of nature or the vicissitudes of history, the masses have managed to survive their misfortunes, and one should not overlook these fundamental facts when one sees the conditions in which so many Chinese live.

This work was produced not so much for the purpose of instructing you as to enlighten you, in the hope that your sojourn in China will be enjoyable. What is probably most important is the capacity to adapt to situations which, after all, is the corollary to an open mind. Combine these two qualities with sensitivity and a lively sense of adventure, and you can hardly fail to enjoy your stay among the people of China.

Meanwhile, to each and every one of you:

Yílù píng'ān!

APPENDIX

BASIC ELEMENTS

"If you don't scale the
mountains, you can't see the
plains."

This appendix is a summary of supplementary information, designed to avoid repetition in the Rationale and Interpretation portions of the chapters.

As familiarity with the Chinese language develops, the range of meanings and uses ascribed to many words becomes increasingly apparent. The language has long enjoyed a certain structural elasticity, where nouns may function as verbs, and adjectives and adverbs are often used as equational verbs. Characteristically the Chinese developed a logical and ingenious method of employing verbs in sentence constructions in a manner which virtually dispenses with conjugation. However, the treatment of this subject has to be in general terms; only a formal textbook could deal adequately with the subject in its entirety.

NOUNS

1 The Glossary shows that Chinese nouns fall mostly into two basic categories:

(a) The great majority of nouns are formed by compounding two or more words, and thus are usually referred to as compounds. Each word in the compound contributes to its etymology.

(b) A number of basic terms consist of what would be monosyllabic words but for the addition of four common particles which are used as suffixes. This may be illustrated as shown:

    i.   -zi. Primarily, the word **zǐ** means son or child and, by extension, seed or egg. When used as a suffix, -zi is toneless e.g., **míngzi** (name), **yǐzi** (chair), **zhuōzi** (table). When nouns ending in -zi are compounded with other words, the -zi is discarded, as in the case of **míngpiàn** (business card).

   ii.   -er. The word **ér** also has the meaning of child or son; it is toneless as a retroflex suffix. It is often used in North China as an alternative to the suffix -zi, and as such has a diminutive effect, thus **háizi**—child can be expressed as **hár**, in which case it has more the effect of kid or kiddie. This suffix is encountered less frequently in South China where the -zi suffix is prevalent.

  iii.   -chu. The primary meaning of the word **chù** is place; by extension it also means point or part, as well as department or office (being part of an organization). Thus, there are such nouns as **yòngchù** (use or usefulness, good or benefit); **nánchù** (difficulty or trouble); **bànshìchù** (office). Note that this suffix retains its fourth tone, but the stress is on the first syllable of the noun.

iv. **-tou.** This word has a primary meaning of head; by extension it means top or chief. As a suffix its purpose is to indicate an extremity or locality: e.g., **zhítou** (finger or toe); **shāntou** (hilltop). Although ordinarily **tóu** is spoken in the second tone, when used as a suffix it is toneless.

PRONOUNS

2   These are straightforward and simple since gender plays no part. The singular forms are:

wǒ   I, me
nǐ   you (**nín** is the formal style used as courtesy dictates)
tā   he, him or she, her; and it (gender is distinguishable only in the written characters)

The plural forms are created by adding the suffix **-men**, which is usually toneless, and therefore not stressed; it is also never used in conjunction with a number. Thus the plural forms are:

wǒmen   we, us
nǐmen   you
tāmen   they

The possessive case—the only case which applies—is indicated by means of the connective or possessive particle **-de**. Like **-men**, this suffix is also toneless.

SINGULAR		PLURAL	
wǒ-de	my	**wǒmen-de**	our, ours
nǐ-de	your (**nín-de** where applicable)	**nǐmen-de**	yours
tā-de	his or hers	**tāmen-de**	theirs

SPECIFIERS

3   Note that although Chinese make no use of definite or indefinite articles (i.e., the, a, or an), considerable use is made of specifiers, words denoting this or that, which are basically words similar to those used in English:

zhè   this   and   **nà**   that

Both of these are often coupled with the number one (**yī**), as in English, thus:

zhè yīge　　this one　　or　　**nà yīge**　　that one

What is more prevalent is a compressed form, for instance:

zhèige　　this one　　or　　**nèige**　　that one

In order to pluralize these specifiers it is necessary to modify them, either with a specific number or, in general terms, the word **xiē** meaning some or several. For example:

zhè shíwèi kèren　　these ten guests
nàxiē péngyou　　those [several] friends

NUMBERS

4　Numbers have an important role to play in connection with specifiers. (See Section 3). In fact, both numbers and measure words serve an essential purpose together when used to modify a specifier. One particular exception regarding numbers relates to the number 2. Although **èr** is a basic digit, when two is used as a modifier the word **liǎng** is employed, e.g., **liǎngge**. This is the only digit which changes for this purpose. While **èr** means precisely two, **liǎng** can be used as a couple is used in English. **Liǎng** is always followed by a MW. The words are not interchangeable except in rare instances. For the most part **èr** may be considered as a mathematical noun (as for instance in fractions). However, **liǎng** precedes **bàn** (half), **qiān** (1000), or **wàn** (10,000), and also units of quantity or time, such as **nián** (year) or **tiān** (day). (These last two words are never used together with the general MW **gè**.) A typical example of the separate uses of these numbers is **Èryuè** for February, but **liǎngge yuè** means two months.

NOTE: There is one exception regarding the use of **liǎng** in connection with **qiān**. Only **èr** can be used if any **wàn** digits precede **qiān**. For example: **liǎngqiānjiúbǎi** is acceptable for 2900, but for 12,900 one should say **yíwànèrqiānjiúbǎi**. If in doubt on this point, stick with **ér**.

MEASURE WORDS [MW]

5　In place of articles in Chinese, more use is made of numbers and measures closely utilized with specifiers. Such measure words [MW] are sometimes referred to as classifiers. Measure words abound in Chinese!

While not so esoteric as a pride of lions or a gaggle of geese, there are several dozen in common use. For example:

běn (*a volume, a copy*)	MW for a book (**shū**).
jià (*a frame*)	MW for aircraft (**fēijī**), or a screen (**wéipíng**).
jiān (*a space*)	MW for a room (**wūzi**).
jiàn (*an item*)	MW for a thing (**dōngxi**), a matter (**shìqing**), or luggage (**xíngli**).
kuài (*a piece*)	MW for a dollar (**qián**)—being a *piece* of silver, a piece of bread (**miànbāo**), or a stone (**shítou**).
zhāng (*a spread*)	MW for a bed (**chuáng**), a sheet of paper (**zhǐ**), a table (**zhuōzi**), or a picture (**huàr**).
zhī (*a stem*)	MW for a brush (**máobǐ**), a pencil (**qiānbǐ**), or a hand (**shǒu**).

(a)   The most common of all MW is **gè** but there is no exact English equivalent. It may be best considered as designating a piece or an item, or as a general measure word, which can be applied to most nouns or pronouns. **Gè** is sometimes referred to as a bound form, since it never stands alone. **Yíge** (i.e., one) often takes the place of the English article *a* or *an*. Though often considered as piece, it is not to be confused with **kuài** referred to above.

NOTE: **Gè** can never be used together with another MW. As a suffix to a specifier or number -**ge** is always toneless.

(b)   The standard sequence of syntax in terms of specification is:

Specifier—Number—Measure word

Examples of interconnection of these three terms preceding a noun are:

zhèi sānběn shū	these three books
nèi jiàn xíngli	that item of luggage
tā liǎngge péngyou	her two friends

Note that in the last example the pronoun **tā** acts as a specifier in this construction.

6   Pronouns and specifiers have associated question words [QW], which in English would be denoted as interrogatives, demonstrative adjectives or adverbs. Therefore, the QW for pronouns is **shéi** (also pronounced **shuí** in some regions) meaning who or whom, and **shéi-de** meaning whose. In connecting with the specifiers, **nǎ** is the QW meaning which, with **nǎ yíge** or **něige** to denote specifically which one. This QW, when dealing with amounts or numbers, is **jǐge** (how many). **Jǐge** is used where a small or limited number is expected, otherwise the oxymoron **duōshao** (*many few*) meaning how many is more appropriate. Just as the suffix -**ge** is not necessarily an essential part of a specifier, **jǐ** can be used as a QW modifying other MW of a less general nature.

NOTE: The QW for where will be dealt with in Section 8d.

(a)   The Chinese for QW associated with how, what and why question words and their corresponding response words are as follows:

QUERY	RESPONSE
shéi/shuí (who)	**tā** (he or she)
něi (which)	**zhè** (this) or **nà** (that)
zěn[me] (how)	**zhème** (thus)
shén[me] (what)	(numerous)
wèishénme (why)	**yīnwei** (because)

(b)   Generally, the position of QW in Chinese sentence construction is to situate the QW where the corresponding response term or clause would be expected to appear. For example:

Tā shì shéi?	**Tā shì wǒ fùqin.**
(He is *who?*)	(He is *my father.*)
Něixiē shì tā-de?	**Zhèxiē shì tā-de;**
(*Which* are hers?)	(*These* are hers;)
	nàxiē shì wǒ-de.
	(*those* are mine.)
Něijiàn xíngli shì tā-de?	**Zhèijiàn xíngli shì tā-de.**
(*Which* MW luggage is his?)	(*This* MW luggage is his.)
Zhèige zì zěnme xiě?	**Zhèige zì zhème xiě.**
(This character *how* write?)	(This character *thus* written).

Háizi zěnme huí jiā?	**Háizi qí zìxíngchē huí jiā.**
(Child *how* return home?)	(Child *ride bicycle* returning home.)
Nǐ zuò shénme?	**Wǒ zuò mùgōng.**
(You do *what?*)	(I do *woodwork.*)
Nǐ shénme shíhou qù?	**Wǒ míngtiān qù.**
(You *what* time go?)	(I *tomorrow* go.)

(c) Because of the meaning of "manner" or "way" intrinsic in the responses **zhème** (thus), and—by extension—**nàme** (then), the word **yàng** with much the same significance may be compounded with them to give **zhèmeyàng** (in this way), or **nàmeyàng** (in that case). Although in many instances the -**me** is omitted, resulting in **zhèyang** or **nàyang**, this does not materially alter the sense of the terms.

(d) **Wèishénme** can signify in context anything from why or how come to "How is it that. . . ." The Chinese equivalent for because is **yīnwei**. Should the sequence of thought in the response progress to cause and effect, an additional clause would be preceded by the term **suóyǐ** meaning therefore or as a result of. . . . Examples are:

Wèishénme nǐ méi qù?	Why didn't you go?
Yīnwei wǒ méiyǒu qián.	Because I had no money.
Wǒ méiyǒu chēfèi,	I hadn't got the fare,
suóyǐ wǒ bùnéng qù	so I couldn't go to visit her.
zhǎo ta.	

QUESTIONS

7   Apart from stylized formal expressions and elliptical questions using the interrogative particle **ne**, there are basically three different methods of framing a question in Chinese:

  (a) *Using a QW.* Questions may be posed by the use of a question word [QW] as indicated in Section 6.

  (b) *Using the interrogative particle* **ma**. The easiest way to ask a question is the use of the interrogative particle **ma**. All that is required is to take a simple statement and add **ma** to the end of the sentence. For example:

    Statement: **Zhèi shì nǐ-de míngpiàn**—"This is your card."
    Question: **Zhèi shì nǐ-de míngpiàn ma?**—"Is this your card?"

Note that there is no change of word order or other aspect of the statement.

(c) *Using choice-type questions*. Choice-type questions are also known as "Verb not-Verb" (or V. not-V.) questions. With the exception of the verb **yǒu** (to have), all verbs are negated by the word **bú** (equivalent to the English negative not).

To illustrate this type of question, consider the example, "Is she right?" which can give rise to two forms of reply in English.

(i)   Yes / Yes, she is / Yes, she is right   (affirmative)

(ii) No / No, she isn't / No, she's not right   (negative)

The Chinese pattern invites the same two alternatives:

Q: **Tā duì-budùì?**
     She right not-right?
     Is she right?

A: **Tā duì.**
     She right.
     She is right.

   or

A: **Tā búduì.**
     She not-right.
     She is not right.

NOTE: In this instance, **bù** (fourth tone) changes to **bú** (second tone), as it precedes a word in the fourth tone.

There are variants in the use of the choice-type question, depending on the type of verb i.e., whether it is transitive or intransitive, auxiliary or resultative. Should one wish to ask whether one's Chinese acquaintances know any English, the question might be phrased along the lines of "Can you speak English?" using the auxiliary "can," and thus inviting the answer "can" or "not can," since a simple Yes or No is not available. The Chinese reply will generally depend on the verb or verbs used in the question. When the choice-type question is used, remember that:

(i)   A split choice-type question can be used to change the nuance or emphasis of the question, and

(ii) The stress or emphasis is placed on the first syllable of the (V. not-V.) question.

In addition, the choice-type question may offer more than a device between an affirmative and a negative response. The possibility of an alternative may exist. In such cases, where we would say or in English, the Chinese say **háishi** (or, among other meanings).

PLACE WORDS [PW]

8 In Chinese sentence construction it is important to be specific in terms of location and position, particularly as these relate to the speaker, so as not to confuse the listener. Much like the MW -**ge** the PW are bound words: they do not make sense on their own, but need to be tied to a noun or verb in order to convey the appropriate meaning.

shàng	up, on
xià	down, under
qián	front, before
hòu	back, behind
lǐ	in, inside
wài	out, outside
zuǒ	left
yóu	right

(a) While to an English speaker these PW may seem self-evident, in Chinese it is often the practice to add one of two or three suffixes to emphasize direction or location in relationship to the speaker. These suffixes are not necessarily interchangeable.

(i) **biān**—Often rendered also as **biār**, this suffix has the sense of edge, and may be used with all the PW currently under consideration. This serves to indicate the direction of motion; as emphasis may be added by the use of **wàng** (towards, which indicates motion in a specific direction) or **zài** (*to be at*, thus indicating position). For example:

lǐbiar	inside
zài lǐbiar	to be inside
shàngbiar	on top
wàng shàngbiar	upward(s)

This may be further amplified by the use of verbs such as **dào** (to reach or arrive at) and **huí** (to return).

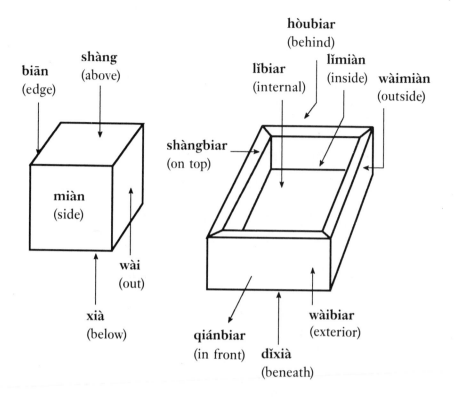

FIGURE 1   FIGURE 2

qiánbiar	the front
dào qiánbiar lái	come to the front
hòubiar	the rear
huí hòubiar qù	return to the rear

(ii) **miàn** means face and, by extension, surface. Should it be uttered as a toneless suffix it would be interchangeable with **biar** but for a subtle difference of meaning:

lǐbiar	meaning interior space
lǐmiàn	meaning internal surface

However, this nuance need not cause much concern, since the context will usually convey the meaning. For example:

tā péngyou zài lǐbiar   her friend is inside
lǐmiàn bù hěn gānjìng   it is not very clean inside

Note that compass points or directions always take **biār** should a suffix be required. Whereas, when a specific aspect of an object is indicated, **miàn** is the obvious choice. For example, **duìmiàr** means the opposite side or facing.

(b) The PW **shàng**, **xià**, **qián** and **hòu** are often compounded with **yǐ**, another bound word that is a preposition generally used to imply "in order to." Examples are:

yǐshàng   more than, over, above
yǐxià   less than, under, below
yǐqián   before, formerly, previously
yǐhòu   after, later; following
yǐnèi   within
yǐwài   beyond; other than, except

Since there are no characters shown here to indicate the difference, note the difference in tones between these compounds where the first syllable is in the third tone (**yǐ**), and those listed in Section 16 where the first syllable uses the character for one (**yī**), with appropriate tonal changes.

(c) Related specifiers use the word **lǐ**, meaning in or inside. Examples are:

zhèlǐ   here, i.e., in this [place]
nàlǐ   there, i.e., in that [place]

In North China, particularly in the vicinity of Beijing, where the retroflex **r** is popular (and distinctive), the -**lǐ** is replaced thus: **zhèr** and **nàr**.

(d) The associated QW with these specifiers is **nǎ** (where), which gives

nǎli or **nǎr**   where, i.e., in what [place]

The QW **nǎr**, by extension, may also be used to mean whence or how come.

This QW is usually preceded by **zài** meaning at, thus:

Tā zài nǎr xuéxí?   **Tā zài yīyuàn xuéxí.**
(She at *where* study?)   (She at *hospital* study.)
Nǐ-de péngyou zài nǎr?   **Wǒ-de péngyou zài Shànghǎi.**
(Your friend at *where*?)   (My friend at *Shanghai*.)

VERBS

9   Verbs are utilized differently in Chinese than they are in English. There is no simple way to define Chinese verb forms using many of the standard English grammatical labels. Not only do Chinese verbs not indicate tense or mood, they also do not alter their form for person, gender or number, since such information is already obvious from the context and the remainder of the sentence. Certain English verbs such as bite, rest, or talk are used also as nouns; this dual function exists much more widely in Chinese. While English verbs frequently rely on the support of prepositions, or the use of the active or passive voice, Chinese verbs in general require only suitable auxiliary verbs. The context is relied on to clarify the meaning. Some certain major differences between Chinese and English verbs may be described as follows:

(a)   Regardless of the person or number of the subject, the verb does not alter its form; instead it is the subject alone which will indicate the singular or the plural. For example:

Wǒ-de mǔqin bùlái.   My mother is not coming.

Wǒ-de fùmu bùlái.   My parents are not coming.

Note that the verb **lái** (to come) remains unchanged; **bù**, like not in English, indicates the negative.

(b)   Tense is indicated by the use of auxiliary verbs and time words or clauses, as shown below:

Yǐqián tā méi qùguò.   She had not been before.

Wǒ xiànzài qù.   I am going now.

Nǐ jiānglái yídìng   You will certainly go in
yào qù.   future.

Note that the verb **qù** (to go) is supported by auxiliary verbs, such as **guò** (to pass) indicating past action or **yào** (to want) indicating intended action. The inclusion of **yǐqián** (before, previously), **xiànzài** (now), and **jiānglái** (in future) as time words indicates clearly the tense required in English. Note also the position of the words indicating time *when*, which are always at the beginning of the sentence, immediately preceding or following the subject.

(c)   The auxiliary verb is what indicates whether the verb is used in the active or passive voice since a Chinese verb alone makes no such distinction.

9.1   ACTION—COMPLETED, CURRENT, AND INTENDED. Verbs in Chinese are in terms of completed, current and intended actions rather than in terms of past, present and future tenses as in standard English.

(a)   *Means of indicating completed action*

    i.   Adverbs of time such as **gāngcái** (just now), **yǐqián** (previously), **qùnián** (last year), or **zuótiān** (yesterday), are used. These precede the verb.

    ii.   The suffix **le** (occasionally pronounced **liǎo**) is used invariably to indicate completed action.

    iii.   Often auxiliary verbs such as **guò** (to pass), **jiàn** (to meet, to perceive) or **wán** (to finish) are used after compound verbs to indicate completed activity.

    iv.   The word **méi** (abbreviation for **méiyǒu**), which may be used instead of **bù** to negate a verb, also indicates completed action.

(b)   *Means of indicating current action*

    i.   Any lack of indication regarding past or future time may be taken as a tacit indication of the present.

    ii.   Adverbs of time such as **xiànzài** (now), **lìkè** (at once), or **jīntiān** (today) may be used, and again these precede the verb.

    iii.   Three words which, by virtue of their meanings, imply continuing or current action, and may be used as suffixes to the main verb, are: **-zhe** (or alternatively pronounced **zháo**), which is roughly equivalent to the English suffix -ing; **zhù** (to hold); and **ne**, which, though used largely as an interrogative particle, may also imply the current state.

(c)   *Means of indicating action to come*

    i.   Use of the verb **yào** (to want) implies an intention to take a particular course of action. Other verbs may perform a similar role. For example, **yuànyì** (to be willing), **xīwàng** (to hope), or **kěndìng** (to be sure to) all support the likelihood of future action.

    ii.   The same role is performed by such adverbial expressions as **jiānglái** (in future), **kěnéng** (possible or probable), or **míngtiān** (tomorrow), which also precede the verbs they modify.

    iii.   Two other indicators of impending activity are **jiù** (then), which relates closely to the immediate future, and **cái** (not until then), which obviously applies to an activity that is anticipated. As usual, these come before the main verb in the sentence construction.

(d) So far only monosyllabic verbs have been used in examples; however, like most other Chinese terms, Chinese verbs are usually compounds of two words (in this case verbs) of similar meanings, e.g., **kànjiàn** (*look perceive*) meaning to see, or **sònggěi** (*send give*) meaning to bestow or to give; or **xǐhuan** (*happy joyful*) meaning to like or to be keen on. One group of auxiliary verbs indicates specific degrees of competence for action, while another group of polysyllabic verbs, known as resultative compounds, indicates potential or actual results. There are also numerous verb/object compounds, such as **chīfàn** (*eat rice*), meaning to feed or to eat; **xiězì** (*write characters*) meaning to write; or **kànbào** (*look report*) meaning to read a newspaper.

9.2   EQUATIONAL VERBS (e.v.). A large number of adjectives are in effect also used as verbs, and are consequently referred to as equational verbs or, sometimes, are known as stative verbs. The verb **shì** (to be) in such cases is implied. That is to say that such words as **hǎo** (good), **lěng** (cold), or **dà** (big) may function alone as verbs. Another feature of equational verbs is that they may be modified by the adverb **hěn**, meaning very or quite.

9.3   AUXILIARY VERBS. Certain auxiliary verbs (sometimes called co-verbs), particularly **yào**, **yuànyì**, **kéyǐ**, **néng** and **huì**, serve to indicate what may be called "degrees of competence." They are essential for expressing an intention or willingness to carry out an action, as well as a person's freedom, physical capacity or ability to act.

yào	to want, to require, to have to; extn.—to intend, be going to . . .
yuànyì	to desire, be willing, ready to; extn.—to like to, want to
kéyǐ	can, may (i.e., permission or freedom to act)
néng	can, be able to (physical capacity)
huì	can, be capable of (acquired knowledge and skills)

(a) Here are some examples to illustrate the differences of meaning and the nuances of these five words.

(i) **Jiē-shang nǐ** yào **xiǎoxīn qìchē.**

You *must* be careful of cars on the street.

Rénrén dōu yào **qián.**

People all *want* money.

Kuài yào **xiàyǔ.**

It's *going* to rain.

These few examples show that there are several distinct ways in which to use **yào**, ranging from stressing the importance of an action, to indicating something which is about to happen.

(ii) **Wǒ xiàyuè** yuànyì **fàngjià.**

I'm *ready* to go on holiday next month.

Tā fùmǔ yuànyì **tā liú zài jiā**

Her parents *want* her to stay home.

Nǐ yuànyì **wǒ jídiǎnzhōng lái?**

What time would you *like* me to come?

These examples are presented to illustrate the use of **yuànyi** to indicate a degree of preference or readiness to oblige with a particular action.

(iii) **Tā kéyǐ gēn nǐ qù.**

She *can* go with you.

Wǒ kéyǐ chōuyān ma?

May I smoke?

Zhège cài zuòde hái kéyǐ!

This dish *is* pretty good!

The range of uses for **kéyǐ** is fairly broad. In English, the distinction between can and may seems to be fading; similarly, in Chinese **kéyǐ** can be used to express either notion. In the third example, **kéyǐ** is used in an idiomatic fashion, indicating a good degree of "can do," i.e., quite acceptable!

(iv) **Tā néng bǐ ní pǎo-de kuài.**

She is *able* to run faster than you.

Wǒ néng shuō sìzhǒng wàiyǔ.

I *am able* to speak four foreign languages.

Nǐ néng gàn shénme?

What *can* you do?

These examples show how the word **néng** is used to indicate a physical capacity to perform an action.

(v) **Wǒ** huì **yìdiǎr Zhōngwén.**

I *know* a little Chinese.

Shénme qìchē tā dōu huì **kāi.**

She *can* drive any type of car.

Nǐ huì **zuò mùgōng ma?**

Are you any *good at* carpentry?

These examples show how **huì** is used to indicate ability to carry out an action, this time in the sense of having the necessary knowledge or skills.

(b) The PW **shàng** (on) and **xià** (under), may also be used as auxiliary verbs to imply ascent and descent respectively. Other auxiliary verbs are often used including:

chū	to emerge, to go out
dào	to arrive, to reach
dé	to obtain
kāi	to open, to start
lái	to come
liǎo/le	to complete
qǐ	to rise
qù	to go
yào	to want
zhù	to hold, to stay

Auxiliary verbs are used generally in the same way as their English counterparts.

9.4   RESULTATIVE VERBS. These verb compounds, known as resultative verbs, are necessary to indicate potential or express potentiality, actual results, or to provide an alternative phrasing for questions about potential.

(a) Examples of indicating potential results are:

> **Wǒ** tíngdejiàn **shōuyīnjī.**   I *can hear* the radio.
> (*listen-obtain-meet*)
> **Liù tiān jiù** wándeliǎo.   [It] *can be completed* in just
> (*finish-obtain-complete*)   six days.
> **Tā-de bàozhǐ** sòngdedào.   His newspapers *can be*
> (*send-obtain-reach*)   *delivered.*

Note the features of these verbs. The first component is a verb indicating the action, while the last component is a verb indicating a potential result of that action. The potential result will be either positive or negative. For example:

listening—potential—to hear or not hear, or
finishing—potential—to complete or not complete.

In all these examples the potential expressed is positive, with **dé**, the middle component, signifying attainment. Should the opposite be the case, **bù** (not) is substituted for **dé** e.g., **tīngbujiàn** for cannot hear.

(b) Using the same illustrations, we can demonstrate how actual results are indicated:

    Wǒ tīngjiànle shōuyīnjī.   I heard the radio.

    Liù tiān jiù wánle.   [It] was completed in just six days.

    Tā-de bàozhǐ sòngdàole.   His newspapers were delivered.

Again the examples are expressed in the affirmative: i.e., an action has been completed. In the event the negative is required, it is expressed by deleting the **le** (which does not apply since no action was completed) and placing **méi** (the abbreviated form of **méiyǒu**) ahead of the compounded verb, e.g., **méi tīngjiàn** for did not hear.

(c) Resultative verbs provide another means of phrasing choice-type questions. Using a Verb not-Verb variant, the variation lies in the omission of the not between the two potential-type compounds which provide the alternative.

    Nǐ tīngdejiàn tīngbujiàn shōuyīnjī?   Can you hear the radio?

    Liù tiān wándeliǎo wánbuliǎo?   Can it be finished in six days?

    Tā-de bàozhǐ sòngdedào sòngbudào?   Can his newspapers be delivered?

This is a somewhat emphatic way of putting a question, as the questions posed above distinctly imply "... or can't it," and "... or can't they," respectively. To be less emphatic choose either of the resultative combinations, and end the sentence with the interrogative **ma?** For example:

    Nǐ tīngdejiàn shōuyīnjī ma?   Can you hear the radio?

or alternatively:

    Nǐ tīngbujiàn shōuyīnjī ma?   Can't you hear the radio?

The change of emphasis is obvious in the questions, but it will not alter the answers.

(d) The function of the verb which is the last component of a resultative verb, as well as the emphasis placed on direction is especially apparent in compound verbs with directional endings, e.g., **názǒu** (to take away), **dàichūqù** (to carry outside), or **sònghuíqù** (to send back). In these compounds, it is possible to express potentiality in a limited number of cases since, by nature of their meanings, only the actual form applies as a rule.

COMPARISONS

10   Because of the affinity between adjectives and verbs in Chinese, particularly in the case of equational verbs, it is appropriate to consider how comparisons are expressed in Chinese. To begin with, it is not as simple as in English, where -er or -est as a suffix for most adjectives will serve the purpose.

(a) For simple likenesses, the expression **gēn . . . yíyàng** (*with . . . alike*) is used. For example:

> **Nǐ-de qìchē gēn tā-de**   Your car is like his.
> **yíyàng.**   (i.e., resembles)

(b) Dissimilarity may be expressed using either the negative form **gēn . . . bù yíyàng**, or the term **méiyǒu**. For example:

> **Nǐ-de qìchē gēn tā-de**   Your car is not the same as
> **bù yíyàng.**   his.
> **Nǐ-de qìchē méiyǒu**   Your car is not as fast as
> **tā-de kuài.**   his.

In most cases, either of these two expressions should suffice. Two other expressions are available: **bùrú**, meaning not equal to or inferior to; or the verb **bǐ**, which means to compare. For example:

> **Nǐ-de qìchē bùrú tā-de.**   Your car is inferior to his.
> **Nǐ-de qìchē bǐbushàng**   Your car cannot compare with
> **tā-de.**   his.
> **Nǐ-de qìchē bǐ tā-de**   Your car is better than his.
> **hǎo.**
> **Nǐ-de qìchē bǐ tā-de**   Your car is far better than
> **hǎo-de duō.**   his (i.e., *by contrast a*
>   *lot [more] good*).

(c) When expressing superlatives, there are several variants to choose from. **Zuì** is the term which probably equates best with -est in English. However **zuì** always precedes the adjective in question:

> **Wǒ-de qìchē zuì hǎo.**   My car is the best.
> **Nǐ-de yé hǎo-jíle.**   Yours is very good too.
> **Tā-de qìchē liǎobudé!**   His car is terrific!

The expression **bùdeliǎo** signifies the very opposite, meaning the worst or disastrous!

DUPLICATIONS

11   Verbs and adjectives in Chinese may be duplicated in Chinese syntax, sometimes to give a certain nuance to the resulting compound. Duplication may be used to indicate the degree of casualness with which an action is performed, or to provide emphasis. It may also take several forms.

(a)   When a word is duplicated, **yī** (one) may be inserted between the two identical components of the new compound, or it may be dispensed with. In either case, the meaning of the original word is subtly altered. For example, **kàn** basically means to look in a variety of senses, from look at to scrutinize. **Kànyikàn** has the sense of "to take a look at," while **kànkan** has just the sense of "to look." Similarly, **shì** is the verb "to try," while **shìyishì** means "to have a try" or "to take a shot at. . . ." These two examples serve to indicate the degree of casualness with which the action is performed. For example, **shāngliang** means to consult or to discuss; **shāngliang-shāngliang** has the sense of "holding a discussion," thus emphasizing the duration of the activity.

(b)   Another form of duplication is illustrated by the compound **jíjimangmáng**. **Jímáng** is an equational verb, meaning [to be] in haste or urgent. Duplication of this term in the form shown serves to emphasize the urgency or the need for haste.

(c)   A third form of duplication involves two changes to the second component of the compound: addition of the diminutive suffix **r**; and the use of the first tone, regardless of the tone of the original word. For example, duplication of the word **màn**, an equational verb meaning [to be] slow, yields the adverb **mànmār-de** meaning slowly or gradually. By the same token, duplication of the word **kuài**, meaning quick or fast, yields **kuàikuār-de**, meaning quickly—thus urging haste or hastening.

ANTITHETICAL COMPOUNDS

12   An interesting facet of the Chinese language is the use of certain compounds consisting of a pair of words with opposite meanings. A prime ex-

ample is **dōngxi** (thing), which is explained in detail in Chapter 7.1. Oxymora include:

TERM	LITERAL MEANING	ENGLISH EQUIVALENT
chángduǎn	long/short	length
dàxiǎo	big/little	size
duōshǎo	more/less	quantity
gāo'ǎi	high/low	height
jìnchū	enter in/go out	business turnover
kāiguān	open/close	switch
kuàimàn	quick/slow	speed
láihuí	come/return (or round) trip	back and forth, a return
mǎimài	buy/sell	business
máodùn	spear/shield	contradiction
nèiwài	inside/outside	about, around
qīngzhòng	light/heavy	weight
shàngxià	up/down	approximately, thereabouts
sǐhuó	dead/alive	fate
sōngjǐn	loose/tight	elasticity
yīnyáng	darkness/light	the Taiji philosophy
záowǎn	early/late	sooner or later, someday
zhēnjiǎ	true/false	true or false
zuǒyòu	left/right	approximate, anyhow

USES OF **-de**

13   The character **-de** performs several useful functions in Chinese.

(a)   The most common function of **-de** is to indicate the possessive. For example:

>   **tā-de péngyou**   her friend
>   **wǒmen-de fángzi**   our house
>   **nǐ péngyou-de máobǐ**   your friend's brush

In the last example, you might expect to see **-de** added to both **nǐ** and **péngyou** since there are actually two possessives. But repetition sounds awkward, so the -de retained is usually the one attached to the noun.

(b) -De is also used to form relative clauses, in which case it is the equivalent of which or that in English, e.g.,

nǐ kànguo-de dìfang	places which you have seen
zhèr zuò-de dōngxi	things that are made here

(c) Duplicated adjectives with -de suffix become compound adverbs, for example:

haǒhāor-de	properly
kuàikuār-de	hurriedly, quickly

Note how the repeated second syllable takes on the first tone, and also the stress.

(d) Participles require the use of -de, as well as Verb-**de** compounds. For instance:

Kāi qìchē-de shì wǒ péngyou.	The car driv*er* is my friend.
Qí zìxíngchē-de shì tā érzi.	The bicycle rid*er* is her son.
Zhè shì tā huà-de huàr.	These are the pictures [of which] she is the paint*er*.
Zhè búshi wǒ zuò-de.	This isn't my work (i.e., of my do*ing*).

(e) The suffix -de may be added to create certain participial nouns, a practice which is prevalent in Chinese. Consider these few examples:

jiāoshū-de	teach*er*
màibào-de	newsvend*or*
shuōhuà-de	speak*er*
zuò mǎimai-de	merchant, trad*er*

Similarly, -de may be used as a suffix to a noun to create an adjectival form:

mùtou-de	wooden (of wood)
tiě-de	metal (of iron)

Thus, -de also follows any numerical expression modifying a noun, e.g., **shíkuàiqián-de piào** for $10 tickets.

(f) Certain characteristic expressions take on -de as a suffix, the best known being **biéde**, meaning another or other, and **shìde**, meaning correct or "That's right." In particular cases, -de may also be considered to mean "the...one," e.g., dà-de (the big one), hóng-de (the red one), or Zhōngguo-de (the Chinese one).

(g) The expression -de shíhou may invariably be translated as when or while in time clauses.

USES OF le OR liǎo

14 (a) The basic meaning of the word liǎo is to complete; and since le is the common alternative pronunciation for liǎo, a Chinese verb will take -le as a suffix to indicate past or completed action. Consider these examples:

Kèren láile.	The guests have come.
Wó màile fángzi.	I sold the house.

(b) In addition to this, -le may be used at the end of a sentence to indicate an anticipated change of situation. This is done to give emphasis, and also to give euphony to what otherwise would be considered too abrupt or bald a statement in Chinese.

Yào xiàxuě-le.	It's going to snow.
Kuài wán-le.	It's nearly finished.
Bié nào-le.	Don't be naughty.
Gāng zuò dé-le.	It has just been done.

(c) Thus -le may often be encountered twice in the same sentence—not only after the verb, but also at the end of the sentence for the sake of the rhythm, which the Chinese refer to as kǒuqì signifying tone or a manner of speaking.

Tā yǐjīng xiěwánle nèifēng xìn le.	She'd already finished writing that letter.
Tā líkaile jiā le.	He had left home.
Wǒ fùle sānge yuè-de zūqian le.	I've paid three months' rent.

Note that here the time clause follows the verb, since it is modifying the object.

(d) Le may appear in the Verb-not-Verb form of questions. For example:

Nǐ kànle-méikàn wǒ-de huāyuán?	Have you seen my garden?

Here le is a suffix to the first element in the Verb-not-Verb construction regarding a possible past action, but not to the second (re-peated) element should the action not have taken place after all.

(e) -Le is often used in an idiomatic capacity, e.g., **duìle** (Right!), **déle** (That's it!), or **hǎole** (O.K.).

(f) The word -le, when pronounced **liǎo**, takes on a somewhat different role, particularly in connection with resultative compounded verbs. **Liǎo** is used generally for potential purposes only, while its -le counterpart is confined to use in the actual instances. Consequently, **liǎo** is used mostly with **dé** or **bù**, and occasionally with both.

USES OF **jiù**

15 **Jiù** is a particle which is used more than a dozen different ways in spoken Chinese, but there is no an exact English equivalent.

(a) **Jiù** signifying "as soon as" or "then":

Wǒmen chīwán-le fàn jiù **qù kàn diànyǐng.**	We will go to the movies *as soon as* we have eaten.
Kànwán-le shū wǒ jiù **shuìjiào.**	Having finished the book, I shall *then* go to sleep.

In both these instances, **jiù** implies an action in the near future. When used to indicate an action in the immediate future, **zhè** (this) may precede **jiù**. For example:

Huǒché zhèjiù dào.	The train will be arriving shortly.

(b) **Jiù** signifying "only" or "just":

Nèige háizi jiù **yǒu tā fùqin.**	That child *only* has a father.
Wǒ yìtiān jiù **chī yídùn fàn.**	I have *just* one meal a day.

(c) **Jiù**, in combination with **shì** (to be), giving a different sense of "just" or "the very one":

Nèijù huà jiùshi **tā shuō-de.**	He's *the very one* who said that.
Tā zhīdao, jiùshi **tā bù gǎn shuō.**	He knows, it's *just* that he dare not admit it.

(d) **Jiù**, compounded with **shì** (to be), signifying "even if":

Jiùshì **wǒ mà tā, tā hái bù tīng.**	*Even if* I scold her, she still won't listen.

USE OF yī *COMPOUNDS*

16 While there are no articles as such in Chinese, considerable use is made of the number one (yī). Though not an actual replacement for a or an, yī is often used in a similar context as such. Yī also serves wider purposes, as shown below.

yìdiǎr	a little [quantity], a bit
yìhuěr	a while, a short time
yíkuàr	together, at the same place

In all, there are several dozen compounds which start with yī. The following examples are those which occur most frequently. (Note that the tone may alter depending on the tone that follows, i.e., *fourth* tone before first, second or third, and *second* tone before fourth or toneless.)

yìbān	generally, ordinary, usual[ly]
yídìng	certainly, definite, fixed
yígòng	altogether, in all, total
yíjùhuà	in short, in a word
yìqǐ	together, in company (alternative to yíkuàr)
yíqiè	all, every, everything
yíxià	once, all at once, one time
yìxiē	a few, some, a number of...
yíyàng	alike, equally, the same
yìzhí	straight, continuous[ly], all the way

COMPARING THE USE OF bǎ *WITH* jiào OR ràng

17 Bǎ is used for the active voice, while jiào and ràng are used for the passive voice. To prevent any confusion between the voices, consider the following examples. Note the word order in each case.

ACTIVE CONSTRUCTION

Tā àirén bǎ méi chī-de cài dàihuí jiā qù-le. His wife took the uneaten dishes back home.

The standard S-V-O order is altered by the bǎ construction to the extent that the object is placed before the verb.

PASSIVE CONSTRUCTION

Méi chī-de cài ràng tā àirén gěi dàihuí jiā qù-le. The uneaten dishes were taken back home by his wife.

Note that the object (i.e., uneaten dishes) now occupies the subject position.

(a) Sentence constructions using **bǎ** have certain other characteristics:

  (i) The principal verb is followed by -**le**, or such final auxiliary verbs as **dài, huí, lái, qù** or **zǒu**.

  (ii) Should such verbs as **gěi** or **gàosu** occur, an indirect object must follow.

  (iii) If a verb is followed by **zài** it must be completed by a PW.

  (iv) The sentence may end with a duplicated verb.

  (v) The sentence may end with a MW or other quantifying expression.

The following examples illustrate these features in the same sequence:

  (vi) **Tā bǎ cài dàizǒu-le.**   She took the dishes away.

  (vii) **Tā bǎ huār gěi tā àirén le.**   He gave the flowers to his wife.

  (viii) **Wó bǎ dōngxi fàng zài nǎr le?**   Where did I put the things?

  (ix) **Wǒ yào xiān bǎ shìqing shāngliang-shāngliang.**   I want to discuss the matter first.

  (x) **Tā yīngdàng bǎ zhuōzi gěi cā yíxià.**   He ought to give the table a wipe.

(b) **Jiào**, meaning to cause or, by extension, to let is similar to **ràng**, meaning to allow, and thus these two words may be considered interchangeable. Both **jiào** and **ràng** are equivalent to the English preposition by when employed in the passive construction. In general terms the characteristics of passive constructions are as follows:

  (i) An action is initiated by a performer, and the results of the action are felt by a receiver;

  (ii) Any remaining sentence components describe the results in terms of time or extent.

The usual pattern of passive sentence construction looks like this:

NOTE: While the English sentence construction may vary according to circumstances, the Chinese syntax remains constant—even when the sentence is phrased as a question. The main difference is that the preposition and performer are placed before the verb in Chinese, instead of after the verb, as in English.

Receiver	Preposition	Performer Elements	Action	Other
(Subject)	(Jiào or ràng)	(Object)	(Verb)	(Subordinates)

Wǒ-de qián   ràng   tā   tōu   zǒule.
(My money was stolen by him.)

Nàxiē
  bàozhǐ dōu jiào   da fēng gěiguā   chūqùle.
(Those newspapers were all blown away by a high wind.)
Guógēr   ràng   xiǎohár   chàng-de zhēn hǎo.
(The national anthem was beautifully sung by the children.)
Nǐ-de qìchē jiào   chēchǎng xiūli   jǐ tiān-le?
(How long has your car been under repair by the garage?)

SUGGESTED READINGS

"After three days without reading, talk becomes flavourless."

There is an abundance of reading material on the many facets of the culture and history of the Chinese people. The following books are my personal recommendations and are divided into subject categories. Most of the material relates to twentieth-century China.

Culture
Lau, D.C., trans. *Confucius—The Analects*. New York: Penguin Books, 1979.
———. *Mencius*. New York: Penguin Books, 1970.
Williams, C.A.S. *Outlines of Chinese Symbolism and Art Motives*. New York: Dover Publications, Inc., 1976.

Social
Bloodworth, Dennis. *The Chinese Looking Glass*. New York: Farrar, Straus & Giroux, 1980.
Bonavia, David. *The Chinese*. New York: Penguin Books, 1989.
Butterfield, Fox. *China: Alive in the Bitter Sea*. New York: Times Books, 1983.
Clayre, Alasdair. *The Heart of the Dragon*. London: Collins, 1985.
Mathews, Jan and Linda Mathews. *One Billion: A China Chronicle*. New York: Random House, 1984.
Mosher, Steven W. *Broken Earth*. New York: Free Press, 1983.

Biography and Politics
Coates, Austin. *Myself a Mandarin: Memoirs of a Special Magistrate*. Hong Kong: Heinemann Educational Books (Asia) Ltd., 1975.

Fathers, Michael and Andrew Higgins. *Tiananmen—The Rape of Peking*. New York: The Independent in association with Doubleday, 1989.

Liu Binyan. *Tell the World*. Translated by H.L. Epstein. New York: Pantheon Books, 1989.

Rodzinski, Witold. *The People's Republic of China: A Concise Political History*. New York: Free Press, 1988.

Ronning, Chester. *A Memoir of China in Revolution*. New York: Pantheon Books, 1975.

Seagrave, Sterling. *The Soong Dynasty*. New York: Harper & Row, 1985.

Taylor, Charles, ed. *China Hands: The Globe and Mail in Peking*. Toronto: McClelland and Stewart, Ltd., 1984.

Thurston, Anne F. *Enemies of the People*. Cambridge, Mass.: Harvard University Press, 1988.

History, Geography and Travel

Chin, Manley. *China the Beautiful*. Hong Kong: The Readers' Digest Association, 1987.

Gernet, Jacques. *A History of Chinese Civilization*. Translated by J.R. Foster. Cambridge and New York: Cambridge University Press, 1982.

Journey into China. Washington, D.C.: National Geographic Society, 1982. (Various well-known authors on behalf of the publisher.)

Lin Yutang. *The Gay Genius: The Life and Times of Su Tungpo*. London: William Heinemann Ltd., 1948.

Loewe, Michael. *Imperial China*. New York and Washington: Frederick A. Prayer, 1966.

Samagalski, Alan and Michael Buckley. *China: A Travel Survival Kit*. Victoria, Australia: Lonely Planet Publications, 1984.

Sinclair, Kevin. *The Yellow River*. Los Angeles: International Publishing Corporation Ltd., The Knapp Press, 1987.

Literature and Philosophy

Birch, Cyril, ed. *Anthology of Chinese Literature*. Vol.1—From early times to the 14th century; Vol. II—From the 14th century to the present day. New York: Grove Press Inc., (Vol. I) 1965; (Vol. II) 1972.

Chan Wing-Tsit, trans. & comp. *A Source Book on Chinese Philosophy*. Princeton: Princeton University Press, 1963.

Lin Yutang, comp. *The Wisdom of China: An Anthology*. London: Michael Joseph, 1949.

Wu Cheng'en. *Monkey*. Translated by Arthur Waley. Woking: George Allen and Unwin Ltd., 1953.

Fiction, Poetry and Drama

Buck, Pearl S. *The Good Earth*. New York: John Day, 1931.

Gu Hua. *A Small Town Called Hibiscus*. Shanghai: Panda Books, Chinese Literature Press, 1987.

Hsiung, S.I., *Lady Precious Stream*. London: Metheun & Co., Ltd., 1956 (Play).

Lao She. *Camel Ziangzi*. Beijing: Foreign Languages Press, 1981.

Pai Hsien-yung. *Wander in the Grade, Waking from a Dream*. Bloomington: Indiana University Press, 1982.

Waley, Arthur, trans. *Chinese Poems*. London: Unwin Books, 1961.

Weekly Publication

For anyone interested in being well-informed with up-to-date developments in the Far East generally, as well as Chinese affairs in particular, the *Far Eastern Economic Review* is highly recommended. This weekly publication is printed by the South China Morning Post, Ltd., GPO Box 160, Hong Kong (Telex: 62497 Revad Hx) and is available by subscription only.

GLOSSARY

> "One who has ambition will succeed, but ambition should be tempered with humility."

This glossary will assist the reader in locating terms used in the chapters. The terms are listed in alphabetical order under the primary character or syllable. The secondary or subsequent syllables are also shown, indicating the compounds to which they belong. The numbers in bold print indicate the page of the dialogue in which the term or compound occurs. Many terms occur elsewhere in the book and these are noted to help show the variety of ways such terms may be used.

a – exclamatory or interrogative particle   **137**
àiyā – exclamation   **155**, 159, **249**, **250**
ài – love, affection   198, **204**, 208
    àihào – hobby; to be keen [on doing]   **197**, 200
    āirén – spouse   **246**, 247
ān – peace, quiet (see **píng'ān**)   113
    ānpai – to arrange   **121**, 125, 231
    ānquán – secure, safe   **129**, 133
ànzhào – in accordance with   **175**

ba – suggestive particle   **137**, 139
bā – eight   **20**, **54**, 56
    bāyuè – August   58
bǎ – to hold, grasp; MW   **120**, 124, 125, 281
bái – white, a surname   27
    báigār – potent white wine [from sorghum]   163
    báihuà – vernacular   48
    báitiān – daytime   57, 74

băi – hundred   21
   băihuò – general merchandise   98
   băihuò-[shāng]diàn – a department store   **96**, 98
băi – to place, arrange, set in order   **167**, 169, 173
bài – to do obeisance, (see **lǐbài**)   176
   bàifǎng – to call on, visit   **175**, 177
bàn – to do, attend to   **69**, 70, 73
   bànfǎ – means, method, way   **214**, 217
   bàngōngshì – office, personal work place   103
   bànshìchù – office, agency   **100**, 103
bàn – half, semi-   **69**, 70
bàn – companion, partner (see **huǒbàn**)   232
bāng – to help, assist   123
   bāngmáng – to lend a hand   **121**, 127
bāo – to wrap; a bundle; surname (see **píbāo, yāobāo**)   130
bǎo – to protect; guarantee   146
   bǎocún – to safeguard   **145**, 146
   báoxiǎn – insurance   146
   báoxiǎnguì – a safe   **145**, 146
   bǎozhòng – take care   **244**, 245
bǎo – replete (see **chībǎo**)   166
bǎo – to report, declare (see **diànbào, rìbào, shēnbàodān**)   91
bàoqiàn – to apologise   **245**, 246
bēi – cup; extn.—a glass (see **jiǔbēi**)   176
běi – North   50
   Běidà – Beijing University   **49**, 51
   Běifāng – the North, northern   110, **167**, 172
   Běihǎi – the Winter Palace   **107**, 109
   Běijīng – Peking   105, 110, **166**
   Běi-Měizhōu – North America   92
bèi – to prepare (see **yùbèi, zhǔnbèi**)   122
běn – origin; MW, volume   56
   běnnián – this year   **54**, 62
   běnrén – oneself   **197**, 201
bǐ – Chinese calligraphy brush; pen (see **máobǐ, shuǐbǐ**)   86
bǐ – to compare   123
   bǐfang – for instance   **121**, 127, **204**
   bǐjiào – comparison; relatively   **174**, 177
   bǐsài – competition, match   **197**, 201
bì – currency (see **rénmínbì**)   81
bì – must, surely (see **búbì**)   75
   bìyào – necessary   177

biān – edge, side; surname   101, 266
biàn (alt. pron. **pián**) – convenient (see **fāngbiàn, suíbiàn**)   81
    biànfàn – a simple meal, potluck   166, 169
biànlùn – to argue, debate   **175**, 177
biànxìfǎr – conjuror, juggler   204, 210
biāo – to label, mark   81
    biāomíng – to indicate clearly   81, 83
    biāoqiār – a label   128, 131
biǎo – outside; to show; chart; watch (see **dàibiǎo**)   45
bié – don't; to leave (see **tèbié**)   97
    biéchù – another place   **245**, 246
    biéde – other   121, 127, **190**
bīng – ice   198
    bīngchǎng – ice rink   201
    bīngqiú – ice hockey, puck   197, 201
bìng – together; (before a negative) by no means   **64**, 65
    bìngqiě – besides, moreover   121, 123
bìng – ill; sickness (see **kànbìng**)   215
bō – to turn; to dial   142, **149**, 150
bù – not (2nd tone before 4th)   33
    búbì – no need to   **74**, 76
    bú cuò – not bad [i.e., pretty good]   **214**, 218
    búdàn – not only   **183**, 185
    bù gǎndāng – not deserved; too kind   **64**, 67
    bùguǎn – regardless   **197**, 200
    búguò – however   **166**, 171
    bù hǎo-yìsi – embarrassing   **231**, 234
    búhuì – unable   **231**, 235
    bùrú – inferior to, not as good as   275
    búshì – is not; no   **32**, 34
    bùtóng – dissimilar   **55**, 56, 62
    bùxíng – unsatisfactory, unacceptable   **81**, 83
    bú xiàng – unlike   **64**, 65, 68
    bú yàojǐn – never mind; unimportant   **17**
    bùyídìng – uncertain   **137**, 139
    bú zài – not at home, not in   **152**, 153
bù – ministry; part, sector (see **gànbù, quánbù, wàijiāobù**)   122
    bùfen – part, section   **120**, 124
bù – step, pace (see **liúbù, sànbù**)   197

cā – to rub, wipe   **167**, 169
cái – wealth   **123**

cáiwù – financial affairs   **122**, 128
cái – just now, then only; talent   **142**, 145, **219**, 221
cài – vegetable; course, dish [of food]   161, **166**, 168, 171
   càidān[zi] – menu   93, **219**, 221
cān – to eat; extn.—fare, meal (see **xīcān**)   175
   cānjù – tableware   **174**, 177
cān – to take part in   190
   cānguān – to visit, to look around [a place]   **190**, 192
   cānjiā – to participate, to take part in   **197**, 200
cāochǎng – sportsground   **237**, 241
céng – layer, storey   114, **115**
cèsuǒ – toilet, washroom   **18**
chákàn – to observe, look over   **120**, 124
chá – tea (brewed ready for drinking)   162
   chádié – saucer   176
   cháwǎn – teacup   **174**
   cháyè – tea (dry goods)   162
chà – to differ from; fall short of   **74**, 76
   chàbuduō – almost, nearly   **97**, 99
chǎn – to produce   183
   chánpǐn – product   **183**, 185
cháng (alt. pron. zhǎng) – long; strong [point]   113
   Cháng'ānjiē – Chang'an Avenue   **112**, 113
   Chángchéng – the Great Wall   151
   Chángjiāng – the Yangtze River   151
   chángtú – long-distance   **149**, 151
cháng – often, ordinary; (see **fēicháng, píngcháng**)   168
cháng – to taste   168
chǎng – factory, works (see **gōngchǎng**)   190
chǎng – place to gather (see **cāochǎng, qiúchǎng, shìchǎng**)   198
chàng – to sing   238
   chànggē[r] – to sing songs   **237**, 240
chē – vehicle (see **huǒchē, qìchē, zìxíngchē**)   122
   chēpiào – ticket [bus or train]   134
   chēshēn – car body   250
chéng – city wall; extn.—city, town   95, 97
   chéngshì – town   **96**
chéng – order; procedure (see **gōngchéng**)   44
chéng – to become; extn.—result (see **fēnchéng**)   122
   chéng wèntí – be a problem   **183**, 185
chī – to eat   **74**, 75, 76
   chībǎo – to eat one's fill   166

chīfàn – to have a meal   76, 271
chóng – lofty, sublime, a surname   112
   Chóngwénmén – a street name in Beijing   111, 112, 113
chū – to come (or go) out; to appear, to produce   70
   chūfā – to start off, departure   69, 72
   chūqù – to go out   114, 115
   chūshēng – to be born   65
   chūshì – to meet with an accident   243, 245
   chūzū – to hire or lease [e.g., a taxi]   183, 185
chú – to eliminate; besides   138, 139
   chúle . . . yǐwài – apart from   138, 141
chúfáng – kitchen   174, 177
chǔfāng – prescription   219, 221
chù (alt. pron. chǔ) – place, office (see bànshìchù, biéchù)   101
chūn – spring   64, 65
   Chūnjié – Spring Festival, i.e., Chinese New Year   60, 64, 68
   chūntiān – springtime   64
cíqì – chinaware, porcelain   174, 177
cí – to take one's leave (see gàocí)   248
cóng – from; extn.—to follow   107, 109
   cónglái – at all times, from the start   71
cún – to accumulate, store (see bǎocún, zhùcún)   183
   cúnhuò – goods in stock   185
cuò – fault, wrong   214, 218

dá – to extend, to express (see liúdá)   205
dá – a dozen   86, 88
dǎ (alt. pron. dá) – to hit, strike; make   149
   dǎ bīngqiú – to play ice hockey   197, 201
   dǎ diànbào – to send a telegram   155, 158
   dǎ diànhuà – to make a phone call   149, 151
   dǎsuàn – to intend, reckon   249, 250
   dǎtīng – to make enquiries   229, 230
   dǎ xíngli – to pack luggage   183, 186
dà (alt. pron. dài) – big, great, major (see Jiānádà)   39
   dàbàn – the greater part; very likely, mostly   204, 210
   dà bùfen – the greater part   121, 125
   dàduōshū – the vast majority, the bulk   210
   dàgài – generally, probably   183, 185
   dà hòutiān – the day after tomorrow   63, 66
   dàjiā – everybody   204, 206
   dàjiē – main street, avenue   100, 102

dàshǐ – ambassador   225
dàshíguǎn – embassy   229
dàifu – doctor [of medicine], physician   214, 217
dài – generation; substitute, instead of, (see xiàndài)   45
   dàibiǎotuán – delegation, mission   44, 49
dài – belt; zone; to carry, bring (see xiédài)   130
dài – to entertain (see zhāodài)   123
dài – to put on, to wear   219, 219, 221
   dài yǎnjìng[r] – to wear glasses   219, 221
dān – single; bill, list (see jiǎndān, qīngdān, zhàngdān)   45
   dānwèi – unit   43, 44, 47, 118
   dānzi – list; form; bill   93
dānwù – to delay, hold up   223, 224
dānxīn – anxious, to be concerned, worried   69, 73
dàn – but, only (see búdàn)   183, 183
   dànshi – but, nevertheless   231, 235
dāng (alt. pron. dàng) – ought; suitable; deserve (see yīngdāng, tuǒdàng)   65
   dāngdì – local   149, 151
   dāngmiàn – in one's presence   90, 93
   dāngrán – certainly, of course   90, 93
dào – road; method (see zhīdào)   97, 227
   dàoqiàn – an apology   246
dào – to arrive, reach; up until   54, 55, 100, 102
   dàodǐ – after all, finally   232, 235
de – possessive particle   277
dé (alt. pron. děi) – to obtain; —able   101, 103
   déle – to be ready; satisfactory, O.K.   153, 154
dé – virtue, kindness   156
   Déguó – Germany   154, 157
děi – must, need to (see dé)   107, 110
dēng – to ascend, mount   130
   dēngjì – to register   137, 140
   dēngjīzhèng – boarding card   130, 133
děng – to wait   17, 114, 115
   děng yìhuěr – to wait a moment   167
   děngzhe – waiting   167, 173
dī – low   189, 190, 192
dǐ – bottom, base; below, (see dàodǐ)   232
   dǐxià – under, beneath   267
dì – Earth, place   45
   dìfang – place   44, 46
   dìtǎn – carpet   190, 192

dìzhǐ – address 99, 101
dì – ordinal prefix 23, 122
dìyī – first; foremost 23, 121
diǎn – dot, spot, [decimal] point; a little, suffix indicating comparative degree
(see yìdiǎr) 70
  diǎn cài – to choose courses from a menu 167, 171
  diǎnzhōng – o'clock 69, 74
diàn – shop, store (see bǎihuòdiàn, shūdiàn) 97
diàn – electricity, electric 150
  diànbào – telegram 155, 158
  diànhuà – telephone 18, 149, 151
  diànhuàfèi – call charge 149, 152
  diànmén – electric switch 143
  diànshì – television 197, 200
  diànyǐng – movies 204, 208
dìng – firm, fixed; extn.—to decide, order (see kěndìng, yídìng) 65
  dìngjià – fixed price 81, 83
diū – to mislay; to lose 218, 219, 220
dōng – East 81
  dōngběi – north-east 109
  dōngxi – thing 80, 81
dōng – winter 64
dǒng – to understand 204, 206, 210
dòng – to move, to touch (see yùndòng) 198
  dòngshēn – set out on a journey 249, 250
dōu – all; even 54, 56
duì – facing, opposite; towards; correct; concerning 33, 265
  duìbuqǐ – Excuse me; I'm sorry 17, 32, 35
  duìle – correct, right 121, 280
  duìmiàr – opposite side 268
duìhuàn – to convert, exchange 90, 90, 92
dùn – MW for a meal 166, 168
duō (alt. pron. duó) – many, more; how [many] 65
  duó dà – how great [e.g., in age] (see duō above) 66
  duōduō bǎozhòng – "Look after yourself" 244, 245
  duó jiǔ – how long for 63, 66
  duōshao – how much 80, 82, 87
  duōzhǒng duōyàng – varied 183, 185

èle – hungry 18
ér – son; diminutive suffix (see yòu'éryuán) 12, 259
  érnü – children 199

érqiě – but also   183, 185
èr – two   20, 22, 261
　èryuè – February   58

fā – to issue, deliver; start (see **chūfā**)   70
　fāshāo – to run a temperature   214, 218
　fāsōng – to relax   209
　fāxiàn – to discover   219, 221
　fāzuò – to have [effect, e.g., heart attack]   223, 224
fǎ – law, method (alt. pron. 2nd or 4th tone) (see **bànfǎ, zuòfǎ**)   175
　Fǎguó – France   96, 240
　fázi – method, way   217
fānyì – interpreter   18
fàn – cooked rice; a meal (see **chīfàn**)   75, 161
　fàndiàn – hotel   99, 108
　fànguǎn – restaurant   96, 99, 166, 169
　fàntái – dinner table   167, 172
　fàntīng – dining room   138, 219, 221
　fànwǎn – food bowl   174
　fànzhuōzi – dining table   172
fāng – square; place, (see **bǐfang, chúfāng, dìfang**)   45
　fāngbiàn – convenient   183, 185
fáng – house; room, a surname   139
　fángfèi – room hire or rental   137, 140
　fángjiān – a room   136, 138
　fángwū – buildings, houses   138
fǎng – to call on, visit (see **báifǎng**)   45
　fǎnghuá – to visit China (formal)   44, 48
　fǎngwèn – to interview, to visit   236, 238
fàng – to release; give way to, to put   56
　fàngjià – to have a holiday, or a day off   54, 60
　fàngxīn – be at ease; rest assured   223, 225
fēi – to fly   130
　fēijī – an aircraft   129, 132
　fēijīchǎng – airfield, airport   249, 250
　fēijīpiào – airline ticket   130, 133
fēicháng – special, unusual   166, 168, 170
fèi – fee, expenses, charge; cost; (see **diànhuàfèi, fángfèi, yóufèi**)   139
　fèi shì – to give [or take] a lot of trouble   140
　fèi xīn – thanks so much   142
fēn – to divide; a unit   75
　fēnchéng – to separate   120, 124

fēnzhōng – a minute [time]   76
fèn – share, portion; MW—copy (see **yuèfènpái**)   55
fēng – envelope; MW (see **xìnfēng**)   156
   [yì]fēng xìn – a MW letter   **154, 156**
fēng – wind; scenery (see **guāfēng**)   215
   fēngjǐng – landscape, scenery   182
   fēngshuǐ – geomancy   55
fǒuzé – otherwise, or else   **223, 224**
fū – man; husband (see **dàifu, gōngfu**)   183
   fūrén – madame   **249, 251**
fú – clothes; serve (see **shūfu, yīfu**)   142
   fúwùtái – reception desk   **229, 230**
fù – deputy, vice-; MW   91
   fù-jīnglǐ – deputy manager   **152, 153**
   fùshǔ – to countersign   **90, 91**
fùjìn – nearby   **229, 230**
fùzé – to be responsible for, in charge of   **218, 219, 220**

gāi – ought, should; deserve, owe (see **yīnggāi**)   **243, 244**
   gāisǐ – damned, wretched   **244, 245**
gài – approximate (see **dàgài**)   183
gān (alt. pron. **gàn**) – dry, empty   142
   gānbēi – "Bottoms up!", "Cheers!"   145
   gānjing – clean, neat and tidy   144
   gānxǐ – dry-clean   **142, 144**
gǎn – to catch up, overtake; hurry   169
   gǎnbàn – to expedite   **223, 225**
   gánjǐn – hastily   **223, 225**
   gǎnkuài – quickly   **167, 173**
gǎn – to dare, make bold; venture (see **bù gǎndāng**)   65
gǎn – to feel, sense; feeling   75
   gǎnjué – feeling, sensation   **74, 77**
   gǎnxiè – to be grateful   **232, 235**
gàn – to do, work; able, capable (see **gān**)   142
   gànbù – cadre, functionary   **43, 145**
   gànhuó – to work [manually]   **204, 206**
   gàn-ma – why?   **204, 206**
   gànshénme – what for?   **197, 198**
gāng – a short time ago   **120, 122, 124**
gāo – high, tall, a surname   **27, 238**
   gāoxìng – glad, happy; delighted   **237, 241**
gào – to announce, report, tell   38

gàocí – to take leave [of one's host]   **247, 248**
gàosu – to inform, tell   **38, 39**
gē – to sing; song (see **chànggē**)   **238**
gé – squares; patterns, structure (see **jiàgé**)   **81**
gè – piece, general MW   **38**
gè – each, every, various   **169**
   gèchù – everywhere   **204, 208**
   gèrén – everyone; oneself   **204, 206**
   gèwèi – everybody, each of you [formal]   **167, 173**
gěi – to give; to cause; for, to   **50, 51**
gēn – to follow; and, with   **44, 45, 47**
gēngchí – spoon   **174**
gōng – work; industry   **44**
   gōngchǎng – factory   **190, 191**
   gōngchéng – engineering   **44**
   gōngchéngshī – engineer   **44, 46**
   gōngfu – time [lapse]; leisure   **182, 184**
   gōngyè – industry   **45**
   gōngyèpǐn – industrial products   **191**
   gōngzuò – work   **46**
gōng – public; general; a surname   **56**
   gōnggòng – public   **204, 208**
   gōngshìbāo – briefcase   **129, 132**
   gōngsī – company, firm   **249, 250**
   gōngyuán – Anno Domini (A.D.)   **54, 62**
   gōngyuán – park, public gardens   **108, 111, 197, 199**
gòng – common, altogether (see **gōnggòng, yígòng**)   **130**
   gònghéguó – republic   **48**
gòu – enough; quite   **69, 70**
gùyì – to make a point of; deliberately   **237, 240**
guā – to scrape, shave   **215**
   guāfeng – to blow up a wind   **214, 215**
guān – to close; barrier; Customs, (see **hǎiguān**)   **56**
   guānxi – connection, consequence; relationship   **43, 55, 62**
   guānyu – concerning, with regard to   **120, 124**
guān – to look at, outlook (see **cānguān**)   **190**
guǎn – inn; hall; office (see **dàshíguǎn, fànguǎn**)   **97**
guǎn – pipe, tube; to manage   **123**
   guánlǐ – to supervise   **121, 126**
guàn – to be in the habit of (see **xíguàn**)   **176**
guàng – to ramble, stroll (see **yóuguàng**)   **206**
   guàng shìchǎng – to wander around a bazaar   **204, 209**

guīzé – regulations; rules [as for sports] **122**, 128
guì – costly, dear; valuable; honorable 29, **80**, 83
    guìxìng – what is your surname? **28**, 30, 32
    guìzhòng – precious, valuable **145**, 146
guì – cupboard, cabinet (see **báoxiǎnguì**) 146
guō – [cooking] pot, "wok" (see **huǒguō**) 168, 174
guó – nation, a surname (see **wàiguorén**) 56
    guógē[r] – national anthem 240
    guójì – international **100**, 102
    guónèi – home [affairs], internal 101
    guóqìng[jié] – national [day] celebration **54**, 60
    guówài – abroad, overseas **155**, 157
    guóyǔ – national language [i.e., Mandarin] 4, 101
guǒ – fruit; consequence (see **rúguǒ**) 215
guò – to cross, pass; part, after; exceed 39
    guòzhòng – overweight **129**, 132

hái (alt. pron. **huán**) – still, yet; even more 39
    háishi – or; still **243**, 245
háizi – child **236**, 239
hǎi – sea; lake; a surname (see **Běihǎi**) 109
    hǎiguān – Customs **129**, 132
háng (alt. pron. **xíng**) – series, business firm; trade (see **yínháng**) 97
háng – boat; to navigate 156
    hángkōng – aviation **154**, 157
hǎo – good; so that; indicates completion of action **32**, **33**, **34**
    hǎochī – delicious **166**, 170
    hǎo-jíle – extremely good; great! **231**, 234, 275
    hǎokàn – attractive 170
    hǎowár – amusing, fun 170, **237**, 241
    hǎoxīn – good intentions; kindness **175**, 178
hào – number, date 55
    hàomǎ – number, figure 61
hēzú – to drink sufficiently 166
hé – gentle; and (see **xiéhé**) 223
hé – to close; combine 232
    hétong – contract **231**, 233
    hézuò – to cooperate **231**, 233
hè – to congratulate; a surname (see **zhùhè**) 65
hēi – black; (abbreviation for **Hēilóngjiāng**) 181
    hēitiān – night-time 57, 74
hěn – very; quite 34, 271

hén hǎo – very good   **32**
hòu – behind; after   **64**, **266**
    hòutiān – day after tomorrow   **63**, **66**
    hòubiar – behind, the rear   **267**
hòu – to wait; to ask after (see **qìhòu, shíhou, wènhòu**)   **69**
hútòng – alley, lane   **111**
hù – to protect   **91**
    hùzhào – passport   **90**, **93**
hù – door; household (see **yònghù**)   **156**
hùxiāng – mutual, each other   **231**, **235**
huādiāo – a yellow wine popular in China   **165**
huá – China (literary form); Sino-   **45**
    Huáběi – North China   **110**
    Huáqiáo – overseas Chinese   **95**
huà – spoken words, speech (see **diànhuà, liúhuà**)   **86**
huà – to plan (see **jìhuà**)   **123**
huà – to change, transform; [i.e., suffix "-ize"]   **139**
    huàxuéjiā – chemist   **47**
huà – to paint; picture   **198**, **202**
    huàbào – illustrated periodical   **202**
    huà huàr – to paint pictures   **202**
    huàjiā – an artist   **202**
    huàjuǎn – a pictorial scroll   **202**
    huàkān – pictorial magazine   **197**, **202**
    huàtú – picture   **202**
huān – glad, joyful (see **xǐhuan**)   **115**
    huānyíng – to welcome   **114**, **116**
huán – to return; to repay (see **hái**)   **90**
    huán zhàng – to pay an account   **89**, **91**
huàn – to exchange, change (see **duìhuàn**)   **90**
    huànhuàn nǎojīn – change of topic or scene   **204**, **207**
    huàn jùhuà shuō – in other words   **204**, **207**
huáng – yellow; a surname   **32**, **34**
    Huánghé – Yellow River   **110**
huí – to return; turn   **142**
    huíguó – to return to one's country   **223**, **225**
    huíjiā – to return home   **243**, **244**
    Huíjiào – Islamism   **166**, **169**, **242**
    huítóu – later, shortly   **175**
huì – to meet, assembly; [to be] able, opportunity (see **jīhuì, yànhuì, zàihuì**)   **115**
hūn – to marry (see **jiéhūn**)   **64**

huó – alive; movable; work (see **gànhuó**) 204
huǒ – meals; companion (see **jiāhuo**) 139
  huǒbàn – partner 231, 233
  huǒshi – food, meals 138, 141
huǒ – fire 168
  huǒchē – train 125
  huǒchēpiào – railway ticket 125
  huǒchētóu – locomotive 125
  huǒguò – fire-pot 166, 170, 171
huò – goods (see **bǎihuòdiàn**) 97
  huòwù – merchandise, goods 183, 185
  huòzhě – either, maybe, perhaps 121, 127

jī – machine; chance (see **fēijī, xiàngjī**) 130
  jīhui – chance, opportunity 237, 239, **247**, 248
  jīshēn – aircraft fuselage 250
jí – extreme (see **tàijíquán**) 168
jí – anxious; urgent (see **zháojí**) 215
  jíshì – an urgent matter, emergency **222**, 224
jǐ – how many, [QW]; several 75
  jǐdiǎn[zhōng] – what time 74, 75
  jǐge – how many; a few 86, 87
  jǐhào – what date, what number 54, 56
  jǐkuàiqián – how much [money] 86, 87
  jǐ tiān – how many days; a few days 137
jǐ – one's own, personal (see **zìjǐ**) 130
jì – boundary (see **guójì**) 101
jì – to record; era (see **jīngjìrén**) 65
  jìniànrì – anniversary 63, 66
jì – season, a surname (see **sìjì**) 64
jì – to fasten, to tie 130
  jìshang – to tie up **129**, 131
jì – to calculate; idea 123
  jìhuà – plan 121, 126
jì – to entrust, to mail 156
  jìxìn – to mail a letter **154**, 157
jì – to remember; to register (see **dēngjì, wàngjì**) 139
  jìzhù – to bear in mind **218**, 220
jìshì – as; now that **229**, 230
jiā – to add, to augment, to increase (see **cānjiā**) 39
  Jiānádà – Canada 38, 39
  jiā yóu – "Press on!" **253**

jiā – family; home; specialist (see **rénjia, shíyèjiā zhuānjiā**)   45
   jiāfàn – home cooking   163, 164, 173
   jiāhuo – implements   **174**, 177
   jiājù – furniture   **190**, 193
jiǎrú – if, supposing; false (see **jià**)   **236**, 238
jià – price (see **dìngjià, jiǎngjià**)   81
   jiàgé – price   81, 83
   jiàqián – price   81, 83
jià (alt. pron. **jiǎ**) – holiday; (see **fàngjià**)   56
jià – harness; to drive (see **láojià**)   142
jiān – between; room; MW (see **fángjiān, shíjiān**)   139
jiǎn – simple; brief; to select   175
   jiǎndān – simple, uncomplicated   **174**, 176
jiàn – to see; to meet (see **yìjiàn, zàijiàn**)   39
jiàn – common MW for numerous items (see **tiáojiàn**)   130
jiàn – to recommend (see **tuījiàn**)   123
jiànkāng – good health, healthy   251
jiānglái – before long, in [the] future   **249**, 250
jiǎng – to speak, to tell; to discuss   81
   jiǎngjià – to bargain, to haggle over a price   **81**, 83
jiāo – to hand over; relationship (see **shuāijiāo**)   142
   jiāogěi – to deliver, to put into one's hand   **141**, 144
jiāojuǎr – film, a roll of film   237, 240
jiǎozi – dumplings   161, **174**
jiào – to call; to cause, to let   **29**, 29, 281
jiào – to teach; religion (see **zhǐjiào**)   50
   jiàohuì – Christianity   230
   jiàoshī – teacher   **237**, 240
   jiàoshì – classroom   **237**, 240
   jiàoshòu – professor   **49**, 51
   jiàotáng – church   230
   jiàoyù – education   51
jiào – to compare; fairly, rather (see **bǐjiào**)   176
jiē – street (see **dàjiē**)   101
   jiēdào – road, street   111
jiē – to connect, to receive (see **zhíjiē**)   150
   jiēdài dānwèi – host organization   43
   jiēxiàn – to make a [telephone] connection   **153**, 154
jié – festival (see **guóqìngjié**)   56
   jiérì – holiday   **54**, 60
jiéhūn – to marry   **63**, 66
jiě – elder sister (see **xiáojiě**)   34

jièshào – to introduce, to recommend 38, 41
jiè – to borrow; to lend 156, 158
   jiè jīhuì – to take the opportunity, opportune 231, 233
   jièyòng – to have the use of 155, 158
jīn – present day 55
   jīnnián – this year 62
   jīntiān – today 54, 56
jīn – muscle (see nǎojīn) 205
jǐn – tight; urgent (see gánjǐn, yàojǐn) 64
jìn – near (see fùjìn) 97, 97, 99
jìn – to advance, to enter 223
   jìnrù – to get into 223, 224
jīng – capital [of a country] (see Běijīng) 109
   jīngcài – Beijing dishes; northern cooking 163
   jīngxì – Beijing opera 204, 209
jīng – to manage; to deal in (see yǐjīng) 142
   jīngjìrén – agent, broker 189, 192
   jīnglǐ – manager 152, 153
jǐng – scenery, view; a surname (see fēngjǐng) 109
   jǐngshān – Prospect Hill [in Beijing] 105, 108, 111
   jǐngtàilán – cloisonné 187, 189, 191
jìng – mirror; lens (see yǎnjìng) 219, 219
   jìngtóu – lens 219, 221
jiǔ – nine 20, 55
   jiǔyuè – September 54
jiǔ – for a long time 33, 63, 65
jiǔ – wine; any alcoholic drink 167, 168
   jiǔbēi – wine cup, wine glass 174
   jiǔ-cài – food and drink 167, 172
jiù – at once; only; then 32, 34, 35, 58, 280
   jiùshi – simply, truly 112, 280
jú – office, bureau (see yóujú) 97
jù – sentence; MW 86
jù – implement, tool (see cānjù, jiājù) 175
jù – drama, play (see xìjù) 206
   jùyuàn – theatre 204, 209
juǎn – to roll up; a roll; MW (see jiāojuǎr) 238
jué – to feel, sense; be aware (see gǎnjué) 75

kāi – to open; to begin, to start or to drive 90
   kāifàn – to serve a meal 175, 178
   kāiliè – to make a list 145, 146

kāizhàng – to make out a bill　91
kān – to publish (see **huàkān**)　198
kàn – to look at, to see; to consider (see **chákàn**)　56
　　kànbào – to read a newspaper　202
　　kànbìng – to see a doctor　214, 217
　　kàndejiàn – can be seen, visible　100, 103
　　kànshū – to read a book　202
　　kànyikàn – to take a look at　96, 98
kǎolǜ – to consider　120, 124
kào – to depend, to lean on (see **kěkào**)　183
kēxuéjiā – scientist　47
kě – can, may; "-able"　109
　　kěbushì-me – "So it is", "That's right!"　54, 60
　　kěkào – dependable, reliable　183, 185
　　kěnéng – possible　137, 139
　　kěshi – but, however　63, 66, 86, 88, 149
　　kěxī – a pity　214, 216
　　kéyǐ – can, may　108, 111, 149, 272
kěle – thirsty　18
kè – guest, visitor　65
　　kèqi – polite　64, 68
　　kèrén – guest　167
kè – to carve; a quarter of an hour (see **líkè**)　70
kěn – to consent; be willing (see **nìngkěn**)　65
　　kěndìng – definitely　63, 67
kōng (alt. pron. **kòng**) – empty; sky; (see **hángkōng**)　156, 167
　　kōngyóu – air mail　154, 157
kǒngpà – [I'm] afraid, uncertain　69, 72
kòng[r] – [empty] space [see **kōng**], (see **xiánkòng**)　167, 172
kǒu – mouth; entrance; MW (see **lùkǒu, ménkǒu, wèikǒu**)　101
kuài – piece; dollar (see **yikuàr**)　45
kuài – quick; sharp; pleased　101
　　kuàile – cheerful, happy　251
kuàizi – chopsticks　174

lái – to come　38, 39, 40, 41
　　láixìn – incoming mail　249, 251
lán – blue, a surname (see **jǐngtàilán**)　190
lǎn – to view (see **yóulǎn, zhánlǎn**)　101
láojià – excuse me!　141, 142
lǎo – old; of long standing　50
　　láobǎixìng – name for Chinese folk　27

lǎoshī – teacher, tutor   **50, 51**
-le (alt. pron. **liǎo**) – perfective particle   55, 279
lè – to laugh; happy (see **kuàilè, yúlè**)   198
lèi – tired; to toil   18, 74, 75, 77
lěng – cold   142
   lěngqì – air conditioning   141, 143
lí – to part from; without   97
lǐ – plum, a surname (see **xíngli**)   39
lǐ – inside; lining   146, 266
   lǐbiar – inside   167, 172, 266
lǐ – to regulate (see **guánlǐ, jīnglǐ**)   123
lǐ – ceremony; gift   183
   lǐbài – to worship   **229, 230**
   lǐwù – a present   182, 184
lì – to establish; vertical; immediate   115
   lìkè – at once, immediately   114, 116
lì – calendar (see **yánglì, yīnlì**)   56
lì – benefit; profit (see **shùnlì**)   123
lián – link, even   123
liáng (alt. pron. **liàng**) – to measure (see **shāngliàng**)   184
liáng – cool (see **zháoliáng**)   143
liǎng – two, both   39, 40, 261
liàng – capacity, quantity (see **zhìliàng**)   184, 185
liàng – to forgive (see **yuánliàng**)   247, 248
liǎo – to complete; to understand (see -le above)   **69**, 73, 279
liè – to line up; MW (see **kāiliè**)   146
líng – zero   81
   língmài – to retail   **81**, 83
   língqián – loose change   92
   língshòushāng – retailer   **189**, 191
lǐng – collar (see **zháolǐng**)   219
lìng – other, besides   130
   lìngwài – in addition   **129**, 132
liūda – to go for a stroll   **204**, 208
liú – a surname   33
liú – to remain; to detain (see **suǒliú**)   146
   liúbù – "Don't see me out"   **247**, 248
   liú huà – to leave word   **153**, 154
liù – six   **20**
lóu – a storied building   100, 101, 103, **114**, 115
lù – road; journey   101
   lùkǒu – intersection; street corner   **100**, 103

lùyīn[jī] – sound recording   **237, 240**
lǚ – to travel   90
   lǚguǎn – hotel   **97**, 99
   lǚtú – a journey   251
   lǚxíng – to travel, journey   **89,** 91
   lǚxíngshè – travel agency   **96,** 98
   lǚxíng-zhīpiào – travelers' cheques   **89,** 91
   lǚxíng-zhǔnbèi – travel arrangements   **121,** 125
lǜ – to consider, to ponder (see **kǎolǜ**)   122
lùn – to talk about, discourse (see **biànlùn**)   176

ma – interrogative particle   264
máfan – to bother; troublesome   **100,** 103
mǎ – number; MW (see **hàomǎ**)   56
mǎxì – a circus   **204, 210**
mǎi – to buy   86
   mǎimai – business   88
mài – to sell   81
mǎnyì – contented, pleased   241
màn – slow   244
   mànzǒu – "take care"   **243,** 244
máng – busy, hurry (see **bāngmáng**)   **69,** 69, 70
   máng shénme – "What's the hurry?"   **69,** 70
máo – dime; hair; a surname   81
   máobǐ – a [writing] brush   **86, 87,** 88
méi – not [before **yǒu** – have not]   39, 92
   méi fázi – "It can't be helped"   217
   méi guānxi – "Never mind"   17, **246**
   méi nèi huíshì – "Nothing of the sort"   **174,** 176
   méiyǒu – there isn't, haven't   **38,** 40, 92
měi – beautiful   91
   Měiguó – U.S.A.   92
   měiyuán – U.S. dollar   **90,** 92
meìmei – younger sister   **223, 225**
mén – door; switch, a surname   112
   ménkǒu – doorway, entrance   **246, 246**
-men – plural suffix   39
mìshū – a secretary   **153,** 154
miàn – face; side   91
mín – people (see **nànmín, rénmínbì**)   81
míng – name, fame   29
   míngpiàn – calling card   **29,** 31

míngzi – [given] name   29, 31
míng – bright; to understand; surname (see **shuōmíng**)   75
   míngtiān – tomorrow   74, 75
mú – tree, wood, a surname   49, 50

ná – to take hold (see **Jiānádà**)   39
nǎ[r] – where [QW] (see also **něi**)   44, 263
nà (alt. pron. **nèi**) – that, then   260, 261
   nàme – like that, in that case   54, 100
   nà[r] – there   97, 99, 268
   nàxiē – those   261
nán – male   198
   nán háizi – a boy   239
nán – South, a surname   108, 113
   nánbiar – south side   108, 111
nán (alt. pron. **nàn**) – difficult, unpleasant   214
   nánguò – to feel badly   249, 250
   nánshòu – to feel uncomfortable, to feel pain   214, 215
nàn – calamity (see **nán**)   214
   nànmín – refugees   215
nǎojīn – brains; mind; way of thinking   204, 207
nàoshì – downtown (see **rènào**)   95
ne – interrogative or exclamatory particle   30, 32
něi (alt. pron. **nǎ**) – what, which [QW]   263
nèi – that [one] (see **nà**)   38
   nèige – that one (abbreviation of **nà yíge**)   38, 39
nèi – inner, within   150
   nèiháng – "insider", experienced person   189
   nèixiàn – inside [telephone] line   149, 150
néng – to be able; capacity   130, 271
nǐ – you [singular]   29, 30, 31, 43, 44, **149**, **152**, 260
   nǐ hǎo – hello   16
   nǐmen – you [plural]   40, 50, 155
nián – year; harvest; a surname   56, 63, **107**
   niánjì – age   **197**, 200
niàn – to study; think of (see **jìniàn**)   65
nín – you (formal or polite form of **nǐ**)   28, **32**, 260
nìngkěn – would rather   204, 210
nóngmín – peasantry, farmers   254
nǚ – female, woman   198
   nǚ háizi – a girl   239
   nǚshì – Miss, Ms.   35

pà – dread, fear (see **kǒngpà**)   70
pāi – to snap [a photograph]   238
pái – tablet, card (see **yuèfènpái**)   56
pái – to arrange; to exclude (see **ānpai**)   122
 páiqiú – volleyball   197, 201
pànwàng – to hope for   237, 239
péi – to accompany; to take care of (see **quánpéi, shīpéi**)   183, 184
péngyou – friend   38, 41, 42
pí – skin; hide, leather   130
 píbāo – small bag; travel bag   129, 131
 píer – dough skin [dumplings]   174
piányi – inexpensive   81, 83
piàn – a thin slice; MW (see **míngpiàn, zhàopiàn**)   29
piào – ticket, note (see **chēpiào, fēijīpiào, xínglipiào**)   90
pīnyīn – transcription; to spell   8, 9, 14, 15
pǐn – article; product (see **chánpǐn, gōngyèpǐn, shāngpǐn, wùpǐn**)   146
píng – flat, calm   156
 píng'ān – peaceful   251
 píngcháng – ordinary, usually   219
 píngyóu – surface mail   154, 157
píngzi – a bottle   175, 177
píng – a screen (see **wéipíng**)   190
pǔtōnghuà – Chinese vernacular [i.e., Mandarin]   4, 14, 15, 16, 20

qī – seven   20, 22, 55
 qīdiǎn – seven o'clock   74, 76
qī – period of time, phrase; to expect (see **xīngqī**)   55
qí tā – apart from [which], besides, other   122, 128
qí – to ride [on a saddle]   206
 qí zìxíngchē – to ride a bike   204, 208
qǐ – to rise; to begin   34
 qǐlái – to get up, to stand up, to rise   74, 75
qì – air, gas; weather; (see **kèqi, lěngqì, tiānqì**)   65
 qìhòu – climate   238
 qìxiàngxué – meteorology   238
qì – steam, vapour   183
 qìchē – motor car   124, 183, 185
 qìyóu – gasoline   253
qì – implement, utensil (see **cíqì**)   175
qiàhǎo – luckily   221
qiān – thousand   21, 261
qiān – to sign (see **biāoqiār**)   91

qiānding – to sign a contract   231, 232
qiānmíng – to autograph   90, 93
qiānzhèng – visa   121, 127
qiānzì – to sign one's name   90, 94
qián – ahead, [in] front   50, 266
  qiántiān – day before yesterday   57
  qiánbiar – in front   267
qián – cash; money (see jiàqian, xiànqián)   18, 81
qiàn – apology (see bàoqiàn, dàoqiàn)   246
qiě – while (see bìngqiě)   123
qiè – to correspond to (see yíqiè)   123
qīnrén – relative   223, 225
qīng – clear; clarified; distinct   105, 122
  qīngdān – inventory, itemized list   120, 124
  qíngxing – circumstances, situation   120, 124
qǐng – to invite, request; please   29, 30
  qǐngjìn – do come in   17
  qǐngtie – invitation   231, 235
  qǐngwèn – may I ask; please tell me   18, 28
  qǐngzuò – please be seated   17
qìng – to celebrate, congratulate (see guóqìng)   56
  qìngzhù – to celebrate   63, 67, 231, 233
qiū – autumn   64
qiú – ball, sphere (see bīngqiú, páiqiú)   198
  qiúchǎng – games field, ball ground   197, 200
qiú – to beg, to request (see yāoqiú)   238
qú – area (see shāngyèqú)   97
qǔ – to obtain   190
  qǔxiāo – to cancel, to eliminate   189, 192
qù – interest, delight (see xìngqu)   190
qù – to go [away], to leave   97
  qùnián – last year   59
quán – complete, whole (see ānquán)   130
  quánbù – entire   137, 140
  quánpéi – national guide   80, 118, 184
quán – fist (see tàijíquán)   198

rán – so (see dāngrán)   91
ràng – to allow, to give way   238, 281
rè – heat, hot; popular   64
  rènào – active, bustling, lively   63, 65
rén – person; mankind (see nánrén, nǚrén)   38

rénjia – people   153, 154
rénmínbì – RMB currency   79, 81, 83
rèn – to admit   38
   rènshì – to recognize   38, 39
   rènwéi – to consider, deem   174, 176
rì – sun; day (see shēngrì; xīngqīrì)   56
   rìbào – daily newspaper   197, 201
   rìqī – date   65
   rìzi – a day   63, 67
ròu – meat, flesh (see yángròu)   168
rú – if, as if, such as (see jiǎrú)   215
   rúguǒ – in case   214, 217
rù – to enter (see jìnrù)   223

sài – competition, contest; game (see bǐsài)   198
sān – three   20
   sānkè[zhōng] – three quarters of an hour   71
   sānyuè – March   23
sàn – to disperse; to scatter (see sòngsàn)   197
   sànbù – to take a stroll   197, 199
sǎngzi – throat   214, 215
shān – hill, mountain (see jǐngshān)   109
   Shāndōng – Shandong [Province]   192
shāng – business, commerce   97
   shāngchǎng – shopping mall   205
   shāngdiàn – shop, store   180
   shāngliang – to discuss   214, 218
   shāngpǐn – merchandise   191
   shāngyè – business, commerce, industry   98
   shāngyèqū – business district, downtown   95
shàng – to ascend, to climb   75, 266
   shàngjiē – to go shopping   182, 184
   shàngbian – on top   266, 267
   shàngwǔ – morning; A.M.   73
shāo – to burn (see fāshāo)   215
   shāoxiāng – burn incense [before an idol]   230
shǎo – few, less, little   81
shào – to continue (see jièshào)   39
   shàoxīng [jiǔ] – a well-known yellow wine   177
shè – agency; society (see lǚxíngshè)   97
shè – to establish   123
   shèbèi – equipment, facilities   137, 140

shéi (alt. pron. **shúi**) – who, someone 38
shēn – to declare, to express 91
    shēnbàodān – declaration form **90**, 93
    shēnqǐng – to apply for **121**, 126
shēn – body, one's person (see **dòngshēn**) 215, 234
    shēntǐ – body; health 214, 217
shén – what? 263
    shénme – any; what, whatever 29, 31, 263
    shénmede – and so on **129**, 132
shēng – to give birth to; (see **chūshēng, weìshēng, xiānsheng, xuésheng**) 33
    shēngrì – birthday **63**, 65
shěng – to economize; province 196
    shěngqián – to save money **189**, 192
shèngxià – [to be] left over, remain **232**, 235
shī – teacher, master (see **jiàoshī, lǎoshī**) 44
shī – to fail, to lose 219
    shīpéi – to excuse oneself **245**, 246
    shīwù – lost property 218, 220
shí – to know; knowledge (see **rènshi**) 39
shí – fast; truth 45
    shíyè – industry **45**, 47
    shíyèjiā – industrialist **44**, 47
    shízài – honestly, truly **245**, 246
shí – ten **20**, 21, 22, 55
    shíyuè-fèn – the month of October **54**, 59
shí – time; days 69
    shíhou – [duration of] time **69**, 69, 70
    shíjiān – [concept of] time 70
shí – to eat; food (see **huǒshi**) 139
shǐ – to send; envoy (see **dàshǐ, dàshíguǎn**) 223
shì – to be; correct; used to indicate affirmative 30
shì – market; municipality, town 39
    shìchǎng – bazaar, market **204**, 205, 209
    shìzhǎng – mayor **38**, 40
    shìzhèng – municipal **44**, 46
    shìzhèng gōngchéng – municipal works **44**
    shìzhōngxīn – town center 95
shì – affair, matter; work (see **chūshì**) 45
    shìqing – happening, matter 176
    shìwùsuǒ – general office 103
shì – room (see **bàngōngshì, yùshì**) 139
shì – to test, to try 169

shì – to adorn; decorations (see **zhuāngshì**)   190
shì – to look at, to watch (see **diànshì**)   198, 200
shōu – to receive   146
   shōutiáo – a receipt   **145**, 146
   shōuyīnji – radio [set]   **197**, 201, 274
shǒu – hand   130
   shǒutíxiāng – suitcase   **129**, 131
   shǒuxù – procedure   **129**, 133
   shǒuyì – handicraft   **167**, 172
shǒuxiān – in the first place, firstly   **174**, 177
shòu – to confer; to teach (see **jiàoshòu**)   50
shòu – to sell (see **língshòushāng**)   190
shòu – to receive; to endure (see **nánshòu**)   214
shū – to write; a book (see **mìshū**)   101
   shūdiàn – a bookstore   **100**, 102
shūfu – comfortable, to be well   **214**, 215
shǔ – to sign (see **fùshǔ**)   91
shǔ – category   45
   shǔyú – to belong to   **44**, 47
shǔ (alt. pron. **shù**) – to count   56
shù – figure, number (see **shǔ**)   56
   shùzi – digit, numeral   **54**, 61
shuǎ – to play, to put on an act (see **wánshuǎ, záshuǎ**)   206
shuāijiāo – to wrestle   **204**, 210
shuàn – to dip [as with fondue]   168
shuǐ – water (see **fēngshuǐ**)   143
   shuǐbǐ – pen   87
   shuǐjiǎor – steamed dumplings   174
shùn – along with   123
   shùnfēng – a tail wind   **249**, 251
   shùnlì – success, successfully   **122**, 128
shuō – to speak, to talk; say, explain   153
   shuōhuà – to speak, to talk   **152**, 153
   shuōmíng – to explain; instructions   **138**, 140
sī – to manage; department; a surname (see **gōngsī**)   249
sǐ – to die; fixed (see **gāisǐ**)   244
sì – thought (see **yìsi**)   206
sì – four   **20**
   sìjì – the four seasons, the year round   64
   sìyuè – April   58
sōng – pine; loose, slack (see **fàsōng**)   206
   sōngsan – to relax   **204**, 209

sòng – to deliver, to give, to send   142
   sònggěi – to bestow, to give   237, 241
   sònghuí – to send back   141, 144
   sòngxíng – to send off [on a journey]   249, 250
sù – to inform, to tell (see **gàosu**)   38
suàn – to calculate, to reckon   81
   suànzhàng – to make out a bill, to settle
   an account   91
suíbiàn – casual, informal; at will   89, 90, 92
suì – year [of age]   66
   suìshù – age   66
sūn – grandson; a surname   198
   sūnnü – granddaughter   199
   sūnzi – grandson   197, 199
suǒ – place, MW; where (see **cèsuǒ, shìwùsuǒ**)   146
   suǒliú – [those] left   145, 146
   suóyǐ – so, therefore   124, 219
   suóyǒu – all   122, 128

tā – he, she, it   260
   tā-de – his, hers, its   260
   tāmen – them, they   121
   tāmen-de – their, theirs   260
tái – platform, stage; table (see **fàntái, fúwùtái**)   169
tài – extremely, greatest; too   34
   tàijíquán – T'ai Chi   197, 200, 277
   Tàitai – Mrs., Madam   32, 34
   tàiyángjìng – sunglasses   219, 221
tài – peaceful (see **jǐngtàilán**)   190
tán – to chat, to discuss   248
tǎn – blanket, rug (see **dìtǎn**)   190
tángrénjiē – Chinatown   95
táng – auditorium, hall (see **jiàotáng**)   229
tāo yāobāo – to pay the bill, to pick up the tab   232, 235
tè – specially; unusual   97
   tèbié – special   96, 98, 121
téng – ache, pain   214, 214, 215
tí – topic (see **wèntí**)   90
tí – to carry; to mention   130
   tíchū – to put forward   231, 233
   tíxiāng – suitcase[s]   131
tǐ – body   50

tǐyù – physical culture   **49, 51**
tì – to replace; on behalf of   123
tiān – sky; day (see **hòutiān, jīntiān, míngtiān**)   55
    Tiānānmén – Gate of Heavenly Peace   113
    tiānqì – weather   **197,** 198
    Tiāntán – Temple of Heaven   105
tiāoxuǎn – to pick out, to select   **155,** 158
tiáo – item, MW (see **shōutiáo**)   101
    tiáojiàn – condition, requirement   **121,** 127
tiē – to stick on; to attach   **130,** 130, 133
tiě – invitation card (see **qǐngtie**)   232
tīng – to listen   **152,** 153
    tīngshuō – to hear of   **166,** 169
    tīngxì – to go to the theatre   **204,** 208
tīng – hall (see **fàntīng**)   219
tōng – open, through, communicate   150
    tōngxìn – to correspond   **249,** 150
    tōngzhī – to notify   **149,** 152
tóng – same, together (see **hétong**)   56
    tóngshí – at the same time, meanwhile   **249,** 251
    tóngyì – to agree, consent   **190,** 193
tóu – head, MW   70
    tóuténg – headache   **214,** 215
tú – road, route (see **chángtú, lùtú**)   150
tú – map, picture; plan   190
    tú'àn – design, pattern   **190,** 193
    túxiàng – image   158
tuán – group, organization (see **dàibiǎotuán**)   45
tuī – to push, shove   123
    tuījiàn – to recommend   **121,** 127
tuǒdàng – appropriate, suitable   **123,** 127

wài – outside; foreign (see **guówài, lìngwài**)   111, 112, 266
    wàibiar – outside   **243,** 244
    wàiguórén – foreigner[s]   96
    Wàijiāobù – Foreign Affairs Bureau   121
    Wàishìbàn – External Affairs Office   **121,** 126
    wàixiàn – outside [telephone] line   **149**
wán – to complete; whole   150
    wánquán – entirely   **167,** 172
wán – to play, to have fun (see **hǎowár, yóuwán**)   198
    wánshuǎ – to play   **237,** 241

wárwar – to play 199
wǎn – evening; late 69, 70, 73
   wǎnfàn – evening meal 76
   wǎnshang – evening 73
wǎn – bowl (see **cháwǎn, fànwǎn**) 176
wáng – king; a surname 32
wǎngqiúchǎng – tennis court 201
wàng – towards 109
wàng – to expect, to hope for (see **pànwàng, xīwàng**) 232
wàng – to forget; to neglect, to overlook 219
   wàngjì – to forget, to overlook 218, 220
wéi (alt. pron. **wèi**) – to serve as (see **rènwéi, yǐwěi**) 176
wéipíng – a folding screen 190, 193
wèi – because of (see **yīnwei**) 75
   wèishénme – why 54, 263
wèi – place; position, MW (see **dānwèi, zuòwèi**) 39
   wèizi – a seat, place [at table] 167, 172
wèishēng – health, hygiene 121, 127
wèikǒu – appetite 214, 218
wén – language, culture 29, 112
   wénjiàn – documents 121, 127
wèn – to ask, to enquire 29
   wènhǎo – to be remembered 247
   wènhòu – to extend greetings 246, 247
   wèntí – problem, question 89, 92
wǒ – I, me 28, 260
   wǒ-de – my 29, 260
   wǒmen – us, we 260
   wǒmen-de – our, ours 42, 260
wǔ – noon (see **shàngwǔ, xiàwǔ, zhōngwǔ**) 70
   wǔfàn – midday meal 76
wǔ – five 20
wù – affair, business (see **cáiwù, fúwùtái, shìwùsuǒ**) 123
wù – matter, thing (see **shīwù**) 146
   wùjiàn – items 145, 146
   wùpǐn – articles, goods 145, 146
wù – error (see **dānwù**) 223

xī – west 81, 108
xī – breath; rest (see **xiūxi**) 56
xīwàng – to hope, to wish for 232, 235, 236
xī – to pity (see **kěxī**) 215

xíguàn – custom, habit   175, 177
xǐhuan – to like   155, 157
xǐ – to wash (see gānxǐ)   142
   xǐyīfáng – a laundry   141, 144
   xǐzǎofáng – bathroom   138
xì – system (see guānxi)   56
xì – a drama, a show (see biànxìfǎr, jīngxì, tīngxì)   206
   xìjù – drama, play   209
xià – below; to descend   51, 245, 266, 267
   xiàlóu – to come downstairs   115
   xiàwǔ – afternoon, P.M.   73
   xiàxuě – to snow   243, 245
   xiàyǔ – to rain   245
xià – summer; a surname   64
xiān – earlier, first (see shǒuxiān)   33
   xiānsheng – Mr.; gentleman; husband; teacher   31, 34
xián – idle; leisure   197
   xiánkòng – leisure [time]   197, 198
   xiánshū – light reading   197, 202
xiǎn – danger, risk (see báoxiǎn)   146
xiàn – existing, present (see fāxiàn)   69
   xiàndài – modern [times]   137, 140
   xiànqián – cash   89, 92
   xiànzài – at present, now   69, 70
xiàn – thread, wire (see nèixiàn, wáixiàn)   150
xiāng (alt. pron. xiàng) – mutually (see hùxiāng)   235
xiāng – box, case; (see báoxiǎnxiāng, shǒutíxiāng)   130
xiǎng – to intend, think; consider   86, 86
xiàng – appearance; extn.—photograph (see xiāng)   130
   xiàngjī – camera (see also zhàoxiàngjī)   132, 237, 239
xiàng – towards; a surname   249, 251
xiàng – image; to resemble; like   64, 68
xiāo – to vanish; extn.—to remove (see qǔxiāo)   190
xiǎo – little, small; young   34
   xiǎohár – young children   240
   xiáojiě – Miss; young lady   32, 34
   xiǎoshí – one hour   69, 73
   xiǎoshuō[r] – a novel   202
xiē – a few, little (see yìxiē, zhèxiē)   97, 263
xiédài – to carry, take along   129, 130, 132
Xiéhé yīyuàn – P.U.M.C.   222, 223, 224
xiě – to write   100

xiěxìn – to write a letter **219**, 221
xiè – to thank (see **gǎnxiè**) 34
  xièxie – thanks! **17**, **33**, **35**
xīn – heart; mind, centre 70
  xīnzàng – the heart 224
  xīnzàngbìng – heart attack; heart disease **223**, 224
xìn – true; to believe; a letter (see **tōngxìn**) 123
  xìnfēng – an envelope 156
  xìnyòngzhèng – letter of credit (L/C) **122**, 128
xīng – a star 55
  xīngqi – a week **54**, 58
  xīngqīrì – Sunday 58
xīng (alt. pron. **xìng**) – to prevail; to promote 190
  xīngfèn – exciting, stimulating **197**, 201
xíng (alt. pron. **háng**) – to walk; permissible, O.K. (see **lǚxíng**) 56
  xíng-buxíng – will it do . . .? **54**, 61
  xíngli – luggage **18**, **128**, **129**, 131
  xínglipiào – baggage check **130**, 133
xíng – shape; extn.—to appear (see **qíngxing**) 120
xìng – surname, to have the surname 29
xìng – desire, excitement, interest (see **xīng** above) 190
  xìngqù – interest **190**, 194
xiū – to rest 56
  xiūxi – to take a break, have a rest **54**, 60, **214**, 217
xuyào – to need; necessities **122**, 128
xǔ – to allow; maybe 123
  xǔduō – many **189**, 191
  xúkězhèng – a permit, a license **121**, 127
xù – continues, successive (see **shǒuxù**) 130
xuǎn – to choose 156
xué – to learn, study; school 50
  xuéyuàn – college; faculty **49**, 51
xuě – snow (see **xiàxuě**) 244

yǎn – eye 219
  yǎnjing – eyes 220
  yǎnjìng[r] – glasses, spectacles **218**, 220
yànhuì – banquet, feast **231**, 234
yáng – the sun; positive element 56
  yánglì – solar calendar **54**, 61
yáng – sheep, a surname **166**, 168
  yángròu – mutton 169

yàng – appearance; manner, sort   **54, 56, 61**
  yàngzi – fashion, kind, pattern, sample   **61**
yāobāo – purse; pocket   **232, 235**
yāo (alt. pron. yào) – to require   **240**
  yāoqiù – to request, a demand   **237, 240**
yào – to want; if; must; important (see **yāo**)   **39**
  yàoburán – otherwise   **74, 76**
  yàojǐn – important   **63, 66**
  yàoshi – if   **108, 111**
yào – medicine   **215**
  yàofáng – dispensary, pharmacy   **214, 216**
yě – also, as well; either; too   **34**
  yěshi – also, too   **183**
yè – line of business, occupation (see **gōngyè,
  shíyè, zhíyè**)   **44**
yèli – at night   **74**
yī – one, once, single   **45**
  yībǎisuì – Bless you! Gesundheit!   **63**
  yìbān – generally; ordinary, usual[ly]   **281**
  yìdiǎr – a little   **100, 103**
  yídìng – definite   **67**
  yíge – one [MW]   **100**
  yígòng – all told, total   **129, 131**
  yìhuěr – a little while, a moment   **114, 116**
  yìhuí – once   **166, 171**
  yíjùhuà – in a word   **86, 88**
  yíkuàr – together   **44, 49**
  yìqǐ – in the same place, in company with   **231, 233**
  yíqiè – everything   **121, 126**
  yíwèi – one person   **137**
  yíxià – once   **50, 51, 229, 231**
  yìxiē – a few, somewhat   **189, 191**
  yíyàng – alike   **61, 281**
  yìzhí – straight [on], continuous[ly], all along   **281**
yīyuàn – hospital   **222, 223, 224**
yī – clothes, garment; covering (see **yǔyī**)   **130**
  yīfu – clothing   **141, 144**
yí – appropriate, suitable (see **piányi**)   **81**
yǐ – in order to; to use (see **kéyi**)   **50**
  yǐhòu – afterwards   **71**
  yǐjīng – already   **141, 144**
  yǐnèi – within; less than   **268**

yǐqián – previously **50**, 71
yǐshàng – above, more than, over 268
yǐwài – apart from, outside of 141
yǐwéi – to consider **231**, 233
yǐxià – below, under 268
yì – idea; meaning (see **hǎoyì, tóngyì, zhǔyi**) 123
yìjiàn – suggestion **231**, 233
yìsi – idea, opinion **204**, 209
yì – art, skill (see **shǒuyì**) 169
yì – friendship (see **yǒuyì**) 183
yīnwei – because, on account of **74**, 76
yīn – the moon; negative element 56
yīnlì – lunar calendar **55**, 62
yīnyáng – cosmic principles of philosophy 55
yīn – sound (see **lùyīnjī, pīnyīn, shōuyīnjī**) 198
yínháng – bank **96**, 98
yǐnliào – beverage, drink 165
yìn – to print 238
yīng – English, Anglo- 215
Yīngyǔ – English [language] 18, 96, **214**, 217
yīng – to answer; ought 70
yīngdāng – ought **69**, 72
yīnggāi – should **231**, 234
yíng – to greet (see **huānyíng**) 115
yǐng – shadow (see **diànyǐng**) 206
yòng – to use; need 90
yònghù – consumer, user **155**, 158
yóu – mail, postal 97
yóudiànjú – telegraph office **155**
yóufèi – postage **155**, 157
yóupiào – postage stamp **155**, 158
yóu[zhèng]jù – post office **96**, 98
yóu – oil, grease; fat (see **jiāyóu, qìyóu**) 253
yóu – to swim; tour 198
yóuguàng – to tour 199
yóulǎn – to go sightseeing 199
yóuwán – to amuse oneself, to play 199
yǒu – to have; to exist 39
yǒumíng – famous **166**, 169
yǒudeshì – are to be had **141**, 144
yǒude shíhou – there are times . . . **197**, 201
yǒu yìsi – enjoyable, interesting, significant **236**, 239

yǒu – friend (see **péngyou**) 39
  yóuhǎo – friendly, goodwill 44, 49
  yǒuyì – friendship 183, 185
yòu – right [side] 112, 113, 266
yòu'éryuán – nursery school 236, 238
yú – at, by, in (see **guānyu, shǔyú**) 45
yúlè – amusement, pastime, recreation 197, 201
yǔ – rain 130
  yǔyī – raincoat 129, 132
yù – to bring up, raise (see **jiàoyù, tǐyù**) 50
yù – beforehand, in advance 139
  yùbèi – to get ready, prepare 167, 173
  yùdìng – to reserve 136, 139
yùshì – a bathroom 137, 140
yuán – recreation ground (see **gōngyuán, yòu'éryuán**) 109
yuán – circular, round; a dollar (see **měiyuán**) 91
yuán – primary (see **gōngyuán**) 56
yuánliàng – to excuse, pardon 247, 248
yuǎn – distant, far 101
yuàn – courtyard, designation of some public places (see **jùyuàn, xuéyuàn, yīyuàn, zhùyuàn**) 50
  yuànzhǎng – head of faculty 49, 51
yuànyì – to be willing to; to like to... 231, 234, 270, 271, 272
yuē – to make an appointment 232
  yuēqǐng – to invite 231, 233
yuè – moon; month 55
  yuèdǐ – end of the month 231, 232
  yuèfènpái – calendar 54, 61
yùn – movement, transport 198
  yùndòng – movement; sports 197, 199
  yùndòngchǎng – sportsground 200

zá – sundry; to mix 198
  záshuǎ – variety show 204, 209
  zázhì – magazine 197, 202
zài – to exist; [to be] at, in (see **búzài, xiànzài**) 44
  zàinèi – included 138, 141
zài – again, once more 109
  zàihuì – goodbye 249, 251
  zàijiàn – au revoir, see you again 15, 247, 248
zāng (alt. pron. zàng) – dirty 142
zàng – internal organs (see **xīnzàng**) 224

zǎo – early; in advance   **15**, 70
   zǎofàn – breakfast   **74**, 76
   zǎoshang – morning   73, **74**, 75
zào – to construct, create (see zhìzàochǎng)   190
zé – duty; responsibility (see fùzé)   219
zé – criterion, standard (see fǒuzé, guīzé)   123
zěn – how, why   81
   zěnme – how, how come   **80**, 189
   zěnme huíshì – how it was   **218**, 219
   zěnmeyàng – in what way   **237**, 240
zhǎnlánguǎn – exhibition hall or centre   **100**, 103
zhāng – sheet, spread, MW; surname   91
zhǎng – chief; to grow (see shìzhǎng, yuànzhǎng)   39
zhàng – account   90
   zhàngdān – bill, check   **89**, 91
zhāo – to beckon   123
   zhāodài – to entertain   **121**, 126
   zhāolǐng – finding of lost property   **218**, 220
zháo (alt. pron. zhe) – feel, to be affected by   217
   zháojí – to feel anxious   **214**, 217
   zháoliáng – to catch a chill   217
zhǎo – to call on, to look for   97
   zhǎo jīhuì – to seek an opportunity   **189**, 192
zhào – to reflect; license (see hùzhào)   91
   zhàopiàn – photograph, snapshot   **237**, 239
   xhàoxiàng – to take a photograph   18
   [zhào]xiàngjī – a camera   129, 132, **237**, 239
zhe – suffix "-ing" (see zháo)   169
zhě – suffix (see huòzhě)   123
zhè (alt. pron. zhèi) – this   55
   zhè jiù – directly, right away   **114**, 115
   zhèli/zhèr – here; now   90
   zhème – such   81
   zhèxiē – these   97
   zhèyàng – thus   **189**, 191
zhēn – real, true   64
   zhēnzhèng – authentic, genuine   **167**, 172
zhěng – complete   69
zhèng – administration (see shìzhèng, yóuzhèng)   45
zhèng – just, main, upright   101
   zhènghǎo – just right   **121**, 127
   zhèng zài – in the course of; precisely at   **100**, 102

zhèng – certificate (see **dēngjīzhèng, qiānzhèng, xìnyòngzhèng, xúkězhèng**)   123
zhī – to realize (see **tōngzhī**)   97
   zhīdào – to know   96, 97, 98, 189, 191, **204**
zhī – branch, MW   86
zhīpiào – a cheque   89, 90, 91
zhīzào – to weave, weaving   **190**, 192
zhíyè – profession, occupation, vocation   45
zhí – value   65
   zhíde – to deserve, worthy   **63**, 67
zhíjiē – direct, immediate   **149**, 150
zhǐ – location, site (see **dìzhǐ**)   100
zhǐ – paper   93
zhǐ – finger; to indicate, to point   123
   zhǐjiào – to give advice   **121**, 126
   zhǐnánzhēn – magnetic compass   108
zhǐ – only, merely   139
   zhǐyào – provided that   **183**, 186
zhì – to make, manufacture; to control   190
   zhìchéngpǐn – manufactured products   191
   zhìzàochǎng – manufacturer   **190**, 193
zhìliàng – quality   **183**, 185
zhì – annals, narrative (see **zázhì**)   198
zhìyì – to present one's compliments   **249**, 251
zhōng – centre, middle   48
   Zhōngguó – China   48, 152
   Zhōngguórén – the Chinese people   95
   Zhōnghuá Mínguó – Republic of China (ROC)   48
   Zhōnghuá Rénmín Gònghéguó – People's Republic of China (PRC)   48
   Zhōngwén – the Chinese language   **204**, 210
   zhōngwǔ – midday, noon   73
zhōng – bell; clock   70
   zhōngtóu – hour   **69**, 72
zhǒng – species, type   56
zhòng – heavy, weight; important (see **chóng**)   130
zhōu – cycle; a surname   65
   zhōumò – weekend   **174**, 176
   zhōunián – anniversary   63, **64**, 66
zhōu – continent (see **Běi-Měizhōu**)   92
zhǔ – host, master; primary   50
   zhǔrén – host   **49**
   zhǔyào – important; principally   **122**, 128

zhúyì – idea, plan **121**, 126
zhù – to reside; hold (see **zhuāzhù**) 115
    zhùyuàn – to be hospitalized 224
    zhùyuàn-zhìliáo – hospital treatment 224
zhù – to express good wishes (see **qìngzhù**) 65
    zhùhè – to congratulate **63**, 67
zhùcún – to store, keep in storage **181**, 185
zhuāzhù – to grab, seize **237**, 239
zhuānjiā – a specialist 47
zhuāng – attire; to pretend; to load, pack 130
    zhuāngshàng – to load up **129**, 133
    zhuāngxià – to load into, to pack **183**, 186
    zhuāngshì tú'àn – ornamental designs **190**, 193
zhǔnbèi – to get ready, preparations **121**, 125
zhuōzi – a table **167**, 172
zǐ – seed; son; (see **háizi, sūnzi**) 29, 259
    zínǚ – sons and daughters; children 199
zì – character, word (see **qiānzì**) 91
zì – self; since 130
    zìjǐ – oneself **129**, 132
    zìxíngchē – a bicycle **204**, 208
-zi – toneless suffix 29, 259
zǒng – head; overall 149
    zóngděi – have to, bound to **249**, 250
    zǒng gōngsī – head office **249**, 250
    zǒngjī – main exchange, switchboard **149**, 150
zǒu – to walk, to go [away] 109
zū – to lease, to rent (see **chūzū**) 183
zúgòu – adequate, quite enough **69, 90**, 93
zuì – most, -est (for superlatives) 64
    zuìduō – maximum **154**, 157
    zuìjìn – nearest **223**, 225
    zuìshǎo – at least **137**, 139
zuótiān – yesterday **219**
zuǒ – the left 109, 266
    zuǒbiar – left-hand side **108**, 111
zuò – to do, engage in, to make (see **hézuò**) 44
    zuòfǎ – method **174**, 176
    zuòjiā – author **44**, 47
    zuòliàor – ingredients [in a recipe] 168
    zuò lǐbài – to go to church **229**, 230
    zuòshì – to work **44**, 46

zuòzhě – writer   47
zuò – to sit; to travel (see **qǐngzuò**)   115
    zuò chē – to ride in a vehicle   133
    zuò chuán – to travel by boat   133
    zuò fēijī – to go by air   133
    zuò gōnggòng-qìchē – to go by bus   133
    zuò huǒchē – to take a train   133
    zuòwèi – a seat, a place to sit   133